# I am
# C-3PO

# I am C-3PO

## The Inside Story

## Anthony Daniels

Foreword by
J.J. Abrams

## author's note

A friend of mine is fluent in more than six million…
oh, you know the rest. Personally I'm only fluent in
English, as it is spoken round the corner from where
I live. Since you know my voice, I've made the decision
not to adopt American spellings here, but to keep my
words in the original. I hope that's OK.

(Translations are available on the Internet
or from your local human-cyborg relater.)

First published in Great Britain in 2019
by Dorling Kindersley Limited
80 Strand, London, WC2R 0RL

First American Edition, 2019
Published in the United States by DK Publishing
1450 Broadway, Suite 801, New York, NY 10018

Text copyright © Anthony Daniels, 2019

The moral right of the author has been asserted

© & TM 2019 LUCASFILM LTD.

Page design copyright © 2019 Dorling Kindersley Limited
DK, a Division of Penguin Random House LLC

19 20 21 22 23 24 25 10 9 8 7 6 5 4 3 2 1

001–311506–Oct/2019

Set in New Baskerville ITC Pro 10/16pt
Typeset by Dorling Kindersley Limited
Printed and bound in Great Britain by Clays Ltd, Elcograf S.p.A.

A CIP catalogue record for this book is available from the British Library.

A catalog record for this book is available from the Library of Congress.

UK HARDBACK ISBN: 978-0-24135-760-6
US HARDBACK ISBN: 978-1-4654-8610-3
UK PAPERBACK ISBN: 978-0-2414-2073-7

For
my amazing wife
Christine
with love

and for
Howard
(who is also rather amazing)

and of course for
You

# contents

# foreword

I want to talk about Anthony (as does Anthony). But I need to give this some context. Let's start with the obvious. There's magic in *Star Wars*. In all of it. From the design of the logo — those outlined letters against the stylized star field — to its aesthetic, production design and delicious combination of Flash Gordon space adventure and Kurosawa samurai high drama.

There's magic in its enhanced real-life locations, gorgeously unique props and ships, sound effects and, of course, its breathtaking, instantly-classic musical score. But would we be considering — or continuing — a story that began nearly half a century ago if, at the heart of it all, there wasn't such a powerful sense of humanity? Surely even the genius of the lightsaber and the growl of a Wookiee would have been long forgotten if George Lucas hadn't focused so ingeniously on the souls of the main characters. It was their desires and desperation, their fears and revelations, their love and loyalty that made *Star Wars* a saga for the ages.

The most potent aspect of *Star Wars* is evident from the opening minute of the first film. After announcing that it's a once upon a time fable, after the blast of unforgettably powerful music, after the thrilling crawl gives us its pulpy context, and after the awe-inspiring Star Destroyer passes us overhead and the small Blockade Runner is revealed, we cut inside to see members of the Rebellion, rocked by the attack. But what happens next is what's most important. We fall in love.

Nearly the instant we meet stalwart droids C-3PO and R2-D2, we laugh. They become our way into a galaxy we're so desperate to be part of. Their fear, their bickering, their frantic need to survive is what grabs us by the heart and allows us to be mesmerized, to be taken on the cinematic adventure of a lifetime. Despite all the wondrous spectacle and artistry, the characters themselves are the glue that keeps *Star Wars* together and us stuck to it. Among them all, only two characters have appeared in all nine saga stories. Those two droids I first met when I was ten years old.

While I suspected that bringing Threepio to life was harder than it looked, experiencing it first-hand gave me an instant, newfound respect for the man with the golden eyes. It turns out that being inside that sensory deprivation tank of a costume is a challenge at best.

Moving, hearing and seeing is only part of the problem, as the actor playing Threepio needs to constantly interact with numerous other performers in a scene with deft, seemingly effortless comedic timing. That actor is, of course, Mr. Anthony Daniels. A gloriously witty, keen and spirited man who may be the least-recognizable superstar on the planet. When I first called Anthony about appearing in *The Force Awakens*, I asked if he was willing and able to return as everyone's favorite humanoid droid. His enthusiasm to do so was heartening. But — and I'll put it bluntly — would he be able to fit in the suit? When I met Anthony and saw that he was in better shape than I will ever be, I was enormously relieved — as was he that a new, more comfortable suit was going to be fabricated by costume designer Michael Kaplan and his team.

In *The Force Awakens* — where Threepio remained mostly within the Resistance base — perhaps Anthony's biggest challenge was the red arm (I gave Threepio a new limb to demonstrate that the character had gone through some dangerous adventures since we'd last seen him. Anthony hated it. Hated. Like... hated. As you will see). In *The Rise of Skywalker*, however, Threepio is out on the wild journey with the others. That means ships and speeders, deserts and snowy villages, climbing, crashing, and encounters with some terrifying creatures. With this, the challenges for Anthony rose exponentially. But every time they would remove his mask (wearing the suit, he is unable to do that himself — just think about that), there was Anthony, his face sweaty and smiling.

Much like the droid he so beautifully, artfully portrays, Anthony wanted to be out on the adventure again, too.

The cast and crew of these recent films were well aware of the stakes involved in creating a third trilogy. How important it was to do well by the legions of *Star Wars* fans, continuing and concluding George's remarkable tale. As surreal as it still feels to know that I've directed two *Star Wars* films, I could not begin to imagine what it was like to have been there before, again and again and again, for all of the Skywalker saga. At least I couldn't until I read this insightful, delightful book.

The stories you'll find in the following pages come from one of the most unique perspectives on *Star Wars* that could possibly exist. It is ironic that, despite Mr. Daniels' limited field of vision (peering through those two slit and lit holes is the visual equivalent of breathing through a straw), this book takes a remarkably wide and deep view of the film series. Why is it that we fall in love with Threepio the moment we meet him? My humbling experience on these films has given me the answer: It's because there's a man inside. A most excellent man, who — I'm happy to say — you're about to meet yourself.

J.J. Abrams
Los Angeles, 2019

# 1 love

It was the best job I ever had.

The story came alive every night, in front of thousands of devoted fans. Across countries and continents around the world, I narrated a finely honed script that spoke of the key moments in our beloved tale. This was *Star Wars – In Concert*.

I stood, smart black-suited as myself, absorbing the power of it all. From 2009 – from Houston to Hamburg, Tokyo to Tulsa – I was enveloped in lights and laser beams, dwarfed by the symphony orchestra and choir behind me. The giant screen, backdrop to our arena stage, reminded us all of what we loved, with sequences edited around epic themes. The Villains. The Heroes. The Princess. The Battles. And John Williams' glorious scores played live to picture. It was huge and inspiring. I had the best seat in the house standing there between the orchestra and the audience. I felt the power of the images, the power of the music. But the power of something else, too.

I had never truly understood the devotion of the fans, their adoration of the whole thing. Being so involved, I was too close to really appreciate it all. Now, I began to see past my own myopic stance and view the Saga reflected back to me by the faces filling the arenas. The vibrant sense of respect, of affection, of love, that flowed across the footlights was palpable. Love for the music, love for George, love for the actors on screen and some small element that made me feel loved too. It gave me an understanding of something that had eluded me for so many years.

I wish there were another word for "fan". It's an abbreviation of fanatic. But most fans are simply gentle admirers. They aren't crazy or nerdy. But maybe it is the best shorthand term for all those who really made *Star Wars* the phenomenon that it became. Without the fans, *A New Hope* would have been the beginning – and the end.

It was all I ever wanted to be.

From the time my parents would hold me up to pull the draw strings on the small window curtains at the top of the stairs, I was fascinated by the simple mechanism that opened them. Like the reveal in a theatre's proscenium arch, they gave a hint of the magic beyond; a magic that ended by pulling the other string that closed them. I was allowed to repeat the trick many, many times. If I connected this with acting, it was unconscious, but we did regularly go to the theatre. Maybe that planted a seed. Did five-year old me excitedly running down to the stage to shake the paw of an actor dressed as the Cat in *Dick Whittington*, a Christmas pantomime, did that unrestrained enthusiasm predict my eventual role, acting in a suit? Because that was all I ever wanted to be. An actor.

Time passed.

I was lucky. I had a métier. A calling. A passion. Something I needed to do in life. An ambition. So many young people have no idea what they want to do. I feel for them. I always knew what I wanted to be. It was easy. If only it had been as a doctor, lawyer, banker, teacher – classic professions – then my parents would have approved. They didn't. They gently dissuaded me from such a perilous thought. So I tried to be a lawyer. For two years. Twenty-four long, long months.

Being a member of an amateur dramatic society kept my sanity and my longing alive. Standing in the wings of our tiny stage, waiting for my entrance as the stage manager pulled the strings to part the proscenium curtains, I murmured.

"I wish I were an actor."

John Law looked at me – a teacher by profession.

"If you want to be an actor, be an actor."

We walked on stage together.

It was that simple.

But it would be three more years before I finally had the courage to take his words and admit that my life was unfulfilled, pointless, unless I followed my dream.

I was twenty-four years old before I took myself to drama school.

For three years I learned a little of this and a bit of that. The curriculum was mostly geared towards the theatre. That seemed enough. To have considered film might have appeared presumptuous. Of course there were acting classes and improvisation. The latter still scares me but how useful it would be later. Mime classes too – they were fascinating; isolation techniques, fighting with imaginary forces to restrain an imaginary umbrella in an imaginary gale; trying to deliver emotion, wearing a blank white mask. Then there was voice work; vocal exercises, projection, diction, tongue-twisters, bi-labial fricatives. Stage fighting, ballet, text analysis and growing up.

I graduated with a job with the BBC's Radio Repertory Company. A huge, overwhelming joy to me. Not just the accolade of winning their annual Carlton Hobbs Award and performing in so many of their productions – but the gift of a union ticket – an amazing thing back then. No membership of Actors' Equity, no work – no work, no Equity membership – without struggling for months – years. Now, the acting profession, quite rightly, is open to anyone who has the courage to put themselves forward and try. And of course the opportunities to work in entertainment have vastly increased, for the amusement of viewers and the employment of so many more talented players. Back then there were a few TV channels – no cable – no Internet. Unimaginable now.

Then, my sojourn with the BBC over, I began to clamber forward on stage and television in minor roles. My luck held for the next two years. I was thrilled to be playing Guildenstern in *Rosencrantz and Guildenstern Are Dead,* by the exceptional British playwright, Tom Stoppard.

The phone rang.

I was there to pick it up. To leave the flat unattended was a brave gesture in the days before answering machines. In the decades before mobile phones.

I listened.

"No. I don't think so. Thank you."

"Don't be so stupid. Go and meet him. You never know what it could lead to."

It was 1975.

The 14th November.

12.30.

I hadn't wanted to meet an American film director called George Lucas, to discuss the role of a robot in his low-budget science-fiction film. I wasn't a fan of the genre and probably thought it was beneath me. I was a serious actor – and had been for the two years since I left drama school. But I obeyed my agent and walked through the traffic to 20th Century Fox House in Soho Square. It was only a short distance from the theatre in Piccadilly Circus where I was performing at the time. I had never thought of being in a film. I was comfortable acting on stage. Filming seemed huge, Hollywood and out of my reach. But here I was, pushing open the front door with the famous Fox logo above me, as I entered the marbled interior.

The receptionist had the air of someone who'd seen it all before – especially seen actors entering in hope and leaving crestfallen. I must have seemed an anachronism as I casually said why I was there. She directed me upstairs and I found the appropriate office. I explained myself to the rather more interested secretary who was guarding the man himself. He was behind the other door in her room. She knocked and I entered the lair of, I supposed, a cigar-chomping, overweight, loud Hollywood movie mogul.

There was George.

Jeans. Plaid shirt. Diminutive. Shy. Polite. Exhausted. He was seeing hundreds of actors.

We sat down.

There was a pause.

"So. You're an actor?"

"Err, yes."

"And good at mime?"

"Well, quite good."

I had been brought up in the useless English tradition of self-depre-cation. I was shy too, but feigning polite interest in this weird project. During a rather desultory conversation, I noticed, what I would learn, were concept paintings, decorating the office walls. George led me to one in particular.

I stared.

My world stopped.

My diffidence fell away.

I was entranced.

Captured.

Bonded.

Ralph McQuarrie had created an evocative image that touched my soul.

Standing on a sandy terrain, against a rocky landscape, with distant planets filling the sky, Threepio gazed out forlornly. Our eyes met and he seemed yearning to walk out of the frame into my world. Or, I felt, for me to climb over and join him in his. I sensed his vulnerability. Maybe he sensed mine. It truly was a strange moment.

I went home to rest before the show that night.

They delivered a script the next day.

*The Star Wars.*

There was a small sticker on the front – colourful in blue – triangu-lar – a young man holding a kind of sword. It suggested drama.

I opened the paper cover.

In my innocence, I had never seen a film script before. It was immensely complicated. Obviously nothing was linear, as the action jumped around from scene to scene. And the pages were packed with alarming stage directions and stuff about POVs – points of view. The only thing I really understood was that See-Threepio had been gloriously conceived by George and the scriptwriters. The poor creature was always out of his depth – always in the wrong place and battered by events beyond his control. Programmed for abilities that would rarely be required in such a violent world, his frustrations were increased by his close and loving friend, Artoo-Detoo – Threepio reticent and self-protective – Artoo gung-ho and inquisitive – their affection for each other so clear in its understatement. It was a master-class in odd-couple scripting. Their banter was delightful. Their menial and meaningless place in society was classically tragic.

I was hooked.

Forget it was sci-fi.

Forget Luke and Han and Vader.

Threepio was the one for me.

Back at 20th Century Fox the next day, the secretary asked when I could go to be cast. I was confused. I said that's why I was there. Now. She gave me a rather quizzical look as she opened the door to George's office again.

George looked more relaxed.

On the other hand, I was a little more nervous as we sat and discussed my lack of faith in sci-fi. I admitted that I'd actually asked for my money back when I walked out on *2001: A Space Odyssey*, some years before. The cinema manager had simply but rudely told me to get lost. Quite right. Years later, I would meet Keir Dullea and Gary Lockwood, two of the stars of that film. They told me that a lot of people walked out. But before I had left that theatre HAL had made a lasting impression on me. A red light bulb and Douglas Rain's hypnotic voice – an early warning of the dangers perhaps inherent in artificial intelligence.

George and I talked. An hour passed. Surely we both had things to do.

There was a silence.

Nervously.

"Please, may I play the part?"

George paused.

Then quietly,

"Shurr."

Not even a word. Hardly a syllable. A sound. A small sound above the London traffic.

It changed my life.


# 3 plastered

A chilly day.

Elstree Studios in North London. I parked outside the rather anonymous admin building.

I'd never been to a film studio before. Not sure what I'd expected but I was slightly disappointed. If I thought the admin offices lacked theatrical glamour, they were the London Palladium, Radio City Music Hall compared to the dressing room where they sent me. A bleak, cold cell of a room.

Two plasterers in workers' overalls had laid out an assortment of plastic sheets and buckets and bags of plaster. They greeted me cheerily and suggested I took off my clothes. Ah. Mr Lucas's secretary had been right – her quizzical glance explained. Now I really was going to be cast.

After a discussion about the uncomfortable and adhesive nature of plaster and body hair combined, they wrapped me in kitchen film.

Another first. I stood there, inelegant and self-conscious, like some long-forgotten leftovers mouldering at the back of a fridge. My sense of humour was trying to win the battle over my feelings of humiliation as they stuck strips of rubber down my sides. I would be cast in two halves, my back first.

Two posts were fixed to the floor. I watched them enthusiastically mixing powder and water. They moved faster as the chemical process began to work. When the mix reached critical point, they began to slap it on me. Slap. Smooth. Slap. Smooth. I hung on to the posts, trying to stay still, as the heavy, wet plaster clung to me, dragging me down. To make the whole thing more sturdy, they slathered lengths of timber and attached them to me with pieces of hessian. I began to feel like a construction site. And then we stopped. And waited. It got hotter. The windows steamed up.

Eventually, they decided I could safely wiggle free. I remember making an embarrassing sucking noise as I peeled my body away from the demi-sarcophagus they had just created. And so, on to the other half.

I lay down in the now cold and damp impression of my back. I wondered how bad this could get. Slap. Slap. Smooth. With just my head sticking out, I had an even better view of the process as they slathered plaster up and down my front. It was like being in a one-man Turkish bath. As the chemicals heated up again, I saw a jet of steam shoot out from a gap at my neck. It was one of the most undignified experiences of my life.

It got worse.

They stuck straws up my nose and encased my head in a ball of mortician's wax and gunk. That bit worked. The rest didn't. We had to do it again.

I drove back to Elstree a week later. I knew the form and was slightly dreading it. This time, a comfortable, blue-carpeted dressing room, where Liz Moore was waiting for me – the loveliest and, as I would learn, most talented sculptor. She was charged with making a casting that was a little more accurate. No more chucking plaster at me. She gave me a pair of woman's tights to wear. Then she carefully stuck strips of rubber down either side. She would make the mould in two halves, as before. I lay on a couch. We talked and relaxed. She gently smoothed face cream over most of my body. And then a layer of plaster. She made me feel like a cake being iced. I began to think I was becoming a work of art. It was all strangely serene – and funny.

And what a sweet coincidence – Liz had created the Star Child for the last scene of *2001*. If I'd known, I would have stayed to the end.

Days later, I returned to see the results of her efforts. More embarrassment. A dreadfully accurate, albino plaster replica of my rather unappealing body stood on display in the workshop. But Liz soon hid my nakedness with grey modelling clay. Gradually, she carefully achieved what George had in mind for the "look". She turned Ralph's painting into three-dimensional reality.

With Liz's sculpture as the bible, the Art Department worked to make a viable suit. Over the next six months, I regularly appeared at Elstree to try on a leg, an arm, a chest, a foot – prototypes – cardboard and plastic mock ups. George was often kneeling on the floor in front of me, while he tried to fathom the engineering of Threepio's knee. When it came to the slightly bulging codpiece, he okayed it as an example of "space eroticism".

Most of the pieces were formed out of fibreglass. The chemical smell and the itchiness haunted me on stage every night, where I was wearing a more traditional costume – doublet and hose. I avoid loft insulation to this day. They prototyped a rubber arm. I tried it on. It felt like being trapped inside a giant squid. Disgusting.

In the days that followed, I was merely a mannequin. I stood there for ages, as the team studied my anatomy and pondered how to create a sort of exoskeleton carapace around it. Dr Who's enemy, the

Cybermen, were a doddle compared with what they were trying to produce. Apart from Fritz Lang's Maria, in his dystopian film, *Metropolis*, made some fifty years earlier, nobody had ever really attempted this sort of thing. Maria was Threepio's pin-up, at least for the designers. Photos of the rather haunting figure were stuck on the office walls. George wanted the Art Department to give his robot that same Art Deco look that had made Maria so striking. And they needed me there as the mechanism that would animate their work. It didn't cost much to have me around.

At some point, George organised for me to see *2001*. He wanted me to watch the whole thing so I could hear the voice of HAL again. It might help me come up with a voice for his robot. I sat alone in the screening room at Fox. As the wide, pizza-like plates of 35mm celluloid passed through the projector, I realised that I had been too young to enjoy it before. There were parts that I still can't fathom, even today. But what a marvellous film. I did sit through the whole thing – shocked at my earlier naiveté. I loved it. Especially the voice of the rogue computer. But those wonderfully calm tones would never do for Threepio.

Back at Elstree, standing there in a huddle of designers, I entertained myself by reading fresh redrafts of the script. Threepio's role was becoming more and more prominent in each new iteration. I began to feel involved – and quite special, since I was the only actor on the studio lot at this time. The team was so highly qualified and skilled that their attention made me feel important. Of course their attention was to the suit. But they did seem to care about me. So I was rather shocked when I heard them discussing the heat of the Tunisian desert and the melting point of plastic. I wondered what I had let myself in for.

Now, I wasn't the only actor on the block. How exciting to finally meet my new master – so prominent in the scripts I was studying. Mark Hamill had flown in from fabled California. That alone gave him a sort of special status in my eyes. I had never been to America. Mark instantly charmed everyone he encountered. His full-on, happy personality was a revelation to me. Words just seemed to tumble out of him, in contrast to my slightly reserved nature. His enthusiasm for the project encouraged me every time we met around the studio. And he seemed to like being in England, in spite of the weather. I liked knowing he was around. It gave me a sense of a team growing around me. He was having costume fittings, too. A costume very different from mine.

Air conditioning would be essential. A technician arrived with a miniature system. He stared at me, standing there in the nearly complete tight-fitting suit. He went away. He didn't come back. It would be four decades before they found a solution, of sorts. But for now, my air-con cooling was the tiny letterbox that is Threepio's mouth. Later, I would learn the art of sucking air into the face through the eyeholes and mouth, and blowing it out with my lips fixed to the inside of the letterbox.

Liz had created a number of designs for the head. They sat on a shelf, like the aftermath of a medieval battle. Alien, blank, flat, strange, their clay faces stared out impassively. I liked them all – except the one at the end. Of course, that was the one George had chosen. In my defence, Liz's creation looked very different in its dark, monochrome clay with black gas-mask eyes. When the finished, gilded version eventually arrived, I was enchanted. Liz had created something magical. Lovely in repose, yet blank enough for me to add life and emotion.

Threepio was beautiful.

I was intrigued by Threepio's eyes.

As with humans, his photoreceptors were fundamental to his expressive face. Brilliantly engineered, the honeycombed reflectors were stuck on a mirrored surface. There were tiny light bulbs drilled into them. A layer of black plastic shielded their light from the inside. Thin wires led to a plug that attached to its counterpart, wired to a battery pack on Threepio's back. My head encased, I could peer through the centre holes but was completely blinkered – seeing nothing except straight ahead. Above, below, sideways were all unknowns, unless I adjusted my position and turned to look. I had never appreciated my peripheral vision before.

Of course, they would now provide a mirrored studio and playback facilities, so I could rehearse in the suit. Obviously, I wanted to know how to work around its restrictions. George had guessed that it would need an actor with mime experience to get a character performance through sixty pounds of assorted metal, rubber and plastic. Naturally, it was going to take me some time to get the best results. They promised – I would have days to see what degrees of motion were available to create reactions and emotions. Now, finally, the suit was fit for a first try-out. We moved to the cluttered Special Effects unit where Phil McDonald, "Maxi", my dresser, helper and guardian, had laid all the bits out on a table, very neatly. It did strike me as interesting that, whereas most actors have an assistant from Wardrobe, Maxi was from Props – as if I were a "thing". There were nineteen pieces that would go together to make the complete Threepio. I stood like an Arthurian knight in my black cotton under-suit as Maxi and friends gradually fitted each section around me. At last, for the first time, I was wearing the whole, magnificent outfit.

It felt ghastly.

It was as if I had lost my own body – lost contact with my world. I blundered around the workshop, lightly crashing into various objects. What a relief to take it all off. It had been about fifteen minutes. It seemed longer – a lot longer. But anyway, now please could I take the suit away and rehearse?

No.

It had to be air freighted. At once. I would only see it again, weeks later, in the alien sands of Tunisia.

## 5 ladies

It was like an exciting school outing – touring theatre from my past.

We were flying to Sousse, Tunisia on our own charter flight. It felt quite special. More special, I was sitting across the aisle from Sir Alec Guinness and, I presumed, his wife. How many years had I watched this man on screen? My favourite, *The Ladykillers* – his goofy-toothed, gentleman bank robber. But there were so many other charming, funny, dramatic roles. And Prince Feisal. How could either of us have predicted that, in forty-plus years, filming the ninth variation on the *Star Wars* theme, I would be treading the same shifting sands of Wadi Rum as he did when filming that role in *Lawrence of Arabia*? But now I realised, he was the first famous person I had ever actually encountered. I was in respectful awe – and within arm's reach. Should I say hello? Would that be an impertinent intrusion on his privacy?

It was a long flight. As he folded his copy of *The Times* newspaper, I finally got up the courage to lean across the aisle and introduce myself. He was immediately friendly and charming. In his instantly recognisable rich tones, he introduced me to his wife. Not "Lady Guinness", just Merula. She was, quite simply, lovely – a real lady – no need for a title.

Sir Alec – days later, "Please call me Alec" – was most interested that I was playing the part of the robot. We chatted in bursts, with the service trolley zooming between us – interrupting.

But now we had arrived.

The customs officers were rather suspicious of the box of assorted greeblies that Maxi had packed at the last minute. He explained that this strange assortment of knobs and finials were parts of my costume. A "greebly" being something that looked interesting but actually had no real purpose. The officers nodded, as if they had completely understood. They let Maxi carry on through with his precious luggage.

But now, everything stopped.

The officers were horrified at a copy of *Playboy* magazine, brought along by one of the Sparks – a member of the lighting crew. Some of the officials were most offended by the centrefold. Others, after some study, picked the young lady on page nine, as being a true affront to public decency. I think they retained the offensive item so they could debate each page in detail, at leisure.

A minor delay. Leaving the air-conditioned arrivals hall, we were suddenly exposed on the sun-blasted concrete, in the fearsome heat. The crew bus was close by – nearer was a black limousine. I knew it wasn't for me, even before I saw Sir Alec and his wife getting in. Ducking his head through the car door, he turned back towards me, his hand reaching into his inside pocket.

"Pardon me. But have they given you your per diem yet?"

I was taken aback. I clearly didn't know what he was talking about. I had never been in a film before.

"Your pocket money," he explained gently. "Because they seem to have given me rather a lot and I think you should have some."

# 6 dogs

I didn't imagine I would ever want to return to this arid land – though, of course, I would.

Hot, fly-blown, sand-blown. Just this side of primitive. But that was long ago. Who could have guessed that it would become a major destination, curiously because we filmed there? Now the infrastructure is much improved. But in 1976…

Maxi and I drove for hours across the Tunisian landscape. He had been tending to the costume pieces, and me, since those early fittings at Elstree. Being from the Props Department, his ingenuity, dedication and patience were to be essential in getting me through this undertaking – not that I knew it at the time.

Now we were rattling along together in the back seat. Barely wide enough for the car, the tarmac strip edged and crumbled away into sand and stones. Our driver constantly played chicken with the oncoming trucks; tinny horns blaring from both parties. It was better not to look. But I did see, as if in slow motion, a rock whip up and into the windscreen. Crunch! The rest of the journey was somewhat draughty. Eventually we reached Tozeur. It was a relief to arrive, though it was hardly what they call "a destination".

The hotel was basic, cheerful and clearly, very cheap. The best they had it seemed, though Sir Alec and Lady Guinness were housed at a distance – somewhere more suited to their status. My room was functionally small with a shower, all blue and white, with running hot and cold water and streaming ants. I would eventually divert them out into the corridor with a sachet of sugar, sprinkled judiciously away from my bed.

Everything in this world was covered in the finest dusting of sand. I soon learned its persistent, insistent presence in this region. It seemed to get on and in everything – including the food. The dinner menu was: one day fish, next day chicken, next day fish, ad nauseam. Normally guests only stayed one night. We would be there for two weeks.

Shooting was to start the next day but parts of my costume had yet to be finished – Threepio's hands. Maxi and I sat on my single bed in the bleaching glare of the overhead light bulb. The box he brought along held some black cotton gloves, wires and weird metal shapes. I put on the gloves. Again using me as a living mannequin, Maxi pushed on the elements of each finger, knuckles and tips and thumbs, securing them with lavish squeezes of glue. It was a sniffer's dream and rather messy, and late. But Maxi persisted – as the sky blackened to deep night outside.

The gluing was finished. But now my hands and Threepio's were as one. The adhesive had soaked through the cotton gloves and attached the metal fingers to me. I sensed Maxi would have preferred me to sleep in them. Eventually he managed to peel them off my skin and took them with him. I got into bed and lay there, too exhausted and nervous to sleep.

A dog howled in the distance. It was all rather surreal.

Too few hours later, we were on the road again. Up well before dawn, we were directed to our vehicles and began our first journey to the set. Mark and I shared a car in the chill pre-dawn murk, staring sleepily but wide awake, at our new surroundings. We left the feebly lit streets of the village for the thin road, dusted with layers of sand. At the edges, small dunes and piles of palm leaves shifted as we passed. Eyes stared out, as we disturbed the sleepy inhabitants in their makeshift dwellings.

A dead dog lay close by – gradually becoming another sand dune.

We drove on.

# 7 action

So this is what a film set actually looked like.

We had arrived pre-dawn at the salt-flat location of Lars Homestead – the desolate place where Luke was raised. It didn't look like much. The sheer flatness of the surroundings was the most impressive thing about it. It went on for ever.

In the foreground was a domed dwelling with steps leading down, some mechanical junk, a large crater about three feet deep, more junk in the distance, moisture vaporators, the sandcrawler close by – its hefty tank tracks reaching to a height of around thirty feet, then scaffolding. The rest being up to movie magic.

All that stuff was going to be in front of the camera. Behind it were the assorted accessories of dollies and tracks and things I didn't recognise. Somebody pointed out my tiny caravan in a clutter of tents and trucks. It wobbled a bit as I climbed inside, reminding me of the budget holidays of childhood, with that strange smell of plastic walls and whiff of toilet. My under-suit was already laid out for me. I got changed. Black tights and a leotard that zipped up the back. Fake wires, painted and patched at the knees and elbows would, I learned, cover any gaps in the gold suit. Now, a pair of blue and white rubber deck shoes, a black balaclava hood and a cream towelling robe finished my new look. I was prepared – and a little apprehensive – as I stepped out and down.

The tent was nearby, a sort of scouting jamboree canvas affair, more practical than glamorous. Behind the flaps, Maxi had laid out the unfamiliar pieces of my robot suit with forensic tidiness, on two trestle tables. It all looked rather daunting. I remembered my brief, agonising try-out at Elstree. But Maxi was in firm control. And we had a helper. Then shortly, two more. It was clearly going to be a tougher task than any of us had imagined.

And so we started.

First, the rubber girdle embroidered with wires. It zipped up the side to create a bendable corset. Next, the thin, plastic, golden pants came in two halves, the "space eroticism" pieces stuck together with gold tape. So far so good. But now came something far trickier.

The right leg.

Thigh and shin were attached by a sort of bungee cord that allowed the pieces to move, yet remain connected. I took off my shoes. Now a strange manoeuvre, devised by Maxi, had me sliding my foot in and down the backward-facing piece, before he revolved it to allow my foot to slip out the other end. My deck shoe back on again, he slid over a thin, plastic, gold cover and taped it in place. Next, the calf piece was pinned tightly to the shin. Too tightly. Ouch! One leg to go. It had already taken a while.

Now I was standing upright, on two legs, complete from the waist down. Another helper was called in. I slid my arm through the proffered shoulder, attached to the chest. The other shoulder, attached to the back, was eased on. The team gently brought these two torso pieces together, sandwiching me inside. I squeaked in pain, the edges pinching my neck. It didn't end there.

As the growing squad wrestled the two halves into one, onto me, I tried not to vocalise the nipping and scratching from the fibreglass shell. They weren't trying to hurt me. The costume was doing that.

Finally the cuirass locked into place and four screws imprisoned me – literally. If the crew were to be abducted by aliens, I would have to beat myself against a rockface to smash my way out. But now, the arms slid on, held up by the addition of my new-minted gloves. The neck slotted into the torso's collar. Maxi held up the face and connected wires, now taped to my hood, that led from the battery pack on my back to Threepio's eyes. More hands offered up the back of the head. A mighty tussle began.

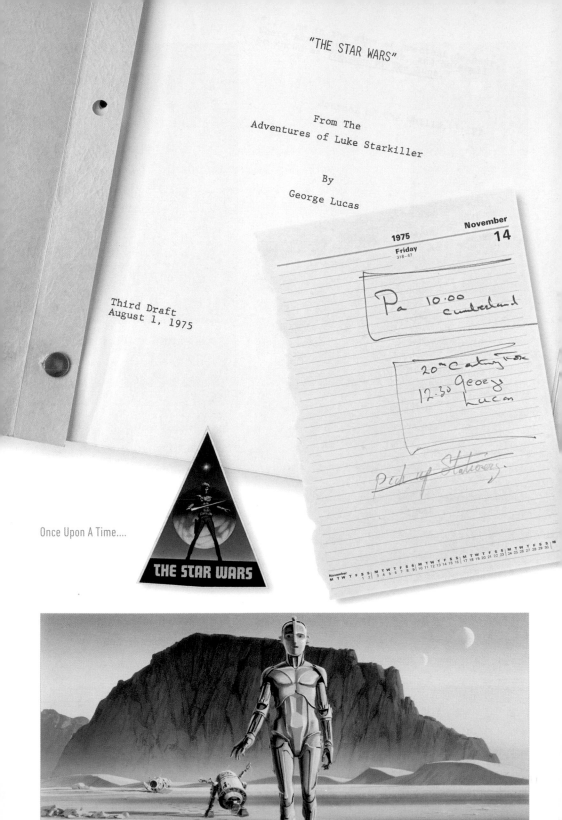

"THE STAR WARS"

From The
Adventures of Luke Starkiller

By

George Lucas

Third Draft
August 1, 1975

1975                    November
Friday                      14
318—47

Pa  10:00  cumberland

20ᵗʰ Century Fox
12:30 George
Lucas

Pick up Stationers.

Once Upon A Time....

THE STAR WARS

Maria – the inspiration

Liz Moore – the sculptor

Feet of clay

Progress

John Barry and George Lucas

Norman Reynolds

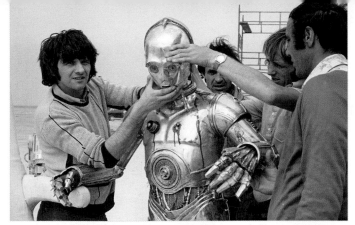

Maxi and Jim struggle

Leaning

Lost in a dune sea

The message not
the medium

3PO IS HUMAN!

My wires are showing

Some days I was hot

Some days I was cold

Some days I was just too shiny

Some greeblies

Transports

Dead Jawas

Jim stands in

Peter Diamond

Ouch!

Live Jawas

Towel

Sewing Bee

Who?

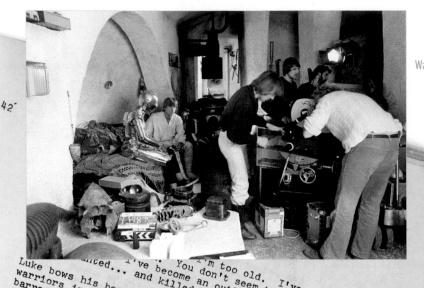

42

Waiting

I'm too old. I've
...ted... and killed.
You don't seem to
I've become an outlaw, to be

Luke bows his head in sorrow for one ...
warriors in the galaxy and a fallen ...
barrassed and makes a needless adjustm...
belly thermal heater, which radiates a ...
out the room. Little Artoo begins to p...
of the old man's arm and reassemble the...
dented Threepio breaks the awkward silen...
standing up.

                    THREEPIO
        If you'll not be needing me any mo...
        I think I'll shut down for awhile.
Luke nods his head. Old Ben leans back in...

                    BEN
        Son, I'm sorry I lost control.
        Perhaps we should talk about this in...
        the morning.

INT. CAVE DWELLING - SLEEPING AREA - NIGHT

uke tosses and turns in his sleep. Threepio sleeps
racefully. Luke keeps hearing the voice of Prince
ia calling out for help. Suddenly he sits ...
rt. He hears Leia's voice coming f...
ing area. Luke climbs out of bed an...
way through the darkened dwelling.
ance to the main room.

Shut down

CAVE DWELLING - MAIN LIVING AREA - N...

sitting before the flickering holog...
s Leia. The old man rests his head ...
n. His back is to Luke, but he sens...

ke, come here... sit down.       BEN

43

                                        (CO...

Game

If the chest had been a challenge, it was nothing compared to this. Like an Easter egg, the head was in two parts that slotted together fairly easily. The real drama came with the two bolts that locked the thing into one and joined it to the neck. Three holes had to be in perfect alignment to close the bolts on either side. The whole team got stuck in.

They seemed to forget I was inside as they pushed and pulled Threepio's head and mine. A hand covered the mouthpiece making it hard to breathe. I made mooing sounds from the inside, alerting them to the problem. I heard a muffled "sorry" as the hand changed position. But trying to locate the bayonet fitting in the plastic neck that kept moving away was clearly a nightmare, especially from where I was standing. But finally, a satisfying Click. They had done it. At last. There were no more pieces left on the tables. It had taken two hours – twenty minutes for the head alone. The six-month preparation had clearly not been long enough. Certainly, a try-out period would have ironed out some of the glitches. But now Maxi flipped the tiny switch under the battery pack. I saw a corona of light around the edges of my vision. I could see the tent flaps being pulled aside. I wobbled forward.

Threepio stepped out into the world, for the very first time.

I sensed that the newly risen sun was burnishing the golden outfit. I could see the crew around me, gazing, amazed, in awe. Even the hardened professionals were impressed – very. The locals were stunned – totally. I stood there enjoying this rare attention. It didn't last.

Standing still was one thing. Within moments of trying to move to the set, my left foot felt like it was being sawn off by the, now crumpled, gold cover on my deck shoe. The weight of the fibreglass leg was crushing it into me with my every step. I finally got to my mark, after Maxi had stuffed some foam padding up my ankle. A foretaste of what was to come. But that wasn't the end of the indignities.

Standing where I had been placed, I felt little bumps and knocks. Twisting my head as much as possible, I saw what was happening.

"Just dirtying you down a bit. OK?"

It was the stand-by painter, dabbing and daubing on my bright new suit. He dipped his brushes and cloths in various pots of shoe polish and wax to get the required effect of used beaten-upness that George wanted. It seemed such a shame to mar the beautiful factory finish, but of course, I had no say. That was fine by me, but at least I knew why someone was besmirching my costume. Worse was the camera crew coming over. They'd already decided I was too shiny.

"Hold your breath, Tones."

There was a swishing sound as they sprayed me in the face. The slight chemical odour of dulling spray haunts me still.

Before they rolled, I asked Continuity, Ann Skinner to take a Polaroid picture of me, or rather, of Threepio. I needed a reminder of what he looked like, because it was a very different view from the inside. She held up the little photo in front of me, eventually getting it into my limited field of vision. I stared at the eloquent face blankly gazing back at me. I was ready. Except I clearly wasn't.

EXT. TATOOINE – DESERT – LARS HOMESTEAD – AFTERNOON

ACTION!

"My first job was programming binary load-lifters."

It wasn't my first line but my lips and my memory just couldn't do it inside the distractions of my crazy new outfit. After the third attempt at trying to say the line as written, George walked over to me, clearly rather irritated at my time wasting.

"Don't worry about the voice. We can fix it later. You can say anything you want."

I was amazed – and a little confused. I was used to the discipline of, eventually, saying what was in a script. But I was new to the world of movie making.

George stepped back behind the camera.

ACTION!

"Why sir, my first job was bewawa bewawa bewawawa."

CUT!

"Terrific."

Actors often forget the words but rarely the rhythm.

"You look amazing!"

I was a movie star – a thrill to behold. How many of the crew came up to admire me in my fancy dress. They beamed into Threepio's face. They tried to look me in the eye, as they smilingly congratulated me on my appearance, but tended to end up addressing my nose, or an ear. They meant well. They were really impressed. All the attention took my mind off my new world – mine alone for the next twelve weeks.

Shooting distracted me, too, but in the minutes and hours between set-ups, it was more difficult to ignore my isolated situation. Time passed. When not actually shooting, I stared out at the endless flatness around us. A whistle blew. I turned toward the sound. Lunch. A lemming flow of crew was moving towards the shaded area, with its tables and chairs and buffet of hot and cold offerings. It was some way off. Maxi came into view.

"Can I bring you something?"

Given my enclosed situation, what did he have in mind? I mumbled that I would quite like to be with the others. He looked doubtfully at the distant gathering. I wobbled over. They sat. I stood. As the crew ate, I stared out at the flatness. We shot until the sun was gone.

They began to gently unhinge me from the suit. I almost fell to the ground, squatting down, bending my knees for the first time in eight hours. Sitting was a forgotten luxury – peeing, too. Wiping my face. Breathing easily. None of these simplicities had been possible for so many hours. I remember gently weeping, unobserved, at the range of emotional and physical assaults on my body and mind. Without any real guidance, I had been required to offer up an acceptable performance of – to say the least – an unusual character. I had probably made a complete fool of myself. Without feedback, I felt my performance must have seemed ridiculous. And I had been locked away from human society and tormented – unintentionally. In my shower, I was shocked to see the wealth of cuts and scrapes and bruises on my skin – in some very sensitive places. I wished my cell-like room had a bathtub to soak my aching limbs.

It had been a long time since breakfast but I can't remember what I ate that night – the chicken, or the fish. I don't think I had much appetite.

This had only been Day One.

Perhaps I should have been a lawyer.


# 8 object

We were bumping along in the dark again.

The dog still lay there, gently rotting. Mark and I shared notes on our experiences so far. It seemed his room had a bathtub. Of course he'd let me borrow it tonight, to soak away the strains of the day. The gloom gradually lightened around us as we started to rehearse each other's lines. How could Mark say such rubbish with a straight face?

"Your lines aren't any better."

"But I'm hidden behind a mask. Nobody knows it's me saying them."

Prophetic words.

Back in my caravan, the nurse put plasters on my worst abrasions from the day before. Then the team and I returned to the struggle that was getting dressed up. It took nearly as long to complete the task as the day before. I asked plaintively, and they did break me out for lunch – a welcome relief – even though the dressing struggle had to be endured again, afterwards. Those six months spent creating my remarkable out-fit clearly hadn't been quite enough.

Various parts of the costume didn't fit each other. Various pieces didn't fit me. But I'd signed on for the duration, and Maxi became ingenious with tape and padding. As time moved on and pain levels continued to build, I grew more and more protective of my damaged skin, he remained a calm, and patient, and kind companion. He was meticulous in the way that he cared for the costume, and for me. I know I wasn't an easy ride.

They constructed a leaning board, a device employed on shoots of a historical nature to help folks in crinolines and fancy robes take the weight off their feet – a sort of padded ironing board with arm rests. The whole thing was angled backwards from the foot plate. A kind gesture, but eventually I found that the weight of the costume still bore down on my ankles. It would have been a lot kinder to undress me between set-ups but that would have taken too long. And by now, it was evident that my glamour factor had totally worn away. I was no longer an object of admiration. I was just an object. Perhaps, I contributed to the phenomenon by barely moving when we weren't shooting. I stood silent and still to conserve my energy and avoid pinching myself. It was understandable that people forgot me and treated Threepio as an inan-imate object. Weeks later, at a studio party, I distributed shiny black matchbooks. I certainly didn't want to encourage smoking. The books were the medium for my message – in gold lettering.

### 3PO IS HUMAN!

They were snatched up. Nothing changed.

Ironic that I would go on to write an anti-smoking spot for the US Health Department – Threepio catching Artoo with a cigarette. Typical.

But before that…

EXT. SANDCRAWLER - DAY.

CUT!

This wasn't the first time.

George came up close. His angry face stared straight into Threepio's. And mine. It was hard not to feel that his ire was directed at me. Of course it wasn't. It was aimed at the fragile connection that joined the eyes – in the mask's face – to the six-pack of batteries below Threepio's shoulders; that same pack that was to give me a problem too, years later. Since the eyes were mounted in the face section, they had to be connected at the last moment to the small plug attached to the battery wires. These needed to be in place before Maxi and Co closed the back to the chest piece. In several shots in the finished movie, I was shocked to see them dangling outside Threepio's head.

He's standing by the sandcrawler, boasting about his ability with Bocce and vaporators, and Luke is whingeing about going to Tosche Station. Maxi was probably being rushed to get me ready at the time. In his haste he hadn't threaded the wires up inside the back. He connected them on the outside, assuming no one would notice the brown wiring sticking out. Back then, audiences didn't have time to study each frame of film. The movie whizzed by as a whole. No one could pore over every moment, no matter how many times they went to the cinema. Video had barely arrived and Blu-ray was science fiction.

But now George's eyes peered through the centre of Threepio's photo-receptors and straight into mine. I felt his frustration at another wasted take and further delays. It wasn't personal. But it seemed like it.

There were many subsequent hold-ups, as bits fell off my arms – or a leg suddenly burst open and I hobbled to a halt. The suit was certainly more fragile than was intended. But never as fragile as me. The arms were made of tougher stuff – hand-beaten metal in the style of medieval armour. They looked fully functional with their motivating pistons. Of course it was me, motivating the arm, motivating the greebly – not the other way round. The hazard for me was at the elbow and under my arm. Here, the metal edges caught my skin and scissored it painfully – or caught me between the upper tube and the shoulder hole. Ouch! Every time I knew I was going to make a dramatic arm gesture, I would wince in advance.

As if that helped.


## 9 control

We had finished the shot outside the sandcrawler.

Threepio had been sold off by the Jawas and I was following my new master – Master Luke. Now I was walking some distance in the suit, for the first time. There had been no rehearsal period. I was making it up, improvising on film, exploring the limitations and possibilities of my outfit as the camera rolled. It was a steep learning curve. I already felt I was a disaster, by fluffing my lines about moisture vaporators. I had peed-off the director on day one. I didn't want to trip up in my new plastic pants and fall flat on my face, as well.

I managed to arrive at Uncle Owen's domed home without incident. Mark skipped down the steps into the interior. The interior was not quite what it looked from the exterior. The natural phenomenon that was the water table, a vast reservoir, lay just a few feet below the sandy surface. There was no standing room. Once out of sight, Mark had to squat down on duck-boards, trying to keep his feet dry.

The gold droid had been sad when Luke and Owen bought the red one, and not the blue. Kenny Baker, the diminutive actor, cast to animate some of Artoo's scenes, wobbled inside the unit as soon as Red exploded. Threepio quickly suggested that the two humans should purchase the blue droid. So Kenny was swapped out, and now I waited for the mechanical, remote controlled unit to trundle forward and join me at the dome entrance. It rolled up.

EXT. TATOOINE – LARS HOMESTEAD – AFTERNOON

ACTION!

"Now don't you forget this. Why I should stick my neck out for you is quite beyond my capacity."

I turned, as if to go down the steps into the dome. I stopped on my end mark, at the top. Threepio does not do stairs. Had I continued, it would have been a huge risk to my kneecaps and other parts.
CUT!

I heard them yell from the camera some fifty yards away, where the crew member stood, thumbing Artoo's remote control. Maybe he couldn't see. Later, I would ask to have a go at driving the unit. It was much harder than I thought – which certainly explained what happened next. A heavy thump from behind, against my legs. I was suddenly being rear-ended by my counterpart. Our first scene together and it was trying to kill me. I braced myself against its rather powerful motors. I didn't want it to be destroyed by crashing down the stairs. Perhaps more important was my sense of self-preservation. They ran the fifty yards and found the off switch. We tried again.
ACTION!

"Why I should stick my neck out for you is quite beyond my capacity."

I turned, took a pace, and stopped. Artoo didn't.
CUT!

Its motors whined in distress, as I prevented us tumbling over and down. They ran. They found the switch. I got the idea. For the third time, I said the line, took a pace towards the drop, then turned and politely ushered Artoo ahead of me. He stopped... dead on his mark.
CUT!

Standing by the sandcrawler was one thing.

Walking away was quite another. I was definitely in learning mode when I strode across the flat land after my new master. Perhaps "strode" is a bit of an exaggeration. With the suit adding a load of around sixty pounds, I became aware of my increased weight and the strange new forces exerting themselves around my body. The torso made me top-heavy. I needed to adjust to the combined weight distribution of my costume and body. Walking normally, shifting the top weight from side to side, gave the character a rather threatening style – lumbering like a monster. Years later, I would meet Robert Kinoshita. Back in the fifties, he'd designed Robby the Robot for the movie, *Forbidden Planet*. He spoke of his disappointment that his creation had come to life with a Frankenstein gait. I was so pleased that such a professional artist had understood what I had tried to do with Threepio's bearing.

As filming continued, I had realised that a more considered gait would add something to the character. I developed a kind of geisha shuffle, Threepio's forearms pointing forward. This had benefits. My feet were always reassuringly in contact with the planet's surface. I felt slightly more secure in my physically challenging world. Fortunately, my core strength helped me keep stiff and upright. The projected arms shifted my centre of gravity forward over my feet. It helped me balance. The pose also implied a kind of servitude. Threepio looked friendly, harmless and ever ready to be of service. Ultimately his stance was as if perpetually carrying a tea tray.

I soon found that I could only turn my head about twenty degrees from the centre. Looking sideways was a problem, an impossibility, without always twisting from the waist or revolving on my feet. I worked out that turning my torso in preparation, gave me an extra twenty degrees. Adding the two together gave me more options.

In the finished film, Ben Burtt provided a further element – noises. During filming, my suit made all sorts of irrelevant squeaks and bangs and groans. If it sounded bad on the outside, the cacophony was uncomfortably well amplified for me on the inside. I learned to ignore the noises I was creating. It didn't really matter if it intruded on anyone's dialogue. The other actors would later be revoicing their roles, in the more controlled environment of a dubbing studio.

George liked everyone's dialogue to be separated. No overlaps. It allowed him to keep control. But no one in my life waits for me to finish a sentence. I certainly don't. In post, I would eventually offer to slip in "shutting up, sir" inside Uncle Owen's lines. It seemed the right thing to do.

In post too, Ben gave Threepio servo motors. A member of his team devotedly watched all Threepio's footage. Each movement got its own sound effect. Walking – zer, zer, zer. Head turns – zih, zih, zik. Hand movements – well, listen to the film and you can work it out. But each sound was created by Ben and added by hand, all contributing to Threepio's believability.

As I followed Luke Skywalker in my clunky outfit, I noticed his neat shoes, custom-made from the softest doeskin, topped by folds of sand-defeating cotton bands, the gentle texture of his creamy pants and tunic, carelessly draped across his frame, his blond hair ruffled by his easy progress across the sand. He looked as though he felt relaxed – comfortable. And me?

I felt envy.

# 11 tricks

It was barely a town.

Like an invading army, the production had unloaded the assorted baggage of crew and equipment needed to bring the Twentieth Century to this ancient world. Umbrellas to shield us from the sun, reflectors to move the sun around, lamps to light the shadows, boards to smooth the way. Droids. Cameras. Food. Water. Styrene cups. Mars Bars. Most of the many loads borne by teams of patiently enslaved donkeys. They had already trudged us up a mountain to look down at Mos Eisley far, far below. And hauled us down again. Now our braying caravan had arrived in Mos Eisley Central to be unburdened. It was an extraordinary juxtaposition of ancient and modern. Techno running on primitive. Not till the Ewoks' triumph over the stormtroopers would such a contrast be manifest. But no one had heard of Ewoks back then.

Having nothing to do for a while, I wandered off, down the gritty street, exploring. This was a real village but there wasn't much to attract the eye of a passing stranger like me. An all-purpose store with a myriad of domestic necessities piled in dusty heaps. A butcher's shop – its wares loudly buzzed by flies. Days before, I had ridden on a camel. Not the loveliest experience – for me or the camel. It spat. Here was less of a threat. A row of its brethren's severed heads hung from hooks, silent in the window. They looked so calm in repose. Their long, languid eyelashes the envy of any Hollywood film star. I didn't linger. But I was in an antique land. The clutter of oasis life against the bright blue skyline of this bizarre place. Some of the clutter was ours. A strange plastic creature was immobile in the unforgiving glare. It was a dewback. It was ours. The Cantina was Ahmed's.

It was at the far end of the fly-blown road. Dome-shaped, in keeping with much of the local architecture, it was bleached and weather-worn, as was Ahmed. He stood proudly outside. This was the bit we were going to film, the outside. It was his family home. But today, for us, it was the Cantina exterior.

We smiled at each other. His grinning friends crowded around. He was obviously a popular man. We managed a passable conversation in a smattering of common words and gestures. I think I understood Ahmed. His enthusiasm and fascination with our visit from another planet was evident. He was personally in contact with a techno-world he could only have dreamed of. He was very happy – particularly so, since he was receiving rent for the use of his home. The film production was paying him location fees. Eight dollars a day, in local currency. I was appalled. It was a rip-off.

No.

The producer, Gary Kurtz, patiently explained the socio-economic effects of paying location fees above the local rate. First, inflation would eat at any savings the villagers had set aside. Secondly, it would jeopardise future film location work as a source of national income.

Thirdly, my smiling new friend would be a wealthy man during our visit. It would dramatically improve his social status. But he risked losing his place in the natural order of local society. Once we departed, the income stream would dry up. He would find it hard to readjust to normality. So – far from being mean and tight-fisted, they were being kind, generous and responsible by paying Ahmed eight dollars a day.

At the other end of the street, the famed landspeeder was baking in the sun. A fact I didn't realise until I took my position and sat on the back. My uncostumed rear instantly overheated. I got off again. Fast. Some foam padding helped. I perched myself next to the Artoo shell, which was firmly strapped to the back. I steadied myself with my ungloved left hand. The other was in gold and, therefore, fairly useless.

This was my first ride. I'd been amused to see the speeder parked, as if hovering, its supporting leg hidden behind Artoo or a convenient rock. I had already watched Mark being quaintly swung into shot on a scaffold arm, as if on some cheap fairground roundabout – the camera artfully ignoring the manpower crew pushing at the other end. This was the real thing. This was horsepower. Sort of.

Sir Alec and Mark were in front. I gathered that we were sitting in, and on, a converted three-wheeler car. Its original incarnation was as a "Bond Bug" – a bargain form of self-transport in the 1970s. The light-weight body had been replaced by a more sturdy shell. But the chassis was just as fragile as before. I was interested to see what a ride on the speeder would feel like. I noticed a piece of carpet pinned beneath the rear. I imagined that this old rug had something to do with the rather battered appearance of everything in the movie. In contrast, the long, thin mirrors were sparkly clean. They fringed the bottom edge of the car, on the driver's side – the camera's side, to my right.

Finally, everyone seemed to be standing by for a take. I removed my sunglasses and was bolted into the ultimate sunscreen that was Three-pio's head. The crowd artists hovered on their start marks. The camera crew watched and waited. The inhabitants of this archaic world paused to look. Ahmed watched and smiled, anticipating the techno-miracle about to happen. After Sir Alec had pulled off a Jedi mind trick, we were on our way.

EXT. TATOOINE – MOS EISLEY – STREET – DAY

ACTION!

Mark gripped the steering wheel. I noticed it was on the right. Good – in the unlikely event that it would ever again be driven on a British road. But now, no gentle rising up from the ground. Just a throaty grumble. I had the sensation of being stuck in a traffic jam. Funnelled by the ancient rug, exhaust fumes streamed up and into Threepio's small rectangular mouth. I blew them out and nearly fell off the back of the now lurching speeder. Mark had found second gear. I managed to grab Obi-Wan's seatback but Mark accidentally hit the brakes. I shot forward, heading for a soft landing in the Jedi Master's lap. I steadied myself as, unrestrained in second gear, Mark steered us round the corner and we swept down the street.

There they were. The camera, the crew, the crowd artists and locals and Ahmed – all marvelling at our peculiar progress. I was precariously perched over the throbbing exhaust and hovering was not at all the smooth experience I'd imagined. The vehicle's frail suspension echoed every rut and bump on the planet's surface. The fumes were still getting up my nose as the old rug, trailing in the dirt, brushed out our tyre tracks, but we were making progress. Not for long.

I thought Mark must have found the brakes again, as we slowed in the centre of the street. But this wasn't in the script. We weren't even within smelling range of the Cantina. Mark wrestled the gently coughing vehicle to a hiccupping stop. My lungs breathed the clear desert air. Silence. Charlie rushed in with a jerry can. Our landspeeder was clean out of fuel.

Of course, we did it again until we got it right. The magic had slightly worn away for the onlookers but was finally scuppered when the mirrors fell off. They had been concealing the vehicle's tyres. Using old stagecraft techniques, they reflected the sand in front. The audience's brain would assume it was the sand behind. The landspeeder would appear to defy gravity. Simple magic.

The sun was falling fast as we packed up our umbrellas and reflectors and bits of gold. They watched us go with all our techno-trappings. I think we must have already become a part of their folklore. I waved goodbye to Ahmed. He smiled back. Happy to have met. I suspect, even happier with his eight dollars.

## 12 tears

EXT. TATOOINE - MOS EISLEY - STREET - DAY

ACTION!

"I can't abide these Jawas. Disgusting creatures!"

But the gang of Jawas gave me some kind of distraction from my own costume problems. Their tiny, monk-like shapes would scuttle busily around, trying to act mean. This effect was sometimes thwarted by the rather random behaviour of their eyes, caused by their design.

A battery pack around the waist was connected to two torch bulbs, attached to wires on their wool-covered faces. Trouble was that the flimsy wires kept shifting. So, so did their eyes. Many a take was cut midway because Jawa Number Five looked a little wonky, with one eye shining off the end of her nose. An endearing look, but just not menacing enough. The odd disconnection would cause Number Three to go monocular during scenes, while a flat battery made it seem that Number One was gently nodding off. But the real problem with Jawas was something else entirely.

Some Jawas were little people. Several were children. They were thrilled to be playing dressing-up. They excitedly put on their battery packs, their monk-like habits, bandoleers, woolly face masks and torchbulb eyes. They urgently pulled the thick wool cowls up over their heads. They were ready for anything.

The sun was high as we started the scene. We filmed it again to avoid the rather blatant wink of Jawa Number Three. We did it again because a bit of my costume fell off. We did it again, since I nearly fell over a Jawa who was out of position because she suddenly couldn't see. We did it many times. I was hot and uncomfortable. As usual. In a pause between takes, there was a sound. Nearby. A sort of sniffle – a kind of sob. I lurched nearer. Yes. It was a Jawa. Crying. It's very hard to give comfort to anyone when you're wearing layers of metal and plastic, but I tried.

"What's the matter?"

I mumbled sympathetically in the direction of the woolly, sobbing face mask and fading light bulbs. They gave a random flicker, as if of deep sadness. A voice muffled back.

"It's hot! And I hate it!"

I sidled closer, sharing that I knew how it felt, and that it would all be over very soon. I tried to put a comforting metallic arm around the trembling heap of wool. It was slightly below my reach. Given that, and my limited vision, my kindly gesture became a sort of karate chop across its left ear. I don't think I can have helped much.

"I don't wanna be a Jawa anymore!" it wailed.

But now I was just watching.

The Jawas had zapped Artoo and hoisted him in the air, to carry him back to the sandcrawler, like pall-bearers at a rather bizarre funeral. The original gang had been expanded. There were still some children but others were older actors, who weren't going to grow any taller. Mustapha was 16 years old. He was the smallest, destined to stay tiny for all his life but he had a huge, delightful personality. He dressed up with the others, his monk-like robe brushing the ground at his tiny feet.

As rehearsed, the gang hoisted Artoo and carried him off, each lending a helping hand. Except Mustapha. He tried. He stretched both his hands in the air towards the now moving load, just beyond his reach. He followed. He reached again. He gamely followed the cortege, trying to participate. And then I noticed something strange. Mustapha was growing smaller. As the others moved ahead, he came to a sort of swaying stop. Held by an invisible force.

His tiny feet had caught the trailing hem of his costume. He had walked up the inside of the flowing robe so far, that they had reached the battery pack at his waist which stopped him in his tracks. He crouched there powerless and abandoned. His torch-bulb eyes flickering with a wounded bewilderment.

The truth is, I am rather fond of Jawas.

EXT. TATOOINE - WASTELAND - DAY

So it hurt a little, when I had to dump a few dead ones on the fire – fake dead ones, of course. Principally it hurt because, with my limited sight, I was unable to see my own feet. I walked into the flames. Fortunately, Maxi's sight was fine. He was watching out for me. As ever.

# 13 damage

EXT. TATOOINE - ROCK CANYON - RIDGE - DAY

Threepio and Luke out searching for the absconding astromech, Luke scanning the terrain with his binocs, Threepio peering from behind. Suddenly. A fearsomely masked Tusken Raider rears into vision. Luke is startled. So is Threepio. He falls off the cliff. Luke is left to battle the Raider and his gruesome gaffi stick. He survives. But something is missing – his golden new friend.

EXT. TATOOINE - SAND PIT - ROCK MESA - DAY

Mark and the camera found me lying on the desert floor. Attentive audiences would have noted the new detail on Threepio's head. Where a human would have suffered a nasty bump, Threepio's left temple had a painful dent, with another on his chin and some painful scratches along the jaw line, all beautifully conceived and executed by the Art Department.

But it wasn't only the head that was damaged. His left arm was detached. Completely. It lay on the sand, some feet away.

The golden chest piece, with one half the neck ring, was strapped to my body. There was no back panel, no other half of the neck. I clung onto the straps, with my spare arm twisted up behind me, out of shot.

Where Threepio's left arm should have been, was a prosthetic prop – an early glimpse of his inner workings, the totality of which would be revealed some thirty years later. At this point it was a heavy metal ball and socket and wires, all attached to the shoulder of the chest piece. The prop was so heavy it dragged the chest sideways and down, opening a space between me and the half neck. The other piece of neck was attached to the unused back plate. Now the camera could see my black cotton hood. So they piled sand into the space to disguise the costume failure. And more sand. Some of it sidled underneath. It felt horrible, trickling down inside.

Mark helped me to sit up in shot. Maxi helped too, as I did a stomach-crunching sit-up. Off camera, he was holding down my feet, on account that my top half weighed rather more than usual. However, what worried me most, was that Sir Alec moved closer to help me up off the sand. I was concerned that a Knight of the Realm, and all round rather terrific person, was helping me to stand. He might not foresee the danger in holding Threepio's right arm – that he could get his fingers caught in the brutal metalwork of my costume.

I now sat with my legs crossed. As Mark and Sir Alec helped me up, I scissor–lifted myself, lifting my own weight. In the final edit, George transitioned many scenes with rather old-fashioned wipes. Left. Right. Diagonal. Here, the scene wiped upwards, with my waistband. Otherwise you would have seen my spindly legs, dressed in less-than-elegant black tights. That day, I was only droid from the waist up.

Earlier, I had felt rather concerned when they wanted to dress someone else in the whole gold suit for the fall. They were taking away a part of my role. No. It was a health and safety issue. They were just being cautious. If I did the stunt, I could be severely hurt. I would be unable to continue filming. Of course they were worried for my safety. But possibly more worried about the shooting schedule that any accident might jeopardise. So I helped them dress Jim Marlow from Props, who'd volunteered. I think he'd volunteered. He was about my size – and plucky.

EXT. TATOOINE – ROCK CANYON – RIDGE – DAY

ACTION!

Dressed in the Tusken Raider's costume of a Sand Person, Peter Diamond attacked. Mark parried. Jim fell back. But then. No spectacular screaming free-fall to a death, hundreds of feet down, no blood dripping from tangled joints, no ominous silence from the wreckage. Just a backwards lean of about twenty degrees, out of camera shot and onto a soft mattress and boxes at his feet. Of course Jim was unhurt. I could have done that. But it was nice that they were protective of my health. Or was it that they really needed me in one piece for longer.

I took a look through the Raider's head piece. Amazing. Peter could barely see daylight down the tube eyepieces with their distorting lenses, just vague shapes out of focus. Yet how viciously he had wielded his gaffi stick in the brutal attack. How energetically Mark had writhed and parried from his prone position on the mattresses, that softened the rock surface beneath him. It looked brutal but, being a skilled stunt performer, Peter had managed not to actually mangle Mark to a paste.

I will never know how.

I stood deep amongst the sand dunes, near the apparently crashed vessel – the escape pod.

Props had shovelled my "footsteps" down, away from the pod into the depression below. Maxi and Co had dressed me up as usual. Then they abandoned me, brushing out their footprints as they backed away to the very distant camera. At my side, Props had placed an empty Artoo shell on skis, attached to a long piano wire which disappeared into the haze, towards the crew.

I was alone. Except I had to believe I wasn't by myself. I had to believe in the relationship that I was improvising with my counterpart beside me. If I didn't believe, neither would the audience. Time passed. My eyes wandered away from the crew, still fiddling with their camera. I turned to survey this truly desolate environment that stretched to infinity. A slight breeze whistled soullessly around me. I felt somehow isolated, forsaken.

Suddenly. Close by.

A ragged robed figure stared at me. His sun-hardened face, rigid with disbelief. A local. A real sand person. I felt a momentary sting of panic. But now, he absorbed back into the dunes – he was gone. A startling encounter. For both of us. I turned back. They were waving at me from the camera. And shouting.

EXT. TATOOINE – DESERT

ACTION!

Someone was pulling the piano wire. Artoo moved a little way, before the skis dug themselves into the soft sand surface. The wire snapped. He stopped. I trudged a few paces, wondering what my visitor must have thought. Perhaps, back with his people, he was telling of his encounter with a golden god. They would have thought he was mad. CUT!

EXT. TATOOINE - DESERT

ACTION!

"I've got to rest before I fall apart. I'm almost frozen."

It was only a slight exaggeration. But it had been a long time. Long. I'd expected the desert location to be sizzling. Today, it was witheringly cold. The chill wind found easy access to my body through the metal and fibreglass components of the suit. My underwear gave little protection. The crew in anoraks and goggles, me in tights and tin.

The delay was due to the challenge of getting two tottering droids up into shot, from behind a pile of sand. I could almost do it – Artoo certainly couldn't. Concealed floorboards now flattened the shifting surface. But still Artoo's motors weren't powerful enough to drive upwards. Its rubber wheels simply couldn't get enough traction. They were also stuffed with sand, swirling around us, underfoot and in the air.

We eventually got the scene, the problem solved with a length of ever-useful piano wire; me trudging up as they hauled Artoo alongside. Reaching the top, they had parked another unit over to my right; a little confusing for me but easier than trying to get one to move there on its own. And all the time, the dunes seemed alarmingly to shapeshift around us in the breeze – all grey skies and eerie and difficult. But not as difficult as talking to myself. In the script, Artoo and Threepio were always nattering to each other. But, apart from the whirring of its motors, the unit was silent. Speechless. Back there in the dunes, I admitted I was finding it challenging, to have a one-sided conversation with something supposed to be my best friend. Could George, or anyone, make a sound in response to my lines? A beep, or something, to make it more real for me – George?

"Oh. Err. Shurr."

We began again.

EXT. TATOOINE - DESERT

ACTION!

"Where are you going?"

A long pause. George.

"Oh. Err... BEEP."

I didn't bother him again.

From then on, I learned the dialogues in their entirety, writing in Artoo's responses, as I imagined them. Eventually seeing the finished film a year later was a revelation, a rewriting of history, a changing of the facts, as I knew them. Artoo in full-on conversational repartee mode, beeping, whistling, groaning – blowing raspberries.

I know Ben Burtt. He showed me the inexpensive electronic keyboard he played to create Artoo's articulate sounds. Pure genius. But, genius on genius, he added his own whistling and his infant son's sighs and gurgles to the mix. Those human sounds added so much to the belief that Artoo was a living thing, with a vibrant personality. How different from my on-set experience. I sat in the audience, entranced by the conversation that seemed so real. Movie magic – rightly winning Ben an Oscar.

Back in the gritty, chill sand dunes, it had taken ages to set up the shot. It was really cold and my frustration was growing as the minutes passed. It was almost as though the scriptwriters had known this in advance. The kick that I eventually aimed at Artoo's shins, was done with feeling. But it didn't sound like anything. Ben later added a more satisfying Clunk. It felt good.

A sadness.

The next day, we received the terrible news that Liz Moore had been killed in a car crash. A senseless loss beyond words. It fills me with a real sadness that she died before ever seeing her creation come alive on film – to become such a beloved and iconic figure around the planet. We all leave this world eventually. Artists can only hope to retain a kind of immortality in the work they leave behind. The Star Child. Threepio. They are immortal.

I will always remember Liz as a most beautiful and kind and creative soul.

## 16 tensions

We were leaving the uncompromising desert for the comparative normality of a British studio.

Our Tunisian experience hadn't been easy. For anyone. Not just me. So many things seemed to go awry. The weather had been an ever-changing factor. One day heat, next day cold, next windy. One time, as I stood there in costume, they held a large umbrella over me. I said thank you, but I wasn't hot. They pointed out it was raining – hard to tell inside Threepio's head.

It got worse. I wasn't there to see the Tunisian Army trying to haul our vehicles out of the mud. A once-in-thirty-years deluge got them stuck as well. And the sets were mangled by the rain and the wind.

You had to tolerate the sand, since there was no escape. But it certainly messed with anything mechanical, especially the motorised droids. Frequently, a take had to be abandoned because of the erratic driving of some beautifully designed machine. Beautiful, but not made for this terrain. And the whole shoot had been jeopardised by unusual weather patterns, which were extremely unkind to the schedule. But there were other problems.

I began to sense that there were communication issues. At heart, the crew didn't seem to understand George's vision. I was new to film making, so didn't know what to expect. Anyway, once George had simply told me where to start and where to end up, he left me alone to do my own thing, as he stood next to the camera. But behind the camera there seemed to be growing tensions.

Gil Taylor was the very British DOP, Director of Photography, an important person on set, directing the lighting and camera crews to give a film its visual quality, its look. Gil was hugely experienced in the film industry. He'd shot with Roman Polanski and Stanley Kubrick. He was extremely competent and immensely likeable – an old–fashioned gentleman. But there was something that clearly wasn't working for him on this production. I was picking up a sort of tetchiness towards him from George. And I began to see, and indeed hear, discussions about the look of the whole film that bordered on argument. As far as I was concerned, George was the director and, in my book, it was what he wanted that mattered. Gil clearly thought otherwise.

I watched as they set up the shot where the Jawas would suck Artoo up into the sandcrawler. I learned that they would actually drop the unit down and then reverse the film. I loved the ingenuity of it all. But standing below the crawler in the dusky light, the tensions were palpable. Suddenly Gil boiled over. He didn't appreciate the direction and advice he was receiving from the much younger American, Gary Kurtz. The conversation escalated with him asking, who was lighting the film – him or Gary? If it was him, would the producer please go away. I discreetly moved aside. The expletive-heavy exchange was unforgettable. I never imagined that you could talk to a producer like that. Years later, I would find that Gil wasn't the only professional who didn't like being told how to do his job by Gary.

For the most part, other tensions were kept in check, often by the gentlemanly demeanour of the First Assistant Director, Anthony Way. He was rather like a Head Boy at a posh English school. But the British crew were clearly fazed by the way the film was being directed.

The Americans were obviously used to doing things differently. I did things differently, too.

I learned they often needed to adjust my height for various shots. They would bring me a small wooden box – a "quarter apple", or higher, a "half apple" – to stand on. I quickly got the idea. Peering from the camera's position, I could work out what was needed. One day, I picked up a quarter apple, stacked nearby where we were filming.

Tony Way looked at me and smiled.

"You work in the theatre, don't you?"

He explained that it simply wasn't protocol for me to move my own apple box – quarter or not. That was the job of a union member of the crew. I suddenly recalled, as a stagehand cleaning half the enormous stage of the Drury Lane Theatre in London, being warned by a fellow union member not to mop so fast. I needed to slow down, my mopping union colleague pointed out, or we'd never go into overtime. But here, I was shocked again. I hadn't wanted to bother anyone, by asking them to do something so simple, that I could do for myself. In the sort of shows I'd been in, we just got on with the small practicalities. Next time, I followed Tony's advice. But I still have to suppress my DIY instincts.

So far, we had all been on an alien shore. But now we were back to England – back at Elstree where Threepio was born. Glad to be away from the desert, I felt quite at home at the studio. But now there was another problem. It was the weather. Again.

Newly returned from Tunisia, the chill air of England was quite refreshing and sand-free. Then, suddenly, everything changed. As filming continued inside the stages, outside began to boil. 1976 became the second-hottest year on record. Day after day the sun blazed down. With little air-conditioning, the buildings, already storing heat from the previous day's onslaught, became ovens. The roads became tar pits. As reservoirs began to dry up, the authorities rationed water and put stand-pipes in the streets. And me – I was in a sound stage, no air-con, huge stage lamps competing to throw out more heat than the sun itself – and me – in a tight fibreglass suit. It was horrible.

Less horrible – Wardrobe had remembered to give me back my dressing gown. The long, towelling robe was a pleasant creamy colour. I certainly didn't need it to keep warm. But it was a more modest outfit in which to wander about than my black tights and wire patches, which it covered up.

And at least I had somewhere to sit. Chairs are at a premium on a film set, unless you're a producer or director or a star. But they gave me one anyway. You see them in films about films, normally set in Hollywood studios; simple cross-legged canvas affairs, the name in question painted on a sort of canvas sleeve that fits over the back. And there was one with my name. I was hugely impressed and surprised – such kudos! I sat in it and immediately saw a paradox. The mere act of sitting rendered me anonymous, as I covered my name behind me. Standing next to it rather defeated the original purpose. But it was all rather irrelevant. Once on set I would be quickly called to dress up – and remain so for much of the day. Now, wearing the gold armour, the chair was immaterial, an empty thing. But I still enjoyed seeing it. Then, suddenly, it was gone.

I made enquiries of a stagehand. He willingly went off to solve the mystery. Back soon, he'd found out that Anthony Daniels had never shown up, so they'd assigned his chair to someone else. Subsequent enquiries revealed that the UK crew had not associated me, or my name, with the gold robot. Obviously, they couldn't recognise me in the suit and, since my dressing gown looked slightly like Obi-Wan's robe, they had assumed I was Sir Alec's stand-in.

Whereas Mark and I used to hang out together quite often in the desert locations, here there were other chairs – other names – Harrison Ford and Carrie Fisher in particular. Americans. I had no idea who they were. But they were very friendly and seemed to know what they were doing. In fact, I was rather awed by their ease in front of the camera. I was still learning. I had read their roles in the script and could see the dynamics of their characters coming to life on set, relating to each other, to me, to Threepio. And of course to Chewbacca.

Here was Peter Mayhew joining the cast. His handmade, yak-hair costume looked comfortably floppy, but being brushed into a hair and latex headpiece can't have been fun. His black eye-makeup needed to be waterproof, as he gently steamed inside.

Inside my costume was like standing in a slow-running warm shower. Sweat cascaded in seeping dribbles down to my toes. Whenever they agreed to take off the face, I must have made an embarrassingly unattractive sight. How I envied the human cast in their costumes, made of more forgiving stuff than my own – Mark in his cotton tunic, Carrie in cooling white, Harrison in a shirt. And they were primped and coiffed to look good all day. I looked cooked.

Hot or not, most of us were back on home turf.

But some issues had returned with us on the charter flight from the desert.

The crew had grown much larger. The tensions were there still, and mounting fast. I had heard the phrase, "pull the plug". Now I saw it in action on the set. We usually wrapped – finished up – at five in the afternoon. It must have been hard to judge how long a scene would take to shoot, and sometimes we went over. This had to be with the agreement of the union-heavy crew. In the slightly negative atmosphere that was growing, they were not always predisposed to be helpful.

I was shocked when the lights went out and we had to leave a scene that, but for a few more minutes' work, was very nearly complete. The plug had been pulled. Of course, it reduced the heat output on set, but the evening air still stifled me on the way home. And I wasn't even wearing the suit. Or my robe.

59

INT. DEATH STAR - FORWARD BAY - COMMAND OFFICE

As per the script, the door flew up and Obi-Wan, Luke, Han, Artoo and I quickly entered the room, which was painted, in my opinion, a rather nasty shade of cerise. Apart from that, it was quite impressive – consoles, and knobs, and switches, and a cupboard. That would come in useful later as a hidey-hole for the two droids. But before that, there was a little accident.

Unfortunately, when the door flew up, my astromech counterpart raced across the room and belted the console. He was scripted to inter-face with a computer terminal, not bash the thing up. But the control desk was made of sturdy plywood and easily withstood this unprovoked frontal assault. Artoo definitely came off second best.

I assumed his new-found energy was due to overcharged batteries. Whatever the reason, this unit was not going anywhere today. His severely dented front panels meant that they had to search out a replace-ment model. So we relaxed while Oscar-winning special effects supremo John Stears and crew got one up to speed – actually less speedy, perhaps, than the one that had just limped off set. But John knew exactly what he was doing. He'd invented Artoo in the first place and this wasn't the first time there had been technical hitches. To be fair, I'd had a go with Artoo's remote controls and nearly crashed it myself. It was not easy.

Time passed and we waded through the scene before it suddenly got interesting. Obi-Wan was leaving on his heroic mission – he needed to open the door again. "The door flew up," was a bit of an exaggeration. But what is the thing with doors and *Star Wars*? I have never actually counted the number of door designs in the Saga. Some go up, some down, others sideways. On occasion, they move in a four-piece scissor attack. But I think that, in all those miles of film, there is not one single, simple door that opens inward or outward merely at the turn of a knob.

INT. DEATH STAR – FORWARD BAY – COMMAND OFFICE

ACTION!

The silver-grey surface of the door shuddered. Then it trudged reluctantly upward.

CUT!

A peek round the back of the set showed that the door-drive was Charlie. He was holding the end of a rope which ran over a pulley. On the other end was the piece of silver ply that was the door. A hefty chap, Charlie's strength still couldn't raise the lump of wood fast enough to satisfy George's vision. So George considered. His master plan is best observed as Obi-Wan finally left the scene.

ACTION!

Obi-Wan approached the door. He put his finger on the door-opener button.

FREEZE!

The Jedi Master didn't move.

DOOR!

The door slowly rose up and finally socketed into the ceiling.

ACTION!

Obi-Wan removed his finger, turned and walked through the resulting gap in the wall.

DOOR!

The door fell back into place – greatly assisted by the gravitational forces at Elstree. I would eventually learn what happened next. Real movie magic. There are 24 frames in each second of standard film stock. Months later, George's team carefully removed every other frame from the exposed footage. This left just 12 pictures, out of the original 24, thereby making the filmed door, when projected at normal speed, appear to move at twice the original. Really clever. But not perfect. Something unexpected happened.

The clue to George's trick is seen in Obi-Wan's face. As the door slides swiftly upwards, he remains completely still – except for his eyes. During that sequence, one of England's greatest actors, blinks. Fine. Except that, in the speeding-up process, half his blink was cut out! This suddenly makes for a very surprised expression on those venerable features. As though he had just been invisibly goosed. You don't get that with a door knob. Unless you back into one.

## 18 embarrassments

INT. LARS HOMESTEAD – GARAGE AREA – LATE AFTERNOON

I nervously stood on a small elevator platform, weighted down by my whole costume. It felt rather peculiar, to be lowered into the vat of green-coloured vegetable oil beneath me. Being early in the year and chill in Elstree studios, the crew had thoughtfully warmed it slightly. The effect was not unpleasant as I descended further into the liquid and it slowly, warmly permeated the intimate spaces inside the suit.

The steam rising was not so much the temperature of the oil but the effect of two concealed electric kettles, boiling away behind me. A careful viewer would notice that, after a quick dip, Threepio's left leg was strangely detached from his pants as he rises, Venus-like from the fluid. The sticky tape that was binding the front to the back, had unstuck in the oil. Everything was coming apart. Embarrassing – but not the main embarrassment.

Many years later, a rather unexpected collector's item would appear for sale. The baseball-type card showed Threepio rising from the oil in an unusual state. It transpired that a mischievous employee noticed a fold in the plastic part of the costume, just above where the top of the leg should have been. It was caused by the failure of the tape, allowing my leg to drop down. Very cleverly, if tastelessly, he painted in a quite credible extension. Threepio had never looked so excited.

I have always disapproved of the altered version, which somehow did go into circulation – though it was quickly withdrawn once the offence was discovered. I care less about the poor taste. It's more that it insults and demeans a good friend of mine, who can't speak for himself in this galaxy.

Meanwhile, back in the garage, that same careful viewer might notice the effect on my performance of having no peripheral vision. As the dust contamination slowly eased, I continued the dialogue, a real live dialogue, with my fellow actor, Mark, who was standing to my right. But at some point, I clearly hadn't noticed that he'd moved across the set. He suddenly wasn't there. I was confused. I wondered where he'd gone, as I found myself speaking to a blank wall. I soon found him again over to my left – it wasn't a large set. An unsettling moment, though still not the main embarrassment.

Safely risen from the bath, oil pouring out of my arms, I made the transition out and down to floor level, during an edit cutaway to Luke. Now came the unintentional moment. I had magically acquired a piece of towelling from somewhere. I held it tight and did drying-oneself-after-a-warm-oil-bath acting. I wouldn't see the full effect till later. Understandably, given my sensory deprivation, it was not quite the effect I had intended. That same devoted viewer would notice that Threepio seems to be doing something not normally considered acceptable in polite society. As he courteously talks with his new master, he nonchalantly rubs the towel up and down his "space eroticism".

At least I was sitting down.

You never see that happening in shot. It can't happen. The suit won't let me. So it's always a gesture, as to what I am about to do – then a cutaway – and the camera returns to see me settling into a seat. The audience's imagination provides the in-betweens.

It felt good for a change not to be carrying Threepio's body weight, as well as my own. Maxi had dressed me in the top half of the suit. I sat down. He had a collection of body parts, made of flimsier stuff than the usual bits. He also had a pair of scissors, and some gold and gaffer tape – the latter being the essential glue and cure-all on any film production. He carefully cut and pasted sections of gold around my middle and legs. Ever eager to help, Mark got involved, tearing off pieces of tape and handing them over to Maxi. It was like a congenial sewing bee. There wasn't much I could do but sit there. The results looked convincing, from the camera's point of view. That's all that mattered.

INT. TATOOINE - KENOBI'S DWELLING

ACTION!

"Sir, if you'll not be needing me, I'll close down for a while."

Maxi flicked an external switch he'd rigged earlier. Threepio's eyes went dark. It sounded as though I would have the morning off.

"I seem to have found it."

They were looking into space. Moments before, Props had put a small oil can on the table. Sir Alec and Mark stared at it before it was whisked away. The actors kept gazing at the empty space as they said their lines. Eventually, George would superimpose the classic shot of Carrie's hologram, and Obi-Wan and Luke would be looking right at it. But at the time, there wasn't much to admire, except the strange objects on Obi-Wan's coffee table – weird, trunked, upside-down cups. I asked. Of course – antique silver ear trumpets. Props are ever so inventive.

But I did not get the morning off. I had to sit there while Sir Alec explained about the lightsaber. I remained motionless throughout. It would have been fairly easy were it not for the breathing. Droids don't breathe. Humans do. To survive the numerous takes – it all took quite a while – I really had to give myself a crash course in shallow-breathing techniques.

"Your father's lightsaber."

Sir Alec handed Mark a sort of handle thing. Mark admired it and pressed a button.

FREEZE!

Mark stood very still as a Props person ran in. He slid a stick into the handle and ran out.

ACTION!

Mark waved the stick. It was covered with a reflective coating. Next to the camera was a spotlight. The light bounced off a half-silvered mirror, set at forty-five degrees in front of the lens, straight at the saber. The beam shone off the blade, sending itself straight down through the mirror, back through the lens and onto the film behind it. The lightsaber silently glowed. Movie magic. Until Mark waved it out of the spotlight's beam. Then it was just a stick again.

And all the time I sat there, breathing shallow. It would not be the last time I had to play "switched off".

I remembered Ahmed and his home in that dusty street, a few weeks before.

I bet it didn't look anything like this. I was surveying a particular den in the hive of scum and villainy, from the top of a flight of steps. There were five of them leading down to the bar. Threepio, you might recall, does not do steps. I had rehearsed and counted, counted and rehearsed. Now this was it.

```
INT. TATOOINE - MOS EISLEY - CANTINA
```

ACTION!

Blindly staring ahead, I felt the top step under the sole of my deck shoes. Like a swimmer leaving the security of the pool edge, I allowed myself to fall forward onto the edge below, and below that, and below again. Counting – a miscount would smash Threepio's joints into my kneecaps, breaking both. Counting – all the time, trying not to speed up, to keep control. Counting – until I reached the floor, three seconds later. It seemed an age. Now a relief.

I didn't want to risk it again but George wanted a second take – "for safety".

And there I was with Mark in front of an unlikely collection of bar flies. They'd asked me to recruit my drama-school friends, to perform as alien characters. They wouldn't cost much. I started to phone around. I'd worked with Paul Blake on my first job on television. We'd got on well and he was happy to be involved – potentially. Production called me again. They couldn't afford actors. Crowd artists in rubber heads would have to do. A shame, since there's more to being an alien than wearing rubber. But Paul, I'm glad to say, did make it into the film, as the infamous Greedo. My student friends would have to build their careers from another starting block.

In the end, it didn't matter, since the scene would be partly reshot in California, months later. This time with music. George realised that an alien band number would add considerable dose of whacky-ness, not just new rubber creatures with crazy instruments, but John Williams' beloved music was a glorious extra – once an additional budget had been found. It became an iconic moment in an iconic film – a moment that almost never was.

And here was the moment where the crew adopted another catch-phrase. The arm of the pugnacious thug, who'd been nasty to Luke, lay on the floor, newly severed by the sweep of a Jedi Master's lightsaber. Now the bartender's voice bellowed out the words, which would subse-quently be used to calm any escalating situation on set.

"No blasters!"

I still use the phrase occasionally. People give me a strange look. They weren't there at the time.

For moments, Threepio gazed around the Cantina with Master Luke, but not for long. A medium close-up of the belligerent and heavy-set bartender broke the mood. Like a pro, he had learned his lines.

"We don't serve their kind here. Your droids. They'll have to wait outside."

How cruel – and how funny.

The actor playing our barman friend was obviously not familiar with the sort of vocabulary we were using in this space fantasy. Accord-ing to him, the kind they didn't serve was, "Druids".

Being in this sci-fi film was actually quite interesting.

Being in any film would be interesting to me, at the time. It was my first. Whenever possible, I watched scenes that I wasn't actually in. It helped pass the time and I learned a lot. Here I was observing from a safe spot, well behind the camera. We were staring at a doorway at the end of a squeaky clean white corridor. The crew were all holding plastic shields over their faces. It was already rather dramatic, even though they hadn't started yet. Everyone seemed to be quite tense, especially the Special Effects crew with their pyros, because this was a "live set".

INT. REBEL BLOCKADE RUNNER

ACTION!
BANG!

A really loud one – and I mean loud. At least I could see the cause of the loudness. But people waiting around the fringe of the stage were genuinely shocked, and not in a nice way. So much bang and too much smoke. The pyro charge was perhaps a little stronger than it needed to be. It was only meant to blow the door off. It terrified the bystanders. And the sound would be replaced in post anyway. I would later understand that a certain amount of noise is good – it helps actors react appropriately to explosions. Too silent, and they might not even notice. But this was overkill. Nor was the blast actually intended to mask the arrival of the arch villain, by wreathing him in clouds of dense smoke. It billowed up to the corridor ceiling and down again, rolling towards the camera.

After this experience, it was understandable that I was a little apprehensive, as I stood on one side of a similar corridor. All I had to do was run across to the other side, following Artoo and dodging imaginary blaster fire. Easy. Except that the doorway through which I would run housed a fearsome-looking weapon. It was rather like a wok – a large metal dish pointing outward towards me. I watched them fill it with cork and Fuller's Earth, and explosives. This was the team that nearly wiped out the Dark Lord, before he'd even wagged a finger. I was nervous. They were going to push the button on their bowl of pyros the second I'd gone by. Okay. But what if it were a second too soon? I'd be peppered and blasted, unless I was, for once, paradoxically, protected by my gold suit. It still didn't sound too safe to me.

INT. REBEL BLOCKADE RUNNER

ACTION!

I beetled across the corridor in around three seconds – an eternity of fear. Then the fourth second. I was passing the wok. Pssheeww... I heard the blast. I felt a warm draught. I had survived.

As I write, there is no Oscar or Bafta award for Stunts. There should be. They're often the unsung heroes of any action film. I was slightly heroic myself – once. As Luke and Han prepare to battle with the TIE fighters, Threepio scuttles down a corridor. Cut to the fight in space. Cut to laser fire. Cut to him walking and the explosion that painfully blasts him backwards against the wall.

It wasn't the explosion that hurled me against the wall. It was two hefty Stunts. They were on the other side of the corridor wall, on the far end of pulleys and ropes. These were attached to a wire, running through a hole in the wall and connected, at the back, to a large belt around my waist. They had laid the slack wire out backwards, along the edge of the corridor, to my start mark.

INT. MILLENNIUM FALCON - CORRIDOR

ACTION!

Like a condemned man I walked forward – reluctantly. They gently gathered up the slack until I passed the hole in the wall. I took another step.

Bvisssh!

Cued by the explosion, they yanked the ropes, picking me up off my feet and smashing me hard against the wall, nearly pulling me through it.

CUT! CUT!

Voices yelled in panic. Quickly the crew rushed forward through the smoke. But thank The Maker – the wall was all right!

## 22 trash

Threepio was somewhere else on the Death Star at the time.

That meant I could actually watch the scene being shot. I wanted to see it, because I'd been intrigued, as I walked from my dressing room to various sound stages at Elstree. I had regularly passed a rather fearsome… thing. A mucus-green, suckered tentacle, dressed around a long steel arm that pivoted on a stand. The whole beautifully crafted prop was quite intimidating and very long; something like a limb of the giant squid that menaced in the movie, *20,000 Leagues Under The Sea*. Fine for them – they'd had the whole ocean to play with there. Here, this thing was intended to wreak havoc inside a small and untidy room which, in due course, would get even smaller. There wouldn't be nearly enough room to swing this sucker. So it stayed in the corridor, abandoned – weeks of work, wasted.

Then came idea Number Two. Smaller, ovoid, brown. It wasn't exactly steaming as we stared at it, but George precisely verbalised my own thoughts. This, too, would be abandoned.

Finally, the Art Department came up with something less contentious – a snorkel eyeball thing. This was the dreaded dianoga. Not particularly terrifying, as it popped its eye above the water. But what followed was certainly more interesting.

The crew had opened up the floor in the sound stage and filled it with water and assorted junk. This was the trash compactor. The walls were on tracks that were cleverly motivated by a forklift truck. It was rigged to a complicated series of wires and pulleys. As the truck slowly drove off, the system pulled the two surfaces together – fascinating to watch. Especially as I wasn't getting my feet wet.

INT. DEATH STAR - GARBAGE ROOM

ACTION!

Luke was dragged beneath the grimy surface by a tentacle of the fearsome dianoga. It was a rather smaller tentacle than the abandoned version but it did the job. It wound itself up Luke's leg and yanked him down. Mark sank out of sight. This was actually more due to the efforts of a frogman, hiding beneath the surface. But the bit that most impressed me was the way the tentacle had slithered through the water and up Mark's leg. Because, of course, it hadn't. Mark had stood there, holding onto a nylon fishing line attached to the squid arm, already wound around his leg.

ACTION!

Mark let go of the invisible line and Props pulled on the sucker. It uncoiled and slipped back through the water. Later, George would reverse the shot. Movie magic. Again. I loved it.

Less magically, Mark yelled so loudly that he ruptured a blood vessel in his eye. For several days, he could only be filmed from his best side.

Revenge Of The Dianoga, perhaps.

The upholstery was not quite as soft as it looked.

If the seats were always this hard, it's no wonder Threepio hated space travel. But somehow I felt quite at home in the *Falcon*'s sitting area. It was all rather domestic. There was Mark, practising his new skills with a stick, under Sir Alec's avuncular gaze. Peter Mayhew was playing some holographic match against Artoo, while I observed. We both stared at the table. The black and silver design was really quite smart. The pedestal helped to mask my fake legs, a little. Maxi had, once again, made a gold collage around my lower limbs so I could sit there, watching the game. Except – there wasn't one.

It's a favourite scene of mine but, on the day, the table was bare. Like so many elements in the finished film, those magical characters, clobbering each other across the chequered markings, would be added later by ILM, eventually coming as a complete surprise to the audience, and me. However, the scene became immediately iconic for another reason. Film crews tend to adopt an in-phrase or two. "No blasters" had already leavened the atmosphere on set. Now my "Let the Wookiee win", became a general expression of kinship, for any occasion.

INT. MILLENNIUM FALCON - CENTRAL HOLD AREA

We were now under attack. Blaster fire raked the ship, so it was a bumpy take off. All the little knick–knacks skittered about on the shelf behind us. This was less due to the blaster fire, as to the Props behind the wall, bashing the underside of the shelf with broom handles. A neat effect but a bit noisy – like blaster fire, I suppose.

I'm only occasionally sure of how my performance in the gold suit reads from the outside. I have to think mechanically. At the same time, I do have to use my humanity to give the pieces of plastic some sense of inner emotion. Then I act it a little larger than life, hoping it works. A moment that does get my approval is when Threepio is seated once more in the central hold. The joys and dangers of playing a board game with Chewie had been replaced by tragedy. Obi-Wan, that most noble of Jedi Knights, had sacrificed himself to allow his friends to escape. As always, context helps the audience feel the emotion of the moment but Threepio is clearly moved by Obi-Wan's destruction.

With very, very little movement from me, I can read the sadness on his face.

## 24 fame

"You're not in this scene, so we wondered if you would do him," said Props.

I was loitering, watching the crew set up a shot. They put a plastic head in my hands.

"We call him White Pointy Face."

And I could see why. I was holding the face of a different sort of robot from the one I normally worked in. It was painted white and its features were indeed pointed. Props can be quite literal, at times. But who, or what, was this droid? The eyes gave it great personality. They seemed to be slightly crossed and staring. Whatever this droid was, I decided he was neurotic. Props explained that the character had been modelled on the same basic shape of my gold suit, so it should fit me. Really?

They dressed me up in this new weird garb. It was wonderful. The chest was much larger and actually allowed me to expand my own inside it. But as a fashion item, White Pointy Face wasn't ever going to be a role model. He was not a stylish droid. In fact, he seemed to be wearing oversized underwear and generally, he looked a bit grubby.

But everything was a bit seedy in that street scene. And I was quite happy being weird White Pointy Face. Of course, I wasn't the only one looking weird in this scene. For instance, what was that actor doing perched atop a pair of feathered stilts?

EXT. MOS EISLEY SPACEPORT - ALLEYWAY - DUSK

ACTION!

The giant chicken legs passed directly across the lens. Obi-Wan and Luke hurried forwards, ignoring White Pointy Face, who was twitchily wandering down the street, trying to remember what mission he was on. AND CUT!

That was it. White Pointy Face's day was done – his five minutes of fame, over. Except they weren't. Weeks later, I was back in my normal garb, shuddering inside a different set.

INT. SANDCRAWLER - PRISON AREA

I had to pretend that the whole thing was bumping over the sand dunes on Tatooine. Of course we were at Elstree, in what appeared to be a junk shop. It wasn't actually moving at all. Decades later, I would relive this moment in another cluttered set, that really was getting jiggled about on a different planet – but the "treadible" had yet to be invented.

And as the sandcrawler, apparently, approached the Homestead, there he was, White Pointy Face, slumped in a corner. Since I was inside my other suit, he was lifeless, twitched only by fishing lines attached to his various parts and yanked by the crew. But at least he had five minutes more of fame. Until *Return of the Jedi*.

INT. JABBA'S PALACE - BOILER ROOM

Poor Threepio. About to be sent to Jabba's sail barge, he is surrounded by droids in various stages of cruel destruction and torture.

And as he leaves, there by the door, staring hauntingly, is White Pointy Face. Now fifteen minutes of fame, total. But it wasn't over yet.

Many years later, game creators, Decipher, produced a character playing card. The image was familiar. But the name wasn't. "CZ-3". It seemed White Pointy Face was an insufficiently techno name for the current times. But as part of a card game – he had finally achieved immortality. Of a kind.

## 25 wrap

It was the last day shooting.

After twelve weeks or so, Fox were increasingly concerned at the contents of the dailies they were viewing back in California. They were understandably nervous at the money being spent – their money. So they cut it off. It seemed a desperate moment, strangely reflecting the story we were telling. But we did manage to grab this last sequence. It didn't look much – just a wall with a small round window. I was told not to encroach on this viewport. It would mess up the visual effect shot of the view of the distant *Tantive IV.*

INT. ESCAPE POD

ACTION!

"Are you sure this thing is safe?"

But I had to get in there first. So here was another set – the hatch in the *Tantive's* passage way. Days before, Kenny Baker had trotted inside. He was short enough to pass through the small door, wearing the top of an Artoo shell like an overcoat. He came out again and we shot Threepio side-stepping in.

It was frightening.

INT. REBEL BLOCKADE RUNNER – SUBHALLWAY

ACTION!

"I'm going to regret this."

I took in a breath and bent over, low enough to pass through the doorframe. The bottom edge of Threepio's chest pushed deep into my diaphragm. I shuffled forward and inside. The door slid down. I literally couldn't inflate my lungs. I couldn't breathe. They wouldn't realise outside. It seemed Eternity had truly begun for me.

AND CUT!

The door slid up. I shuffled out. Fast. We did several takes. It was scary. Every time.

But now it was all over. Filming was finished. Suddenly. Stop. It had been a rather peculiar experience. None of us seemed clear on what we had done. I certainly doubted that anyone would watch our efforts. It all seemed a bit of a mess. I'd certainly had enough of the physical side of it all. And the emotional side too. I wonder if I would have agreed to be part of it if I'd known just how much sheer effort it would take. And I could only hope that I had made a reasonable job of the character. Nobody ever said anything either way. Everyone else had worked hard too. It was just that they had the chance to sit down. I had grown fond of some of the cast and crew but the entertainment industry is full of hellos and goodbyes and hugs and promises to keep in touch. Everyone has their own private life. Working together doesn't mean you're wedded at dinner, weekends and when it's all wrapped. And this was a wrap. The purse strings had pulled tight closed.

That was it.

Or so I thought.

Months had passed and I'd put the whole experience of filming *The Star Wars* out of my head.

Then a phone call. They needed me to go to America. California. HOLLYWOOD. To record Threepio's voice for the finished film.

I'd never flown that far, never had jetlag. I was in mild shock – possibly the lengthy wait to get through immigration, the suffocating feel of the warm air, my first sight of the iconic flying saucer restaurant at the airport, the untidy mass of overhead power cables, the huge billboards screaming their wares, the nodding donkeys, eternally pumping oil. I arrived finally, in a rather bland hotel room, with a whirring air-conditioning unit and brown furniture. Barely unpacked, I fell asleep.

Awake, well before dawn, I stared out of the hotel window, hearing the bleakly alien police sirens screaming down the street. I was famished. It wasn't the sort of hotel that had a minibar with snacks. Anyway, they would have cost too much. If there had been room service, that would have been a terrible extravagance. My stomach just knotted itself. Later, I would find a Ships Coffee Shop down the road – open 24 hours. Who had ever heard of that! The rest of the world woke up and I eventually managed to hail a Yellow Cab, a minor miracle – they were going bust and so in short supply at the time. This, combined with my time-zone challenge, made me nervous as I sat in the morning commute. Would I make it in time? It would be distressing to come all this way and be late. Actors are neurotically punctual, or early, or someone else might get the part.

Eventually, we arrived at Hollywood and Vine. I paid the cab driver, carefully sorting the dollar bills, so new to me – all the same size and colour – too easy to make an expensive mistake. I rather tentatively pushed open the office doors of the Sound Producers Stage building. They'd been expecting me, and I wasn't late after all.

The mixing suite was certainly imposing, with its big screen and huge console of buttons and switches and lights – more impressive by far than the *Falcon*'s cockpit. The technician was twiddling things, adjusting other things. He greeted me warmly.

"You must be Anthony."

He pronounced the H in my name. It sounded so odd to me but I let it pass. Everything in this country was going to be a surprise.

"Welcome. You know, it's amazing that you got here. We've spent a couple of months trying to find a voice for your character, 'cos George really hates your perf… Oh. Hi, George."

I was shocked. I didn't even say hello.

"You hated my performance?"

George looked abashed.

"Well, I… err… never thought of Threepio being a British butler."

I was stunned. He could have said something at the time. I could have done it differently. I could have offered something else.

It transpired that thirty actors, including stars like Richard Dreyfuss, had been invited in to dub my on-screen movements. Many talented people gave it their best, but nothing had quite fitted the character as I had physically created him. Finally, a voice-over pro pointed out that my vocal performance was actually okay. Exhausted with the quest, George had generously changed his mind.

This was my first go at "looping". As each line played on screen, with the original guide track, a second film went by a recording head. There were no pictures on this film, just three stripes of magnetic tape. A system of rhythmic clicks told me when to start – on the fourth click – which wasn't actually there. It was imaginary. The film was literally stuck end to end, in a loop, so it could go past the recording head as often as required. However, I only had three goes at syncing my new voice with the projected picture, before they had to over-record a previous attempt. They could always put up another blank loop, of course.

I was fascinated, but it took a few attempts before I relaxed enough not to worry about the mechanics of it all. I was watching my own mechanics on screen. This was the first time I saw what everyone else had watched on set – me – as Threepio. Gosh!

It was a lot easier saying the lines wearing jeans and a shirt. I have always had a non-regional British accent – a bit posh, I suppose. I enhanced it to give Threepio an exaggerated, servant personality. Perhaps, being surrounded by so many American voices gave me a sense of contrast. The script made it obvious to me that the character was nervous, pernickety and uptight. Voices tend to go to a higher range under such circumstance. I sent mine a bit further backwards with a tensed throat. And I would literally make myself uptight. Buttocks, diaphragm, throat – everything clenched. Whereas I slouch a little, like most humans, Threepio is very upright and correct. And tense. And robots don't breathe. In performance I had to get out the words on one lungful of air – when available. Of course, gasps could ultimately be removed in the edit. But part of his personality comes from his impatient, pacey delivery. George always liked things faster.

I also spoke very precisely, making this talking machine sound didactic. It gave the character a pedantic personality that was just a little off human, emphasising his inability to read certain inter-personal situations.

That first day in the desert, they had stuck a small microphone above my face, just before they locked me into the head. A wire ran down my back to connect to a transmitter, ignominiously shoved in my pants, the only place there was any room. The audio results were awful – miles of magnetic tape of nothing but grunts and groans and expletives; the muffled lines almost unusable as a guide track. They soon asked me to re-record the words immediately, without the head on. A wild track. I was more than happy. I replicated my original performance, and the editors held on to their sanity. For me, anything without the head on was a bonus.

Now, finally, it was me standing there gazing at the screen, waiting nervously for the fourth click that would cue me to speak my line. Watching this curious metal man in a silent, black-and-white world of 35mm loops, didn't grab me. It was all rather flat – no sound effects – no atmosphere – just me.

Then we reached a sequence where George had added a temporary music track. A piece of Ravel's *Bolero*. What a transformation. Suddenly the scene had drama, interest, tension. I had never considered why most films add a score. It changes everything. I was amazed by the power of this music to alter the mood. And I hadn't even met John Williams at this point.

George did beg me to do one thing.

"If you say shed-uled, like you did on the wild track, no one in America will understand what you're talking about."

I was surprised. Was there another way to say the word in the English language? Apparently so – in America. As a small gesture of forgiveness for George nearly excising my performance from the film, I wrote a big letter K on my script and held it up in front of the screen. The cueing system clicked at me to start talking again.

"Level five. Detention Block AA twenty-three. I'm afraid she's sKeduled to be terminated."

"Terrific."

George was clearly relieved – and grateful.

Lunch on day one was a crisis. He took me next door to a burger bar, Hamburger Hamlet, I think. Used to the feeble Wimpey offerings back at home, I was astounded at the stuff you could pile onto the standard bun and patty – "fixings". We placed our booty at a table and sat. My finished stack was quite tall. I picked up a knife and fork, to stab the top. George went into amused shock. I was embarrassed. He taught me to grab the whole thing in my hands, squish it together and chow down. It was the best. Rather stuffed, we went back to the studio and I talked for the rest of the day. But then came embarrassing moment, number two. They found a cab to take me home. We drove off into the heavy traffic, as I spoke.

"Please would you take me to the Holiday Inn."

"Which one?"

In my days as a naïve traveller, it never occurred to me that there could be more than one hotel of the same name. I had no concept of the bigness that is Los Angeles. I had been awake since two that morning and was worn away by the day's effort. I rather pathetically said I thought it was towards the sea. We drove west. Eventually I saw an Inn that wasn't mine but we pulled over. The staff were very understanding and phoned around. It seemed I was a guest at the Westwood branch, on Wiltshire. I always get an address card from any hotel I stay in. Well, I do now.

In post-production, Ben Burtt, the brilliant inventive Sound Designer for the whole, and I mean whole, project took my finished vocal performance and added a small electronic element – a little tweaking of the tonal balance and a few thousandths-of-a-second of digital delay. The treatment gave my words a sort of low grade, transistorised quality. He then went to the trouble of playing my voice back into a suitable environment and re-recording it.

At some point during editing, they phoned me. Would I do them a favour? Would I please go to a studio in London and record an extra line? Of course. What was it?

"That's holding the ship here."

"Is that it?"

"Yes. We forgot to say what a tractor beam is actually for."

Ah.

"The tractor beam, that is holding the ship here, is coupled to the main reactor in seven locations."

It was one of the quickest jobs ever but it worked, once they plopped in the new words. The audience would never know the line was compiled over five thousand miles, and many weeks, apart.

I always stand upright in the recording sessions. Guests smile as they watch me in a typical Threepio pose – arms out, bum clenched, attitude. They can see the character, standing before them. The voice became iconic in its own right. Parents often ask me to do it for their children, who don't quite believe them. After all, any old man can claim to be the guy inside the gold suit and kids are rightly sceptical.

"Hello. I am See-Threepio, human-cyborg relations."

Then I see the magic. I watch as the sound enters their ears, it reaches their brain, it gets processed in moments. And suddenly. Smiles of recognition – and love.

## 27 survival

My work was done.

It had taken three full days in the studio but finally I had spoken my last words as See-Threepio. I had no idea what the finished film would be like – or if anyone was ever going to watch it. The black-and-white clips I had voiced seemed rather flat. Music and effects would be added later. Maybe that would help. But now I was flying back to London. My extraordinary American experience was over.

It had been a treat to visit a country that I'd only observed through the movies. Many of the streets looked familiar, from having seen them on TV. The whole of Los Angeles was a stage set, really quite bewildering in its immensity. And yes, there was the Hollywood Sign, a little run down but still iconic. Yes, they had all-night eateries, diners did ask for their eggs "sunny side up", and the TV was nothing but commercials – and people did say "Have a nice day." It had all been rather alien, though the immigration signs at the airport had cast me in that role the moment I arrived, pointing me to the appropriate queue – or "line", as they put it. Now I was going home to a land where I knew the rules and vocabulary. I had finally seen the USA. I think I liked it. I didn't expect I would ever return.

Then – for months – nothing. Complete radio silence from Lucasfilm. I had put the whole mixed-bag experience out of my mind. I would never forget my trip to the States earlier that year but I had moved on, and back to a more normal life of trying to find other work.

I saw it on a shelf in my local newsagent – the cover of *Newsweek*, or maybe *Time*, or maybe both. I forget. I could read the banner headline without even picking up the magazine. It shouted at me. To my surprise, in every sense, the strange little sci-fi film was clearly a colossal hit.

I eventually saw *Star Wars* at a crew screening in London. The huge Dominion Theatre was packed with so many familiar and unfamiliar faces. The crew was fairly large and most had brought along friends and family. I imagine the team were wondering what they were about to see. They'd certainly been dubious at the time of shooting – doubting that this weird American production would amount to much. The atmosphere was jolly enough. The crew were simply waiting to see the results of their hard work.

The lights dimmed as the gigantic curtains smoothly slid apart, the screen widening to its 70mm vastness, the auditorium hushed. In the silence, a strange message appeared on screen.

"A long time ago in a galaxy far, far away...."

John Williams' main theme crashed in. We were hooked.

I marvelled at so many things in the film – the editing, the music, the effects. And me. I hadn't realised how large a part Threepio played throughout. And that I spoke the first lines of dialogue. I think I left the theatre a little dazed – everyone did.

Now I would see endless reviews extolling everything and everyone – the droids especially. Sadly, in the avalanche of press coverage that *Star Wars* attracted, I was all but absent. Threepio became the first non-human to make the cover of *People Magazine*. But without Lucasfilm's shoulder behind me, that quickly faded, as yesterday's news. I was included in some desultory press interviews in the UK but, apart from that, it was Carrie and Mark and Harrison who bathed in the world's attention. As months went by, I became aware of something that would profoundly colour my relationship with the entire *Star Wars* enterprise. I learned that some of the folks at Lucasfilm were intent on creating the impression that Threepio had no human content – other than a voice.

*New Times*, June 1977, Jesse Kornbluth: "A fussy public-relations robot and his all-purpose android sidekick save the galaxy and steal the show from their human allies. Loveable automata? Computers you can trust? That the 70s Tin Man has a heart is *Star Wars*' hidden message." Threepio was endlessly referenced. Me? Not at all. Likewise, two months later in Paul Scanlon's 12 page feature for *Rolling Stone*, he noted that the droids "practically steal the film". Clearly he had been instructed not to mention me by name.

Apparently, whoever was responsible for the marketing of the film, felt it would detract from the believability of the robot, were it to be known that it was, in fact, a costume with a person inside. An actor, responsible for bringing the character to life – for every nuance of performance, every gesture, every reaction, each emotion. An actor, seriously engaged in the pursuit of his craft. And he was me.

The audience were led to believe that Threepio was a true marvel of robotic engineering, that my sole contribution was merely to grace this fully realised character with a voice. It felt as if half my performance was being amputated – denied.

As well as *People Magazine*, the character I had so stoically played also featured on the cover of the journal, *Psychology Today* – under the circumstances, a far more appropriate place for him.

I knew what I had brought to the film set, on a daily basis, working hard in endlessly horrible circumstances. Now my efforts were dismissed by implication. As if I had done nothing. As if I had never been there. I think any artist would have felt disappointed, if not devastated. It would be less than honest to say that it didn't hurt me – deeply.

I might reasonably have become objectified on the set, since I was playing the role of a machine. But to be erased, redacted, ignored, shut out of the success to which I had contributed, was beyond distressing. The casual cruelty of regularly seeing photo captions such as, "Luke Skywalker (Mark Hamill) with C-3PO in a scene from *Star Wars*," was a regular stab to my sense of self-worth. I was in no way a self-publicist, so could do little about the situation other than assume that I must have done something terribly unprofessional to be so negated.

It wasn't just Lucasfilm who were being insensitive. I'd long admired Paul Newman as a fine actor. I watched him being interviewed on television. Was he upset at never having won an Oscar? He responded that, in a world where the biggest box-office stars were a shark and a couple of robots, he didn't care anymore. I took his remark personally. The shark was probably hurt, too.

That summer I flew back to Hollywood to don the costume once again. I was the only person it fitted – almost. They put me up in the Roosevelt Hotel, opposite the famed Grauman's Chinese Theatre. It was quite a view. The outrageous, oriental architecture was like something out of the movies it had screened over decades, for this was a real cinema. Its forecourt was filled with hand prints and signatures – a concrete index of all the famous Hollywood film stars, dating back to the 1920s. And I was about to add my name – well, Threepio's name.

From my window, I had a front-row view of all the preparations, and the huge crowd that was collecting on Hollywood Boulevard below me. I could see an area that had been ceremoniously cordoned off.

There was a patch of newly wet concrete waiting for something joyous – a recognition that *Star Wars* belonged here, with these stars of the movies.

It was a fearsomely hot day. The crowds were quite intimidating as they pushed forward. Guards had been protecting the little patch over-night. Cement writing was more technical than I expected. The first layer had hardened and now the top waited, damply grey, for us to write on. The crimson rope barriers were parted and we began the ceremony. Someone in a Darth Vader costume was the first to write his name. Next, they lifted an Artoo unit and carefully put it briefly in place, leaving neat little machine prints. Then it was my turn.

The budget clearly didn't extend to flying Maxi across the Atlantic. I had a new team from Lucasfilm who were shovelling me inside for this new experience. They ushered me along as I puttered through the mass of fans from a cool dressing area in the lobby of the theatre. It was odd to walk outside as Threepio, in the real world. The crowds seemed to be pushing harder now, trying for a better view of me putting his feet next to Artoo's. Except they weren't really his feet at all. The rather mundane, ribbed soles of my deck shoes were not quite the thing for immortality. The multi-talented creature effects artist, Rick Baker had created fake soles, which they tied to the bottom of my shoes. These plastic pieces had interesting, high-tech designs, made for posterity and photo ops. Rick would later get his own star on Hollywood's Walk of Fame – due to his fancy foot-work obviously. Good for him. He was great to work with, and gave my costume an added flair. But I was so frustrated at never personally being mentioned in anything *Star Wars*, that I insisted I be allowed to write my own name in the mud, next to Threepio's newly designed footprints. I sometimes visit them on Hollywood Boulevard, pick out the odd cigarette butt and move on.

Weeks passed. I was at TV Center in West Hollywood. As Threepio, I was narrating a television special, *The Making of Star Wars*. I was alone on a sci-fi set with an Artoo unit. My monologues to camera were interrupted by the arrival of Harrison, then Mark and later, Carrie. I had to stand around, while they gave enthusiastic interviews about their involvement in the film. When they'd finally gone, I asked when we would be taping an interview with me – about my contribution to *Star Wars*. The director said they weren't planning to do that. That hit me.

I began to feel that, as far as Lucasfilm was concerned, I didn't exist – and certainly had nothing worth saying about my role in their film. Later, in London, I asked Gary Kurtz why they had opened a door to slam it so deliberately in my face. I forget his reply.

My feelings weren't helped by the sheer ubiquity of it all. *Star Wars* was everywhere. I couldn't escape it. Anywhere I went, there were images and sounds and writings about this marvellous film – with a funny gold robot.

My sense of rejection grew dangerously profound and I marvel that I survived it all. I could hardly bear to talk about *Star Wars*. People congratulated me, assuming it must be wonderful to be a part of it all. But I wasn't a part of it all. Out of a strange sense of professional and personal loyalty, I couldn't let my feelings out in public. I didn't want to put a canker in the rose of the fans' delight. It left me feeling like a secret outcast. Supportive friends kept me going, while Lucasfilm, by omission, continued to perpetrate the myth that Threepio was a real robot. Audiences believed it and indeed, that had been my aim. I was pleased, if not amazed, that fans were so convinced by my depiction of a technology that is still far from becoming a reality. But would it really have harmed the box office to admit there was an actor inside the suit?

Nobody seemed to care what I was feeling. For me, it was a difficult time that seemed as though it would never end. Of course it did, in the sense that, eventually, my true role was clarified. It's just that some scars can take a long time to heal. When I found a Trivial Pursuit card with the question, "What part did Anthony Daniels play in *Star Wars*?"

I realized it was official – I truly was a triviality. I had it framed in gold. Hung it in the toilet. I felt I was probably the only person on the planet to know the answer.

Nobody should take up acting to become rich and famous – certainly I never expected either. I simply wanted to act. But, to misquote the brilliant playwright, Tom Stoppard, actors pledge their identities, secure in the knowledge that someone will be watching. Certainly audiences were watching and adoring the funny gold man. Perhaps it would have been kinder back then, if they had been allowed to know that this quaint humanoid robot actually had a real human concealed within him.

A man.

With a name of his own.

## 28 special

It was 1977. An innocent time. At least as far as TV channels went.

Watched by millions, they were delightful. Both of them. I wasn't a disciple but I was certainly aware of the Donny and Marie phenomenon of utter squeakiness, their amazing tooth whiteness, and their niceness. And meeting them, they were indeed lovely, nice, friendly and very, very professional – and with enviable teeth. I could judge because now I was on their show – *The Donny and Marie Star Wars Special*.

Back in that year, most things on earth seemed somehow to connect to George's new film. America's viewing public also loved Donny and Marie's singing, dancing, smiling show that was a paradigm of life in the USA. This was wholesome, Colgate entertainment – iconic in its own right. And now these two beloved pieces of escapist fun – *Star Wars* and the Osmonds – were joining forces for the night.

This spectacular alignment would be hosted by the two smiling stars. And there was another icon, Kris Kristofferson, celebrated country music maker. I'd certainly heard of him. He was lovely, too. Sadly, in a rather different mode, actor and comedian, Paul Lynde, a regular on the show, was playing something Tarkinish. He seemed a bit put-out. It was quite evident he felt that the whole *Star Wars* team was upstaging him, though Peter Mayhew and I and an Artoo unit were the only originals on board. With Kris embodying Han Solo, the two principals were, of course, the world famous brother and sister act, playing Luke and Leia. Who knew?

Nice as it all was, the script was unspeakably awful – to such an extent that I personally cut most of Threepio's lines. Unusual for an actor. But I had already become protective of my golden alter-ego and would not allow him to embarrass himself in public by speaking drivel. However, I remained heavily involved in rehearsals of the drama, such as it was, and in the dancing which, in my case, was limited.

Many of the numbers were performed by a female chorus line of beautiful blonde-haired stormtroopers. I concentrated on not bumping into them – or not getting in the wrong place and have them bump into me. For the most part, I succeeded. But I was never sure if Threepio should be bopping along with this strange assemblage. It all seemed rather undignified – a foretaste of the embarrassment I would suffer on a forest moon, in the distant future.

The real drama occurred as we all boarded the scenic prop referred to as "The Spaceship". It was a simple piece of set construction, tall and slim with a pointed roof. The black-and-white check markings made it look like some kind of traffic bollard. In fact, the design would allow for a feeble joke about it being mistaken for a taxi. No laughing matter, then.

Access was by way of a ramped drawbridge. It was set at an incline that I could manage. So in we went, to set off on our mission to escape some danger or other – Peter, Kris, Donny, Marie and me. Curiously, cruelly, Artoo was abandoned to twirl alone on the studio floor, beeping, I imagined, some droid profanity of fury at being left behind. Truth was, they couldn't get it up the ramp. And anyway, there was no room for it inside – as it transpired, a lucky escape for my angry counterpart.

Once we were all aboard, the drawbridge hinged upwards and slammed decisively shut. Unfortunately, The Spaceship was rather more frail than even I had imagined. The slamming immediately caused its pointed roof structure to collapse and topple down inside – on our heads. There was a brief silence. Then Threepio's, "How... interesting", made everyone laugh. Nobody was injured. Watching the show however, did make me feel slightly nauseous. But it was nothing compared with the horror that was to come a year later.

Only recently, I found it in a cupboard. Hidden. The original script. A weighty black folder with bright silver lettering – my name and the title. It looked important. Having put the whole thing out of mind, I thought it might make an interesting, memory-jogging read. It didn't. But then, it had made a very peculiar viewing experience, at the time. *The Star Wars Holiday Special.*

I was on the shoot for two or three days. I suspect it seemed longer. Certainly "Wookiee Life Day", the climax to the appallingly misconceived event, seemed as though it would never end. It was my only involvement in the, amazing, script.

Anyone watching the whole broadcast would have endured lengthy episodes of Wookiee home life, to get this far. The family didn't exactly break wind together but their dialogue of grunts and growls was equally off-putting and far from entertaining. These incomprehensible domestic scenes were interspersed with some well-known, and much-admired, artists being reduced to mere stooges. Ghastly jokes and wince-making dance acts floundered around them, as Life Day inexorably drew near. As far as I dare remember, Wookiees everywhere were planning to go on some strange celebratory pilgrimage.

Reading the whole script was a challenge – but not as great a trial as trying to watch the finished broadcast. I'm not sure how many viewers survived this variety show mish-mash of the previous two-hour ramble but at this point, we might well have been playing to an empty sitting room.

My part was easy. I stood on a stage, backed by a threatening tree trunk, in some strange nether world. I chatted with Chewie and Artoo, as the area below filled with Wookiee shapes. Eventually, I turned to face the awful sight.

"Happy Life Day everyone."

I've spoken some rubbish in my years but, seeming to confirm Artoo's sentiments, this topped everything as I addressed the furry throng.

"It is indeed true that at times like this, Artoo and I wish that we were more than just mechanical beings and were really alive, so that we could share your feelings with you."

Threepio has always had feelings. But would he rather be a Wook-iee? Doubtful.

But, "The Best Actor In A Turd" award must go to Mark and Carrie and Harrison. They managed to mouth their saccharine lines without once showing their gritted teeth – though they did seem to cling rather closely to each other on stage, for support.

We were all speaking so sincerely, but as if in slow motion, as if we had all been sprayed with "Hint of Valium". The director clearly rated this very, very calm atmosphere. The deadbeat, energy-free perfor-mances were swamped by a morbid layer of greeting-card emotion, as everyone built up to the amazing Life Day experience.

The finished production would sit on a peculiar sound bed. Endless Wookiee grunts and gurgles. The music, clearly intended to be emotionally moving, was just maudlin and depressing – excerpts from *Preludes in a Sanatorium*. Carrie had to sing without musical backing, on the ugliest of cheap sets. She may have had an in-ear orchestra but from where we were all standing, her unaccompanied voice sounded so thin and vulnerable. She got through the mawkish lyrics like a trooper, though her frumpy white dress and big Danish hair pieces didn't help. But the sheer cloyingness of the words was hard to listen to.

The herd of swaying Wookiees looked surreal and slightly sinister. Like some strange religious cult of sleepwalkers, they arrived in a trance-like state, each moving to some vague internal rhythm, completely unrelated to the backing dirge. They walked, zombie-like, seemingly affected by a chemical cosh dispersed through the air-con system. Each one held a plastic ball of fluorescent light. They carried these "glowing globes" as if going to some dreamy bowling alley. But now they lurked before us in the gloom – awaiting my benediction. Quite why I was there was never clear to me. But arriving had not been easy for them, either. Our stage was solid enough. But the shaggy audience was stranded in some kind of outer-space star field. This effect was inexpensively achieved by tossing white Christmas tree lights all over the blackened studio floor. These were stars. Adding a fog of billowing dry ice made the whole thing more mysterious and magical. It also rendered the "stars" invisible to the actors inside their festive robes and ominous Wookiee heads. That strange crunching was the sound of dozens of Wookiee feet, treading on tiny light bulbs. More deadly than an ion-cannon blast, whole galaxies were instantly crushed out of existence. It was hilarious.

The limo driver glanced over his shoulder, as he drove me away from Burbank Studios.

"Why're you laughing?"

"Because I'm off this awful production."

He turned back, his eyes, once more, off the road.

"You an actor? I'm an actor."

Of course. We were in LA.

Fox Studios promoted *The Holiday Special* as a "Two-hour visual and audio delight. A live animated-musical-potpourri of pure entertainment." It was only aired once. A day of infamy – 17 November 1978. Apparently, pirate copies are available. But not for the faint-hearted.

## 29 identity

Forget Threepio's feelings about space travel.

Jetlag is the price you pay for going somewhere far, far away. 1978 and I was back in the almost familiar grounds of Los Angeles. The flying saucer at LAX was becoming an old friend. But I was already feeling the time change and remembering that I'd be off again in just a couple of days. I had returned to LA for the, rather apt, Golden Anniversary Academy Awards. Nothing personal. They wanted Threepio on stage for one of the events – appearing alongside Artoo and our master, Mark Hamill.

Riding in a black stretch limousine was still a major novelty for me. It felt very grand. Then I spotted an empty cigarette packet in a corner of the floor, presumably tossed there by a previous passenger and unnoticed by the driver. So it was just a cab after all. We waded through the dense traffic and eventually arrived to see and hear the lavish trappings surrounding this spectacular night. I felt a little self-conscious in my black-tie outfit, walking down the red carpet.

It was slightly bewildering to see so many giant statues of the famous gold award decorating the space. The figure seemed oddly familiar.

Some distant relative of Threepio's perhaps. I could see all the crowds behind the barriers peering for a brief glimpse of a celebrity. They glanced at me briefly. Eventually I was passed through the numerous security checks, given a badge and shown to my dressing room. A security guard stood outside – my personal minder for the evening. I was being well looked after.

I was horrified at the amount of weaponry backstage. Various officers wielding serious guns. In those days, Great Britain was mercifully free from the sight of armed police. Sadly, that would change over the years but for now, this arsenal added to my slight sense of unease. My private room was a quiet place for me to change into the gold costume lying there, prepared for this gala evening. I'd already recorded my brief remarks and some interplay with Artoo. My lines would be played-in from the production studio, hidden somewhere in the vast auditorium of the glitzy Dorothy Chandler Pavilion.

There was a comfortable green-room area backstage – lots of potted palm and sofas and Perrier, where the guests could relax during the show. Not really being a stargazer, I was however impressed to see Vanessa Redgrave and Richard Dreyfuss. He seemed to have got over any disappointment he might have had, at not being the voice of See-Threepio – especially since he would end the evening with the Best Actor Oscar in his hands. Miss Redgrave would get hers for Best Supporting Actress.

Stargazer or not, I was thrilled at a life-enhancing moment of mutual admiration with Joel Grey, who had so wowed me, at a distance, with his exquisite, Oscar-winning performance in *Cabaret*. And there was Bob Hope, who would soon be traumatised by encountering me and Artoo on stage. I was awestruck to see Bette Davis too, though she didn't appear to be totally relaxed. Things would only get worse.

George's film was honoured with seven Oscars. But sadly, not one for himself. Meanwhile, I was involved in one of the presentations.

At the podium, Mark looked charmingly dapper and confident in his dinner suit. He read a nice, personal introduction for me, standing next to him in my gold outfit, with the formal addition of my own black tie.

My pre-recorded script began to roll. Artoo replied. Threepio spoke. Artoo beeped lengthily. Mark joined in. Quite a sweet little script, which worked well, except for one thing. Maybe the playback system had inherent delays, or perhaps whoever was punching in the pre-recorded cues in Production had the worst sense of timing – ever. Whatever the reason, the long gaps in the dialogue were excruciating. I filled in with Threepio actions but there was nothing I could do to speed up the conversation and make it sound anything like natural. Mark managed to retain his beautiful smile through it all, like a real pro. As the torture trundled on, I was eventually left to mime to one of the most cumbersome lines ever written, outside a *Star Wars* script.

"A Special Achievement Award has been voted by the Board Of Governors upon the recommendation of the Sound Branch Executive Committee for the creation of the alien, creature and robot voices featured in *Star Wars*."

The good news was that the award went to my talented colleague, Ben Burtt.

It was a relief to get off stage. But then the real trauma began. With every distraction amplified inside my gold suit, the shouting was horrible. Like criminals, Ben, Mark and I were herded along thick yellow lines, painted on the black floor. Suddenly we were in a barrage of flashlights from a bank of press cameras. They were behind rope cordons – or we were. It was unnerving, as each photographer yelled for attention. The flashes bounced around Threepio's eyes, blinding me over and over again. Then onto another yellow line and another room and more flashes and yelling. By the third room I'd had enough. Luckily it was the last one. I could escape back to the private quietness of my dressing room. But the evening's drama wasn't done with me yet.

I changed back into my dinner suit. Then I needed a drink. I thought I'd seen a bar somewhere along the yellow tracks, but really didn't want anyone tagging along with me. My personal guard reluctantly let me go off by myself. I left him to watch all my stuff, including the rather unappealing badge they'd given me. It looked like some kind of radiation alarm and certainly didn't go with my smart clothes. I got in the elevator, as I'd learned to call a lift, and pressed a button. It was a button too far. I realised my mistake as soon as I saw the paraphernalia of the stage-door security. I pressed another button that would take me back up to stage level. The door began to close.

"Pardon me, sir."

A boot was stopping the door from closing, so it opened instead.

"Sir. Please step out of the elevator."

I did, and heard the door slide closed behind me with a Thunk. The boot belonged to a fully weaponised police officer.

"Sir. I need to see your ID."

"Oh. Um... I'm actually English. We don't carry IDs."

I sensed the officer was releasing the safety catch on his gun. I spotted the TV monitor on the desk behind him.

"You probably just saw me on stage, wearing the gold robot costume from *Star Wars*."

I felt his trigger finger itching.

"Sir. I need to see some ID."

I noticed he kept respectfully calling me "sir". However, there was nothing polite in his intention. But now my fingers found the one item in my pockets, apart from a white handkerchief. This might satisfy him.

"Look. I have a ticket to the Governor's Ball at the Hilton Hotel."

He was unimpressed.

"Sir. Anyone can have one of those."

"At a hundred and fifty dollars a time, very few of my friends can have one."

It was an instant, possibly flippant, response but true at the time. One hundred and fifty dollars was a lot of money back then. But my uniformed friend had heard enough. He gestured to the open stage door and the street outside.

"That truck's full of gatecrashers like you. Sir, I'm gonna have to arrest you."

Time stopped. My future life flashed in front of me. I'd be hand-cuffed, fingerprinted, imprisoned with who-knew-who, my professional life over, left a laughing stock. And I'd miss my plane.

"Officer!"

He turned around to see what this other drama was he now had to manage. At that moment I heard the lift door open behind me. Without even looking, I stepped neatly backwards and pushed a button. When he turned around, it was too late for his boot to stop my escape. By the time he'd raced up the stairs to the next level, I was clinging gratefully to my personal minder and flashing my badge at everyone.

And now I was back in the green room. It was febrile with reactions to Miss Redgrave's political acceptance speech. The security seemed to have grown even heavier. Standing near to Miss Davis, I somehow found the courage to speak to this real Hollywood legend. I gestured to the guards and all the trappings of the event.

"What do you think of all this?"

She looked at me with her signature, dour expression.

"Well, I remember when it was all so good. Now it's just money. And politics. And sh…"

I was captured by her surprising directness and her real humanity. I became her fan. Eventually, everyone trooped out of the Pavilion and onto the pickup spot. It was a chill April evening, and a great Einstein-ian truth came upon me. Hundreds of stretch limos cannot be in the same place at the same time. With the average stretch being around thirty feet, you don't have to be a genius to calculate the wait time.

As car after car boarded their famous passengers, I remained one of the few waiting, and waiting. Nothing personal, just mathematics and chance. It was no comfort, but I noticed that one of the guests impatiently chilling on the sidewalk was my new friend, Miss Davis.

Eventually I arrived at the Hilton. The security, the chill, the near-arrest, the time zone – it all began to bear down on me. I found my table. It actually had my name on a place card, next to Mark and his wife, Marilou. They were long gone, table-hopping; their extravagant king crab and caviar appetisers waiting moistly for their return. The guest to my right looked accusingly at me.

"Who are you?"

She'd seen my name card. It meant nothing to her. Maybe she had yet to see *Star Wars*. I suddenly couldn't face explaining myself for the second time this evening. Anyway, I didn't like her. I turned away. And now there was a friendly face – our talented and lovely designer, John Barry, was arriving with his team, even later than me. I congratulated him on the Oscar statuette he was proudly carrying. I briefly held it, feeling its weight, and he went to find his table. Shortly, I caught his arm, as he was abruptly leaving. Tears were starting in his eyes.

"I come here, holding the most prestigious accolade this industry can bestow. And I'm told there's no place for us at dinner."

I wasn't the only one feeling stressed. I made him wait while I manhandled the chairs and the Hamills' appetisers, so he and his team could sit and eat. The lady to my right didn't like that at all. As I brutally nudged her chair sideways, to make room, I'd had enough. I found my limo. My hotel. My plane. I wasn't sure how I felt about Hollywood. Maybe Miss Davis was right. Or maybe it was jetlag?

Some years later, I was at the British Academy Awards ceremony in London. I had learned in my childhood that it is better to give than to receive, and again I was there as part of a presentation – not that they had offered me anything else. Of course, it was Threepio that they really wanted. That was fine. Another free dinner. But there was a problem.

The show designer had created a long flight of curved stairs, swirling down to the stage floor – the sort of curve that allows leggy actresses to show off – with the added drama that hopefully someone might tumble down them. Attentive readers will still remember that Threepio doesn't do steps. The show producer thought about it. Perhaps the gold figure could stand on the top landing. Fine. But how to get him there? Of course, that old forklift routine. I would dress behind stage, at floor level and then be ignominiously lifted up, like freight in a warehouse. The ride would take about twenty seconds. My agent told me that I would be insured for £25,000. I was impressed. Then she rather spoiled the moment. It seemed that the suit would be insured for £75,000.

Lucky I didn't fall over then.

## 30 puppets

Like everyone on the planet, I had loved *The Muppet Show* for all of its reign.

Now I was going to be in it. Mark, Peter and I walked across Borehamwood High Street from our studios to theirs, ATV, on 17th January 1980. I was so happy in the familiar, crummy backstage area that was their set. I recognised it from all the shows I'd watched – and there was Kermit on Jim Henson's arm. More prophetically, there was Miss Piggy, attached to Frank Oz. It was all so magical. We had a blast. The crew were completely dedicated to looking after a cast in strange outfits. I felt so at home. The producers were very respectful and thrilled that we were there. The Pig was less reverential, but that was her diva way.

The puppeteers were on the floor, with their arms up in the air. Mark and I stood in the Pig's dressing room, on a raised platform above them. It was even stranger than being in the world of *Star Wars*. Talking to the wildly charismatic porker was one thing; tap dancing was the real challenge. Strange, to find my simple choreography notes some forty years later. "Weight on L – Hop-step R... Drag L (to close) x 4. + Head & arms. Stamp L.R. Brush L toe back. Brush R toe back. Repeat Forward..." and so on. Ending with "BA BUM!" *Swan Lake* it wasn't but unbelievable to think I managed to perform the short dance number six times in all, while wearing Threepio. I remember being exhausted afterwards. Funny, to return to ATV to dub my voice onto the final edit and watch a man at a microphone, hitting a tin tray with a spoon – Threepio's taps.

How magical subsequently to be asked to join the cast of *Sesame Street* in their New York studio – to meet Big Bird in person – because there was Caroll Spinney, showing me how he created his iconic persona on the street. Again, I felt so at home with a cast and crew who were all lovingly on the same page. In front of camera or behind, everyone worked so harmoniously together – entertainment and education, delightfully combined. I could have stayed for ever. It was just a week, but I had the most memorable time. And there were some unforgettable scenes. Dear Big Bird mistook Artoo for a mail box. And my favourite moment – Artoo taking Threepio into the street to meet his very shy and rather short new girlfriend. Ever informative, Threepio explained the truth.

The object of Artoo's desires was a fire hydrant.

No one had cared when we were shooting *A New Hope*.

It was a mid-budget sci-fi film – not on anyone's radar. I had been embarrassed to discuss my role with friends. They were doing proper acting – television, theatre. I was pratting about in a shiny suit, speaking with a funny voice and pretending to be a robot. Then the film opened and everything changed.

Within a year, they called me about a sequel. I was conflicted. Did I want to go through it all again? Not really. Were they offering an amazing deal? Not really.

The first film had been an endurance test. I don't think that anyone at Lucasfilm appreciated what I'd gone through, portraying Threepio in that unforgiving suit. Neither did they realise how neglected I felt, once the film had wowed the world. Why should they? They all had other things to think about now. On the other hand, if I said yes to reprising the role, at least this time I was going in with my eyes open. I knew what I could expect. I was free to choose.

Was I an actor? Was it a job?

But there was another factor, that was perhaps more important. I had grown fond of See-Threepio. I said yes.

We were back at Elstree. Now the security was intense; the production a collection of guarded secrets. I read the script. I wasn't sure about it. It seemed to be slightly disrespectful of Threepio, a character of whom I felt quite protective. I was shocked, too, to find that Artoo would go off on his own mission with Luke. Artoo and Threepio were a team. It seemed sacrilegious to split them up. And to saddle poor Threepio with a human as dismissive of him as Han Solo…

Harrison's, or Han's, disrespect for the protocol droid, to whom he sarcastically referred as "the professor", was evident in the previous film. Looping the original, I had spotted his reaction to seeing Threepio for the first time, outside the *Falcon* – pure disdain. I suggested to George that I add the cheery line, "Hello, Sir," as a stimulus for Harrison's look. It fitted perfectly. But now Threepio was forced to hang out with him.

The edgy relationship would give rise to one of the most quotable moments in the entire Saga. Ever keen to protect others, and indeed himself, from danger, Threepio became the epitome of a health and safety zealot. His warning about the odds of surviving an asteroid field fed Han that most memorable of ripostes. I can almost hear you say it. Curiously, that iconic line didn't appear in earlier drafts of the script.

I had finally made it. I was almost in the driving seat – well, standing behind it, at least. The lounging area was spacious compared with this. But the cockpit of the *Millennium Falcon* is truly iconic – lots of white, red, blue and green lights on the control panels. But on its first outing, in the days before LEDs, I was amused to find that many were just holes drilled into the plywood walls. A couple of sixty-watt bulbs shone through all the variously coloured gels stuck to the back. A good effect from the front, and cheap.

Peeking round the back again, there was a plastic cup, resting on one of the wooden battens of the set's construction. Someone had dumped the remains of their breakfast – cold tea and a string of fat from their bacon butty. Somehow, the prosaic nature of this domestic litter added to the magic of the scene on the other side – what the camera doesn't show you. But I knew it was there. It kept me grounded.

Though there had been an upgrade, the cockpit was still very small. With Harrison, Carrie and Peter in there with me, it was a tight fit. Warm, too, in spite of there being no glass in the window – just a lens pointing our way, framed by the faces of the camera crew. There was lots of fiddling about to get the lighting just right, and many adjustments to this, that and the other. It all took time to get ready. After a while, Carrie, as Mark observed from the sidelines, "Pulled out twenty minutes' worth of hair," from one of her buns. She had to leave the set and be re-coiffed, while we stayed behind, and waited.

Harrison got bored and, perhaps in a throwback to his previous occupation, picked up a carpenter's saw, left lying out of shot. He began to take out his frustration by slicing into the cockpit's sliding door. It was not the metal structure that it looked, but painted plywood, like the rest of the set. The stand-by painter was called in to repair the damage with grey paint. It took time. I was standing there – in the suit. Eventually we took off, in a manner of speaking, straight into an asteroid field.

INT. MILLENNIUM FALCON – COCKPIT

We peered intensely through the front window as we careened past imaginary lumps of rock. To ensure we all fell around in the same direction, at the same moment, the whole set was rigged on scaffold poles that stuck out at the sides. Two strong teams grasped the poles.
ACTION!
UP RIGHT!
The right-hand team shoved their poles upwards. The cockpit dropped and we all swayed to our left.
DOWN RIGHT! UP LEFT!
And we flopped right. We were shifted around like bowling pins, being careful that we didn't actually fall over. Then the final indignity. Being switched off. Carrie put her hand behind my back and Brian Lofthouse – my new, eternally dedicated and patient right-hand man – flicked the remote switch he'd rigged earlier. Threepio's eyes went out. I slumped to my left, one arm hanging limp. As the crew eventually poled the cockpit upright, I made sure my arm followed suit. That wasn't hard. But there I was again. Breathing shallow.

The whole sequence looked very dramatic in the final edit. But I remember the static camera crew peering from their adjacent platform. With arms folded, their faces said they'd seen this sort of stuff before.

They were really waiting for the lunch menu. Catering is a big deal on a film shoot.

Of course, the new pairing of droid and smuggler gave opportunities for more dramatic and comedic tension between the characters. At least the droid was allowed to show equal contempt for that "impossible man".

Others may have found our director, Irvin Kirshner, to be impossible in some ways as well. I found him a total joy. His enthusiasm and energy were infectious. He brought his immense intellect to bear on a script that would end up as the fan favourite. Personally, I still prefer *A New Hope*, as being the most complete and unselfconscious story of the Saga.

Kirsh was always encouraging. Little bursts of praise were followed by small tweaks to the performance. I felt he was always watching and appreciating. It all felt inclusive. I did notice that some shots grew more elaborate as we worked on them. Set-ups would become bigger and wider; more background; more troopers. The schedule expanded. So, apparently, did the budget. Not my department. I was just there to act.

Threepio had new feet. No more deck shoes that peeped out from the gold covers at awkward moments. The new look was one-piece plastic with shoe laces at the back, almost unnoticeable when covered in gold tape. And I had new pants. The two-piece, flimsy "space eroticism" was now a onesie, which I had to wriggle myself into. I had returned to the plasterers' shop and been smeared with gunk and plaster again. But not all over. Just the area of my body in question. To my embarrassment, the resulting cast would sit on a desk in the workshop. It looked like a retail display for Y-fronts. I don't know what happened to it. Possibly, it became a collector's item.

As filming continued, I began to feel an odd sensation in my hands – or rather, a lack of sensation. It was rather disturbing. It grew worse, until I couldn't easily turn my own front door key. At that point I saw a doctor. When I described what I was wearing, he explained that the arms of the costume were pressing on my nerves – the ulnar nerves. I was risking permanent damage, if I kept on doing it. He'd seen it before. Arms draped over the back of a chair, sort of thing – though he'd never encountered a robot with this problem before – probably never encountered a robot at all. Being left in the costume for such long periods, I had to develop a resting stance, to relieve the pressure – arms raised upwards. I must have looked as though I was about to dance a highland fling. In that costume?

I kept reminding myself that no one had attempted this sort of suit before. Its creators had tried their best. I asked them nicely for some alterations to improve the fit but they had other more pressing things to do for the production. I asked several times over the ensuing weeks. But I would see the ugly cuts and bruises and pinches every night. At some point, my frustration and physical hurt got so strong that I took metal cutters to open the tops of the arms like petals. Now they'd have to repair and hopefully enlarge them. It would give me a little more clearance.

It worked, somewhat.

But they weren't happy.

INT. MILLENNIUM FALCON – MAIN HOLD AREA

"I have reversed the power-flux coupling," Threepio proudly boasted, completely unaware of the sexual tension in the air. Finally the Princess was going to get a good kiss.

But no.

I waded into the scene, gatecrashing the steamy moment. It wasn't exactly a crash but as I tapped Harrison lightly on the shoulder, I did hear a Ting! I knew that something had fallen off something of mine. It was getting tedious. I was aware George was frustrated by the suit's malfunctions. How did he think I felt? So, because of the costume glitch, we would probably have to do the scene once again. Not, I think, that Carrie and Harrison would have minded. We didn't do a retake, because you could only hear the Ting. The sound would be replaced in post-production. And you wouldn't notice what happened, unless you watched closely, frame by frame. In which case, you would see a small gold object falling from my arm and exiting the bottom of picture. It was a greebly.

An elbow greebly.

Then there was Hoth. Norman Reynolds, the Production Designer, and team had created a wonderland. A world of ice and snow. Giant frozen icicles were, in fact, elegantly crafted, hand-blown glass sculptures. Inverted and filled with water, slowly weeping through a pinhole at the tip, they were totally convincing, and beautiful. The floor was covered in salt crystals. The ice corridors were carved out of polystyrene blocks. A coating of melted wax and salt created completely believable walls of frosted snow. Convincing – until you touched them, which I did, often – out of a sense of curious wonder.

Now I was shuddering in the huge, icy entrance way.

EXT. HOTH REBEL BASE – DAY

ACTION!

The crew chucked fake snow into the air around me as I was blasted by the huge and extremely noisy fans. I naturally reacted to the dramatic onslaught of the scene and I desperately waved my arms against the snow-laden gale. I yelled at Artoo, to come inside.
CUT!

Kirsh came up close. He patiently explained that, when I came to see the finished film, I would hear a gentle breeze, drifting off the snow field beyond. In other words, I was over-acting. Not for the first time, I fear. It had become a habit. Threepio was taking me over.

But in an ice cavern, I did do a remarkable thing.

INT. HOTH - REBEL BASE - ICE CORRIDORS

Running away from the stormtroopers, Threepio sees a red and yellow sign stuck on a door, set in the ice wall. He pauses in his flight and considers. His circuits processing the information, he niftily swipes the sign off, before rushing onward. The sign was in fact a warning that on the other side of the door was a herd of ever-hungry wampas. In earlier drafts of the script, the poor captured beasts had been teased to fury by a malicious Artoo, incessantly squeaking high-pitched whistles at them. Now, Threepio used his wits, hoping the pursuers would enter the cell and be chomped up, thus allowing him and his friends to escape. That was all scripted. The remarkable thing was that I managed, with my limited field of vision and poor depth perception, to take aim and grab the paper with my all-but-useless hand. A minor triumph perhaps. But for me, a landmark. The scene was cut.

I wasn't feeling great as the rebels frantically evacuated their collapsing base. I chased Han and Leia down a narrow corridor in this world of whiteness; smoke and explosions around me, wearing my body-clenching gold costume, unable to hear Kirsh's shouted directions or see obstacles in my path. It was ghastly. The more so, since I had clearly overdone it the night before. I learned an important lesson that day. Never go to work with a hangover.

INT. STAR CRUISER - MEDICAL CENTER

It couldn't be the end of the story. This was only the second film of a trilogy. Nevertheless, there was a sense of apprehension as we approached the open end of this chapter. We stood there, gazing at the *Falcon* flying away on a mission to find Han Solo. Luke and Leia wore expressions of concern, as they stared out of the giant viewport. So did I – but you couldn't see.

The iconic craft swept across our view and out into the dark reaches of space or, in this case, an expanse of blue screen, the *Falcon* not actually being there at the time. But the gravity of the situation still hung in the air, as a crew member provided a moving eyeline for us to look at. He walked away, holding up a rather bedraggled floor mop. We giggled, briefly. It was a serious moment.

## 32 illusion

There was a new member of the gang. Billy Dee Williams. Lando Calrissian. A seasoned and charismatic actor and indeed, a charismatic character. It can't have been easy for him to join a group of a ready-made cast who'd been there before. And the script cleverly put doubts in the mind. Whose side was he on? Betrayer or benefactor? Either way, quite a gutsy role. It quickly became apparent that here was a cause of some tension. Harrison had been the only real macho hero thus far. Was there room for another one? Were Han and Lando now playing two sides of the same coin? The tensions gently simmered. Perhaps they were bound to explode in the prison cell with Chewie. The fight was eventually choreographed but Harrison's anger was clearly apparent. And matched by Billy's. Method acting at its finest. But not my problem. I had other concerns. I was in pieces.

I turned the page quickly. Having been rudely insulted by a familiar metal face in Cloud City, Threepio's curiosity was about to become his nemesis.

INT. CLOUD CITY - ANTEROOM

Exploring an intriguing corridor, he had just been blastered apart. Horrifying! When the assault actually happened, the Effects crew had simply stuck a small firework, a squib, on my chest. Fine wires led out of frame to a battery. I tensed slightly as I apologised to an off-camera, non-existent assailant. A quick touch of the wire ends...

BOOFF!

Disembodied parts, hurled across the floor, spoke eloquently of Threepio's fate – the details of his destruction, horribly told by implication and the power of the audience's imagination. But now I was concerned to see whether that was finally it, for the protocol droid. Would the next page reveal a funeral or at most, a careless scrapping? I read on, searching the stage directions for what happened next.

INT. CLOUD CITY - JUNK ROOM

Months later, at Abbey Road Studios, I would be thrilled to watch the London Symphony Orchestra scoring the moment with John Williams' iconic music. After a few takes, they turned towards the screen to watch a playback to picture. There were the filmed shots from the ensuing script pages that I had eventually discovered. As Threepio's severed head rattled fatefully towards the maws of a radiant furnace, the musicians let out a cry of sadness. The orchestra had scored *A New Hope* and had clearly grown fond of the metal man. I was rather touched. And, of course, it wasn't the end of Threepio.

INT. CLOUD CITY - LARGE CELL

Chewbacca had come to the rescue and collected Threepio, albeit in pieces. After a thoughtful Hamlet moment, Threepio needed to be rebuilt. Brian lent Props a selection of my second-best parts. They swagged these in a net on Peter Mayhew's shoulders. He could crudely keep the elements alive by tilting his weapon, up and down. Fishing line attached at both ends, threaded through and animated the plastic parts behind him. An excellent effect for a long shot. But a closer two-shot required a different approach.

I knelt at Peter's feet, wearing the torso as normal. Chewbacca was being kind and thoughtful. But clumsy. He managed to put on the head, backwards. Brian had cut most of the back away from a copy head, to allow my face to stick out. I wore the character's face on the back of my head, while my face poked out of the rear. It was more simple than it sounds. I just had to remember that, to glance at Chewie, I had to look away from him. I eventually got the hang of it. But there was a bigger issue. My nose. It stuck out of the back, more than the rest of me. When I turned to the side, it protruded beyond the curve of Threepio's cheek. Brian found the answer. He stuck shiny gold tape on it. All good. But freeze frame and for a moment you can see an odd-shaped "thing" on the edge of Threepio's face. My nose.

Similar disembodied effects were achieved with me sitting on the floor with my hand up through Threepio's chest, animating his head, like a ventriloquist. That was after Peter had attached it as I sat adjacent, talking out of shot. Running down the corridors was even more fun. Wearing jeans and the top half of the suit, I stood on a wheeled luggage trolley. Peter and I were tied together, with a harness around our waists. The camera shot upwards from a low angle, avoiding my state of partial undress. Where Peter dragged me, I followed.

But my favourite trick was safely back in the *Falcon*, where Artoo thoughtfully welded a severed foot onto Threepio's ankle. Sitting on a packing case, Threepio's legs stretched out, complete, apart from his feet. This high-tech film set, in a faraway place and time, was employing an old stage illusionist's trick. I wasn't sitting at all. Wearing the top of the costume, with the lower half artfully arranged in front of me as if attached, I was actually kneeling inside the case. And you can't tell. Magic. Except for two sore knees.

INT. MILLENNIUM FALCON – HOLD

"I'm standing here in pieces and you are having delusions of grandeur!"

A cute line. Easy to say but very difficult to deliver – the scariest illusion so far. Now complete, but for the last unattached shin, I stood on one leg, waving the remaining part in the air. At the same time, I had to bend my real leg up behind me and make sure it was hidden behind my thigh. It only worked from a certain angle. The camera's one eye can't see round the side. But with the weight of the torso pressing down on me, my centre of gravity shifting precariously, it was a real and scary balancing act. These days they'd do it with green-screen effects. Back then they weren't so into green-screen. That would certainly change.

## 33 cake

I knew Frank Oz, a real star, because he was Miss Piggy from *The Muppet Show.*

I had appeared in scenes with her – or rather – him. And I had loved the show. And especially the Pig. And here he was wandering around Elstree but on our side of the street – his show being taped across the road at ATV Studios.

We would chat together, and I soon discovered what he was doing in our sequel. He had laid the world-famous porker aside for a while and had his hand up a character with a totally different personality – Master Yoda. The funny, wise, crinkly green face was one of creature-maker, Stuart Freeborn's best creations. In repose, his features had a remarkable personality but when Frank infused the rubber doll with his energy, Yoda truly lived.

Since Threepio never got to meet the gnome-like Jedi on set, I watched some scenes from the sidelines. But I would regularly see Frank around the studios. One day we were talking about puppetry and character acting, when he asked me an astonishing question.

"How did you come up with a voice for Threepio?"

I was literally speechless. Here was one of the masters of character voices known around the world, asking my advice. Of course he was voicing the puppet during scenes, acting out the whole thing with Mark. But he gathered that George was unsure, to say the least, about Frank's vocal performance. That certainly resonated with my experience. It wasn't the first time that George had failed to see the true connection between body and soul and voice and character.

I murmured that I'd had six months to prepare while they'd been making my costume. I'd thought a lot about the character and the situations he landed in and I admitted that, on the day, Threepio had arrived on set as a complete personality – through some kind of magic. Frank frowned and pottered away. I'm not sure I'd been much use.

Some months later, I was set another amazing question.

"You know Yoda?"

I was sitting at a large, round table, with all sorts of people from Production – people like George and Kirsh and Howard Kazanjian, our new and considerate producer. We'd been working in the Samuel Goldwyn Studios across the street in West Hollywood. Now we were taking a break in the famous, if florid, Formosa Cafe. The food was fine but the restaurant's real fame was due to the amazing cast list of movie stars who had eaten there over the years – Humphrey Bogart, Frank Sinatra, Johnny Depp. And me, sitting there, from a different league altogether. I did wonder who the guest was, sitting next to me. A real star perhaps?

"I'm the voice casting director for Yoda."

"Really? So you're looking for a sort of scrunched-up, squeaky, weird voice?"

"You know Yoda!"

He look stunned. Amazed that he was eating chicken stir-fry alongside someone familiar with the diminutive Jedi Knight. He explained that the character was so secret that he hadn't been allowed even a glance of a design or photo. Really, it felt that Production were giving themselves an extra headache. They were certainly doing that to my rather deflated dinner companion. Of course, there was a precedent – Threepio and me.

"Looping" was long gone. The slightly clumsy way of re-recording sound to picture had been replaced by Automatic Dialogue Replacement. The computer whizzed the digitised material back and forward, at will, vastly speeding the re-recording process. Doing ADR with Kirsh extended the inspirational time I spent working with him. I really enjoyed that. I was back in Los Angeles – in the dubbing suite.

Kirsh was making a fine job of helping me give Threepio the right vocal attitude. Then the producer, Gary Kurtz, began giving his own direction. Lines went by. He joined in directing, more and more. Kirsh left. A few takes later, I wondered what had happened to my director. I went out to the water cooler to see. Kirsh was there. He was irritated – very. He told me. We talked. He wasn't going to direct the session any longer. I was shocked. Out came Gary. I left them to it. Some minutes passed. Kirsh returned. Alone. We carried on, happily working together, just the two of us. He was very relaxed. He lay down on the floor. I continued for a couple of takes. The engineer was encouraging.

"Great. But there was a funny noise at the end of that last one. Let's go again."

The funny noise was Kirsh. Snoring.

George eventually realised that Frank's vocal performance was brilliantly aligned to his physical one. With Frank speaking the lines, Yoda was Yoda. But it would be a long while before I saw Frank's portrayal, and indeed my own, on the big screen.

I had, at last, been included in publicity events in Los Angeles. *The Empire Strikes Back* was madly awaited by the millions of fans across the planet. No doubt, their appetite was stimulated by seeing my name actually on the poster – a gesture from Lucasfilm that they did indeed acknowledge my participation in the film.

I was pleased and excited to feel a part of it all. A mood heightened by the lavishness of my accommodation. And now, after my few days in my luxurious, newly renovated hotel suite, I was flying to Washington for the premiere screening, joining all the other members of the cast. It was all going so well. Mid-flight, I began to feel quite strange. Altitude? Champagne? I checked in to the fabled Watergate Hotel. Another gorgeous suite, but I wasn't in the mood. I was feeling stranger. I phoned down. They found me a doctor.

I had flu. Not a cold. Real flu. Influenza. But what about this red mark on my foot? The medic said it was nothing, a small puncture. I must have trodden on something sharp as I padded, barefoot, around my newly glamorised suite in LA. Nothing to worry about.

I slept.

I called him back the next morning. Urgently. He arrived and was so shocked at what he saw, that he had them drag me out of bed and wheel me to his own car. No time for an ambulance then. We arrived at a hospital. He grabbed a wheelchair and rushed me forward. I learned later that no one had ever seen a doctor push a patient in a wheelchair before, so this must be serious – porters did menial tasks like that. We reached Reception. Everything stopped. Credit card? Fortunately Sid Ganis, Lucasfilm's Senior Vice President, had arrived with concern and the company's card to hand. It would not be the last time he and the card would come to my rescue. Within minutes I was in a private room, in a bed, an intravenous drip spliced into my hand. The flu had weakened my system. The tiny wound had become infected. I had developed blood poisoning. I was in shock.

INT. HOTH - ECHO BASE - MEDICAL CENTER

No. This was real.

INT. WASHINGTON - SIBLEY MEMORIAL HOSPITAL -
ROOM 25 - DAY

I was still in bed when everyone else was sitting in their seats at the premiere. The drugs were killing off the infection but I was so sad. Time passed in mournful thoughts at what I was missing. Instead of dressing in a smart premiere outfit, I was wearing two short daisy-covered nighties for modesty; one split at the front, covered by the other, split up the back. I was sitting up against the rumpled pillows, self-pitying tears wetting my cheeks. It seems antibiotics can cause depression. Also – I was depressed.

Somehow, word of my baleful situation got out. The door quietly opened. Four visitors walked in. These were the only people I'd seen here who were not dressed in white. Complete strangers they may have been but they were also kind and thoughtful and generous *Star Wars* fans. I must have been quite a sight – bed-haired, teary-faced, daisy-covered, attached to a drip. But they were smiling. Knowing I had a famously sweet tooth, they had brought me a big chocolate cake, to cheer me up. They gave me reason to dry my eyes. Such unexpected, thoughtful kindness. A week later, I returned to London. All the festivities had ended. I had missed everything. But I had survived.

And there would be other premieres.

# Christmas

It wasn't my idea. And a lot of people loved it. *Christmas In The Stars.*

1980 – I was rehearsing a stage production in a church hall in London. It was Friday night and we finished around six. I was a little anxious. Tomorrow I was flying to New York but had to be back for Monday morning rehearsals. Even travelling by Concorde, it was going to be a squeeze. Concorde – wow. But it was a very early taxi to Heathrow the next morning.

I gazed out of the window, in the very exclusive lounge. The stunning plane was parked right outside and pointing its elegant nose straight at me, personally. It was beautiful, so beautiful, and slender – inside, too. It was a different sort of squeeze from the one that worried me about getting back for rehearsals. The cabin was really quite slim. Being that way myself, it didn't concern me but there were some businessmen who would be less comfortable than me on the short flight. Short, because we'd be flying at twice the speed of sound. Sadly, that meant that the luxurious food service was over too soon. But what a treat.

Another treat – being met by one of the producers. Bizarrely, due to the time zone, I had arrived before I'd taken off; a paradox that rather added to this out-of-time experience. Another glamorous touch came as we sat in the back of a limo and she poured champagne into a saucer glass. It was all so luxurious – even after the back axle bounced roughly over a rut in the road and I snapped the stem off my dainty glass. I sipped carefully till we arrived at the mid-town studio. Life was not usually like this. But now I had to do some work.

*Christmas In The Stars* had been in pre-production for months. It was riding off the huge popularity of Meco's *Galactic Funk*. Meco was a recording artist who had released a disco version of John Williams' iconic compositions. It was great but wasn't an official tie-in with

Lucasfilm. The cover was all sorts of artwork, but nothing from *Star Wars* itself. This time the disc would be official.

The Robert Stigwood Organisation was famed in the music industry and RSO Records were producing this vinyl record album. It was going to celebrate two great entities coming together – Christmas and *Star Wars*. Maybe three entities, since it was Jon Bon Jovi's debut as a singer.

I was used to being in recording studios and this was no different, except that I usually arrived by bus. We settled in and I put on the head-phones that would play pre-made music in my head. No massed musicians around me. They'd done their thing earlier. Throughout the day, I would plunge through the musical numbers by myself.

"Bells, Bells, Bells".

"Christmas In The Stars".

"The Odds Against Christmas".

Such innocent pieces. The latter was particularly apt, since *Empire* had been released earlier that year. Threepio's obsession with irrele-vant statistics had been one of the main laughs. Of course, the odds against "Christmas being Christmas" were three hundred and sixty–five to one. But there was also some fairly batty stuff about what else December the twenty-fifth could have heralded – the invention of the wheel, perhaps? Really? But the lines I spoke, or half sang – *sprechgesang* being the great helper to the vocally challenged like me – were notable for another reason.

It was the first time real-world planet Earth was mixing its celebra-tions, or anything else, with characters from another galaxy. Threepio and Artoo were part of a droid team making toys for S. Claus in an unnamed location somewhere in space. Strange, as far as it went, but George Lucas had been very clear that Christian dogma could not sit alongside the Force. Yoda, in particular, could only warmly warble rather sentimental generalities about the time of year and goodwill to all things.

My thoughts were concentrated on the pages of lyrics, as I battled through the day. I finally ran out of puff around six that evening. They drove me to the luxurious Plaza Hotel, where I glanced around the suite and immediately sank into bed and sleep. It was after midnight, my time.

I woke up at two in the morning, New York time. But I felt great. I stared out at Central Park, surprised at the amount of nightlife going on outside – the lives of others. I went over the remaining words in my script. I did it again. I wandered about the suite – bored. I went downstairs. The front desk suddenly remembered that they'd forgotten to give me the large floral display, gifted to me from RSO. A generous gesture – just what I wanted for the remains of my one night in Manhattan. So the hours wore on in their mix of opulent loneliness. But eventually the sky lightened and it was time to pack and go. The team had all agreed to be back at work unusually early that Sunday morning. I had a plane to catch. We sped through the day, working on different pieces in the album.

There was even a magical sighting for the golden droid – a sleigh with eight reindeer hauling across the sky. Poor S. Claus would never jump to light speed that way, but I began to feel quite Christmassy. And then it was over.

I sat alone in the back of a limo to Kennedy airport, where I boarded that most beautiful plane. I lived like the elite again, for a few hours, fast but not at light speed either. Then I was safe home once more. I had got away with the madcap trip. Monday morning, I was on the bus to work, back to normal, rehearsing the play. But the real drama was happening in New York.

Production was completed, with the addition of various numbers that did not feature Threepio in sing-speak mode. It might have been an intergalactic mash-up too far, to have him enquiring, "What can you get a Wookiee for Christmas, when he already owns a comb?"

So Maury Yeston sang my favourite piece from the album. And there were several other fun numbers, backed by a choir of fifty school children. Maury had written most of the lyrics and music and would eventually become a famed musical composer on Broadway.

The record was released, in spite of RSO going out of business at that moment. It wasn't my problem but it meant that this musical masterpiece arrived in the record stores without the usual marketing fanfares. The sales were excellent but with RSO gone, there wasn't going to be another issue. Until it was eventually let out again on CD, many years later. But it remains a loved curiosity for enduring *Star Wars* fans. For many of them, it has become a ritual part of the Holiday Season, playing in the background as gift wrappings are ripped apart, or another glass is sipped.

Actually, a glass or two probably makes it all sound rather better.

Sand storms normally happen outside.

Ours would be at Elstree studios. Inside Stage Two, on day one of principal photography on *Revenge of the Jedi* – a last-minute name change would be forthcoming. But yes, they were shooting another sequel and, yes, I was back again in the gold suit.

The sandy painted walls blended in with the tons of real sand spread across the floor. In one corner stood the *Falcon*. On the far side of the stage were huddled rows of dustbins, filled with sand and powder. Silver tubes snaked upward, to vent themselves in front of a curtain of propeller blades, looking like an antique air force; their blades powerful enough to vacuum the binned debris up and out.

I was disconcerted to see Harrison and Mark and Carrie being heavily draped, goggled and protected from the approaching onslaught. I wondered if the little strip of gauze they had stuck inside my mask would work for me.

All we had to do was walk towards the *Falcon*'s ramp. Two cameras. Camera A, by the *Falcon* and Camera B, way off for a wide shot.

EXT. TATOOINE – DESERT – DAY

START THE FANS!
ROLL CAMERAS A AND B!

That was the last I heard – apart from the appalling roar of the propellers. The sound was overwhelming. I could see that the others had begun to move off, as rehearsed in quieter times. I set out after them. I wasn't fast enough – I'd lost them. I began to search. The air was solid with noise and thick with the choking junk, spewing out of the tubes. Earth and sky merged into one mass of sensory deprivation. I was blindly edging along in my suit in the dense, sandy fog, confused by the din. My eyes blurred over. I blew my breath upwards to try to clear the condensation on the plastic gels they had stuck over the eyeholes. It bounced my breath off the interior of the mask and onto the gels. It helped, a little. The noise still pounded but I could see better. I could see B Camera, surprisingly, right in front of me. Its deafened clapper-loader was kneeling before the lens, still waiting to mark his slate, as disorientated as I was. I never saw the rock – not even after I had careened over it and lay pancaked on the sand. The noise whirred to a stop.

Silence – apart from the coughing. They stood me up. I was okay. The scene wasn't. It was cut.

## 36 beep

We landed somewhere in the rocky desert terrain.

It had been a fun flight in a twin-engine eight-seater. George's good mood only spoilt by the pink-iced cake in his packed lunch. I salvaged the situation by swapping it for my chocolate one – George likes chocolate.

We eventually landed and checked in to the Fire Creek Motel, as I remember. It was basic. Very basic. There was no television reception and the food was clearly not memorable at all. But there was a gift shop. George jokingly bought me a souvenir bill-fold of orange hide – a bucking bronco was crudely branded into the cheap suede surface, with the words, "My Little Buckaroo". Nice. I opened it. It was empty. We went to work.

They put the camera in a cave, shooting outwards. I stood outside, with the rock vista stretching out to the horizon behind me. Threepio was on guard. Supposedly, Luke would be in the cave itself, constructing a new lightsaber. He'd lost his original blade at about the same time as he lost his hand. Ultimately the scenes would hit the cutting-room floor and Artoo would prove to have had a new saber all the time – but we weren't to know that yet. We got the shot and moved on. Fast. The shadows were lengthening, which would give the next scene an atmospheric quality. However, it meant the day was coming to an end. No one wanted to spend an extra night at the motel, so everyone in the tiny crew pitched in and carried. We rushed to get the shot.

Several times, Artoo went off-piste, merrily ploughing a completely different path from the one David Schaefer was struggling to maintain with his remote control. Apparently, the little droid was picking up strong radio signals, emanating from Edwards Air Force Base. We just had to keep doing it over and over, as the shadows grew longer. Part of ILM's genius team, David had been my colleague on various live adventures round the planet. Such events were scary, in that they couldn't be edited. If something went wrong, you had to deal with it in front of the audience. Fortunately, with David's skill, that never happened. Filming was different. You could do things again and again.

Earlier, the crew had constructed a hide for the camera. I watched – fascinated. It had a sheet-glass window, a portion of which was being blacked out. They explained that the painted area would cover a part of the film stock. Later, they would expose that area of the film to a matte painting of the palace itself, back at ILM. For now, the clear glass would allow the camera to film only me and Artoo, walking away on our mission.

It had taken a while to set the whole thing up and I grabbed the opportunity to rehearse walking up the track – searching out any rock or pothole that could send me tumbling. Artoo was still in his packing case.

I would just pretend, as usual.

EXT. TATOOINE – ROAD TO JABBA'S PALACE

ACTION!

"Of course I am worried. And you should be, too. Lando Calrissian and poor Chewbacca never returned from this awful place."

Then. Surprisingly. Behind me.

"Beep-beep. Beep-beep. Beep-beep."

It had taken nearly three movies to get to this point. George was following me on the path. Squatting on his haunches, waddling along, making very silly Artoo sounds.

We got the shot. We didn't have to spend an extra night.


It was the happiest day.


## 37 caged

I had never been a fan of Tunisia, as planet Tatooine. Well, I got my comeuppance in *Revenge*.

October 1982.

I landed at the dusty aerodrome in Yuma, Arizona. Mark had been concerned about how to avoid the crush of fans and paparazzi. The place was deserted. But hot. A short drive got me to the Stardust Hotel. I was amused – Robert Watts had teased me since our first days together on *A New Hope*. Here he was for his third stint on *Star Wars*, now promoted to the role of co-producer. I was soon to be promoted, too – to God of the Ewoks. But basically I was still Threepio underneath it all. Back in the early days, Robert had endearingly nicknamed me "Stardust", so I might have assumed the inn was called after me. It wasn't. It had been around a lot longer than me and rather looked it.

Yuma itself seemed to be a mile of neon-bright fast food outlets, stuck together. Burgers and nuggets were the thing – vegetables were fries. Fortunately, we were fed on the set. And the set was in a vast wire cage, plonked in the desert sands. This was where we were filming *Blue Harvest – Horror Beyond Imagination*. The spoof title was intended to kid the townsfolk into believing that this was not a *Star Wars* shoot. Everything to do with the production was liveried in blue and white lettering – the vehicles, hats, jackets, T-shirts, waterproofs and call-sheets all meticulously badged with a fake identity. This, in an effort to keep location costs down, and to allow the production to go ahead discreetly. Fat chance.

It was a half-hour drive out of town, off the main road and through the dunes. What a visual treat, to pass the rippled sand banks that constantly changed in the sunlight and shadows. As the terrain flattened, there was the set. And there was the hill. It transpired that the former had been built without any regard for the crowds who populated the latter. The giant slope was a mecca for dune-buggy enthusiasts. They would zoom noisily down and up again, all through our shoot. Others sat on the top with their telephoto lenses, snapping away at the mysteries below. And indeed, it did appear a strange construction.

It looked rather sinister, with its high perimeter fencing – as if a crazy border containment camp. Its extraordinary centrepiece was fringed with trucks and transits and security guards. To keep ourselves amused in the long periods of waiting around, Mark and I would wander out of our air-conditioned mobile homes to chat with the sightseers, peeping politely through our perimeter. We faced each other through the chain-link mesh. Our new acquaintances seemed fascinated by what we were up to. Especially, they wanted to know why they had seen a very recognisable gold robot in this horror film. So much for secrecy. It was fun and felt like being in a zoo, though I wasn't sure which of us was the exhibit.

We were actually about seventy feet above the fake desert floor. The real desert was about seventy feet below that. In the centre was a giant hole. All the transit vans were parked underneath. It was an amazing set. Timber, canvas, steam vapour and plaster making a living, breathing ship of the desert.

Threepio was standing on deck. Vast sails fluttered and ballooned above me. As a result of Salacious Crumb's spiteful attack, one of Threepio's eyes was left dangling down his cheek. The convincing prosthetic took away half of my, already severely limited, vision and now I was tottering a few feet from the railing – which they had removed.

EXT. SAIL BARGE - OBSERVATION DECK

ACTION!

As scripted, the powerful motorised Artoo mischievously nudged me forward. I remembered how hard it was to control. I recalled the number of times the machine had run into and over my toes in the two previous productions. Now I teetered closer to the edge, ahead of it – and closer. I raised my arms in theatrical and genuine fear, as I prepared to tumble over.

CUT!

I stepped back from the edge, relieved. Then Tracey Eddon arrived. They dressed her in a rubber facsimile of my suit and led her to the unguarded rail at the edge of the deck, as if to walk the plank. I demonstrated my last position. Just watching a fellow human in this perilous moment made me feel nervous.

ACTION!

Tracey mimicked my pose and then toppled fearlessly forward and down, twisting in mid-air. I learned it's what Stunts do, to land safely on their back. Of course she didn't crash to the desert floor, fake or not. Out of shot, some feet below, mattresses were laid on top of a whole warehouse-worth of cardboard boxes. They absorbed the energy of her impact, but it was still an impact – it could still hurt. She landed safely, like the professional she was, and walked off the set in one piece. With the editor's skill, you can't tell it wasn't me. But I knew – it was Tracey.

A few hours later, she reappeared in a wig and a more revealing costume – Princess Leia's bikini. Because it is Tracey, in that iconic outfit, who swings across from Jabba's barge to the skiff. She was small enough to be a stunt double for both Carrie and me. Small, but tough.

But Jabba's barge would have its revenge.

I did a bad thing. In spite of being warned not to even think of riding a dune buggy, I borrowed one – without thinking. My *Blue Harvest* hat squashed down low, I wore a red bandana over my face as a disguise. I zoomed and skidded about with great joy and didn't roll it or threaten my insurance cover. It was exhilarating fun but a risk. Very unprofessional.

Later, sitting in the shade outside my trailer, I was facing away from the barge and the bikers' hill beyond. I enjoyed the empty, sandy landscape. They had torn up the few scrubby plants to make the place more alien than it actually was. Maybe the vegetation would grow back in time – I hoped so. Nature is good at that sort of thing. It was all rather peaceful. The sounds of human activity carrying on without me in the distance were rather comforting. Then a strange noise. A sort of Bang. A kind of Pop. Then the most spine-chilling scream. And again. And again. This was certainly horror beyond my imagination. There was silence. Now running feet. Now the helicopter flying out.

A member of the crew had been working inside the hull of the set. A hose disconnected itself from the effects steam generator nearby. He had been hit by a vicious jet of scalding steam. When he returned from hospital, unbelievably, he was embarrassed that he had cried out in pain. He thought he should have been tougher. If it had been me, I would have yelled for a week.

On a happier note, I was heading back to the Stardust Hotel, very comfortably relaxing in the back of my car. It had been another rather dusty day in the heat. The privacy of the air-conditioned vehicle made the journey back really quite pleasant. There was hardly ever any traffic on the roads, apart from our own production vehicles. So I was surprised that someone was trying to overtake, blasting the horn for my driver to move out of the way. He did. The crew bus slowly came alongside. It was quite a sight. Every window was filled with a bare bum, as the crew collectively mooned at me. I laughed and laughed and laughed. If only I'd had a camera.

Jabba's barge was indeed a magnificent vessel. It really was constructed as a ship – very convincing with its huge set of sails. Convincing and problematic. I was musing in a quiet corner, hearing the wind wiffling against the canvas sheets above me, and the faint groans from the wooden structure below. My reverie was interrupted by David Tomblin. David was our superb, glorious First AD, with a light and humorous touch. His voice was a gravelly mix of W.C. Fields and Captain Ahab. He came with interesting advice. It seemed that the sails really were sails. As such, they were catching the desert breeze. That would have been fine, were they not attached to the barge, and were the barge not attached to the vast, wooden scaffold on which it was planted. It seemed there was a possibility that the entire set might actually drift back to Yuma.

"So, my darling. I think you'd better abandon ship, as they say."

Though I did exactly what he suggested – and fast – the barge stayed put, perched on the huge sandy platform that was the Pit of Carkoon, nesting place of the giant rubber sphincter – the visible presence of the all-powerful Sarlacc. Underneath was the temporary garage, and the exit passage from the monster's digestive tract.

Over several days, the horrible beast claimed many victims – real ones – all stunt actors. I watched them fearlessly tumble off the barge and smack into the pulsating orifice below, before they slithered down and out of sight. Their performance made the whole battle look realistically dangerous which, in fact, it was. The Stardust Hotel took on the aspect of a hospital. Out of action for the time being, several actors lay around the pool, various parts of their anatomy covered in plaster casts and bandages. The others were in hospital, being patched up.

Everyone survived.

But not without a certain amount of pain and suffering.

Which, *Star Wars* experts will know, is what the Sarlacc newly defined.

## 38 gloop

Jabba's palace was never there.

It would eventually be a wondrous matte painting, planted on shots, filmed in a Californian national park where I had walked weeks before. Now I was walking on set, back at Elstree. And this was the real thing. Well, it was real as far as it went – which was about twenty feet. The rest would, as usual, be added later by ILM. The intimidating doorway to the palace was impressive, unless you looked upward. It was really quite a low build.

EXT. JABBA'S PALACE – GATE

ACTION!

Artoo and I approached. I knocked, then made to move off, without waiting for a response. When it came, Threepio was surprised. And so was I. Richard Marquand, the putative director, must have assumed that I had peripheral vision. He must have supposed I could see the giant eyeball when it shot out of the door to my right. I couldn't. I didn't. And he didn't cue me. So I sort of guessed at its arrival. I am still embarrassed by the delay in my mistimed reaction. Then of course, I had another one-sided conversation. The ball didn't speak till later – neither did Artoo. Even for me it was quite a weird three-way non-exchange. But I had become fairly used to that sort of thing by now.

I wasn't sure about the metalwork spider that scared Threepio into running down the hallway. I was concentrating on aiming at the tiny ramp that Props had put into the step-down in the sand floor. If I'd missed it, I probably would have fallen flat – again. The atmosphere in the vast hallway was quite sinister but pig guards are not really very menacing at all. They'd like to be, but wearing inches-thick layers of foam around your body can sap the energy to scare. I really empathised with the team when they were un-velcroed from their sweaty prisons.

And then I met Bib Fortuna.

I'd worked with Michael Carter in the theatre and always admired his acting talent. Here was no exception. He was wonderfully creepy and inventive as he led Threepio round the corner, to meet the illustrious Jabba. Watching the scene in ADR, I spotted an opportunity. I asked George if I could cram in an extra line. Why not? Everyone else had said it. So finally, I did too.

"I have a bad feeling about this."

And I loved Jabba. He was locked into the set and couldn't go wandering away, to have Hair and Makeup. I first met him at Elstree, when he was a clay and chicken-wire construction. Now, thanks to Stuart Freeborn's art, he was a convincing, greenish, articulate, rubber monster. His look was one thing but his repellent body language came from a band of puppeteers, inside and out. Dave Barclay was the right hand and lips, Toby Philpott the left arm and tongue, while hilarious Mike Edmonds gently rolled around inside Jabba's tail. Yet another puppeteer operated the eyes by remote control. Four people creating something remarkable.

Dave and I had personal radio contact. We whiled away the hours, inside our own little worlds, by nattering about things going on around us, in the weirdness that was Jabba's palace. Stuff happened. Carrie found it hard being disguised as Boushh – she didn't like wearing the face mask. There was so much atmospheric smoke, that we felt we were inhaling a pack of twenty each day. The eight-teated fat lady was said to be suffering a bout of diarrhoea. We didn't talk about that, much.

Salacious Crumb was a welcome distraction for me. Wielded on the forearm of Tim Rose, Crumb kept me endlessly amused. His snarky character was a delight. Tim's snarlings and cacklings were wickedly believable. I asked, and he let me have a go. I slid my arm up into the glove and moved the puppet's head. Then the other way. Nothing. The thing was a collection of feathers and plastics. Nothing more.

The critter was beautifully designed but it was Tim's acting skills that made it come so realistically alive.

A moment of tension.

It was long before the abundance of blue and green screen scenes but Peter Diamond was still very much a popular member of the cast and crew. As a stuntman he was no stranger to peril. But this seemed to be going too far. First having appeared as the murderous Tusken Raider, here he was in another bizarre outfit. Trailing electric cables behind him, he walked slowly – and very carefully – across Jabba's throne room. He was garbed in some kind of insulating suit. His outstretched and elongated arms were dressed with rows of fragile light bulbs like some ghastly parade float. His outer glow was mesmerising. So was the thought that he might get electrocuted at any moment. The idea was that he would provide a travelling source of light for some creature character that would be drawn in and added later. It was one of the moments of real suspense on the set. Peter survived but the idea didn't.

The all-powerful Jabba took his revenge on Threepio – or rather the suit. And actually, it wasn't Jabba but his slime that was the problem. Props had perhaps thought to save some of the budget and use an off-the-shelf cleaning product. They could have invented something themselves but found a jar of green gloop that would do the trick – a retail substance for cleaning grimy hands after an oil change. They daubed it liberally on Threepio's golden skin. It looked great on film. The shot was done. They wiped it off. Off too came the gold finish. The product had bleached large areas of the costume. It had to be sent off for resurfacing.

Expensive.

Years before, there were six of us training to become scuba divers in my local sub-aqua club.

Wet suit, gloves, tank, first stage, second stage, fins, mask. We all struggled a bit – me less so. It was just like being on a *Star Wars* film in a gold suit, except that we were all taught a lot about safety and survival. This was going to come in handy.

Now I was lying on the floor in my jeans and trainers. Brian Lofthouse dressed me in gold, just from the waist up. The camera was very close – closer was Salacious Crumb, with his attendant Tim Rose, brilliantly manipulating him as usual.

INT. SAIL BARGE – OBSERVATION DECK

ACTION!

Crumb cackled as he tore at the eye he was trying to wrench out of Threepio's face. All I had to do was writhe and object – so easy. Suddenly. A strange sensation. Panic. Not Threepio's – mine! I couldn't breathe. I was trapped.

"Get me out! Get me out!"

Instantly, Brian dived in front of the lens and undid the bolts around my head. He sat me up. I tried to breathe slowly – it was hard. I realised that, for the first time in my life, I had suffered a moment of claustrophobia. I was in a safe place, with the camera operator and Tim Rose and Brian right next to me – and yet I had been overtaken by a fear – for no reason. I talked myself down; reassured myself that I was okay. More than okay. So Brian tucked me back inside and we finished the scene. But that brief experience gave me a tiny insight into what a phobia feels like – not good.

It was at the ABC Theater in New York. It was 1985. Threepio ran down the aisle and up onto the stage, to join the producers of the animated TV series, *Droids*. It was all quite exciting and great fun. I'd also enjoyed recording the many and various scripts in Toronto. They were aimed at a young audience and told of the further exploits of Artoo and Threepio. At last we were ready to present this breakthrough entertainment to the world. It would be broadcast on the ABC network, which is why I was here. This was the launch extravaganza.

Threepio politely bowed to the executives who were now applauding his energetic arrival. At that moment, I realised that I had used up all my lung capacity by running from the back of the auditorium. I was about to pass out from lack of oxygen. Somehow, my scuba training clicked in. I didn't panic. I calmed myself down. I survived. It was a rehearsal. When the main event happened, later that day, Threepio strolled down the aisle. He graciously shook hands with members of the audience. He eventually joined the others on stage.

I had learned.

Well, I thought I had.

## 40 torment

Threepio's hands had always been useless – from the first moment Maxi and I sat on my bed, in the failing light, gluing them together.

They had little practical value. I had to curl my hands to keep the strange metal pieces from pulling the gloves off. The joints of Threepio's gloves bore no relation to my anatomy. They were mere encumbrances, rather than a useful aid to practical effect or gesture; flopping uselessly off my wrists. Fortunately, I was hardly ever required to hold anything. Except once – many years ago. I was only wearing his left arm and hand. The rest of me was shirt and jeans.

INT. DEATH STAR – MAIN GANTRY – COMMAND OFFICE

ACTION!

I brought my arm into shot, opened my palm over the communica-tion device and slapped it down, closing the dangling finger joints around it. I pulled my arm out of frame, clutching my prize.

CUT.

It is amazing what a patch of double-sided sticky tape can do, stuck in the centre of your palm.

But now, a new design for a new Episode – one-piece gloves made of thick plastic. They looked the same. They had greeblies inserted on the top. But they still bore little relation to my own human anatomy. And I could hardly bend them – until my body heat eventually warmed and softened the material. If I needed to point in a scene, I had to prepare well in advance. I forced my index finger outwards and bent it in posi-tion against my leg, till required. When the moment came, I swiftly raised the arm. The finger stayed pointed long enough for the effect I wanted. It was supremely frustrating. I basically had two ping-pong bats for hands, and the pressure was excruciating as the arms bore down on my wrists, in a sort of thumbscrew effect. But later, on the Forest Moon of Endor, they would cause me a different sort of torture.

Brian laid out my suit in the chill air under the trees. He got the Sparks to rig some lamps over the hands. The heat from the nine-light softened the plastic, making them more pleasant and somewhat easier to put on. It made them easier to manipulate, too. Like a kind mum, Brian would lovingly warm the hands on the trestle table that was my dressing area in the forest. Since they were hardly a pleasure to wear, Brian left them until nearly last – Threepio's head being always the final blow to my comfort and freedom. The inevitable happened.

One day, he left the gloves under the fearsome lighting array for rather longer than usual, possibly distracted by some heavy Ewok action.

But he finally slid them onto my hands. There was a moment before the heat hit me. I yelped at the raging plastic. A new kind of torment.

Finally, I had had enough. I took a scalpel and sliced away all but the barest bones. Apart from the tops, they were now simply my black gloves and some wires. It gave me more functionality. I could pick up anything I liked – almost. It would be decades before I really got what I wanted. What Threepio needed. But my trials by fire weren't over.

By now, Brian and I had worked out a rhythm of getting me ready to film. The arms, the legs, the hands, the feet, the head and, always the last moment, switching on the eyes – still powered by a pack of batteries. I had forgiven him the "hand" moment, so was later surprised at the growing heat behind me. Had Brian left a screwdriver sticking in my back?

He was wounded at the suggestion. On investigation he found the battery pack was shorting out – I was being baked alive!

## 41 bonfires

We were in Stout Grove, somewhere near Crescent City. California.

The trees were impressively threatening. Centuries-old redwoods towered above us; stunning monuments to nature. Lest we should be stunned in other ways, a work gang looked out for "widow makers" – branches that had grown old and tired and were soon to drop off. The wife of anyone standing underneath would get a phone call later that day, hence the name. In spite of acquiring this piece of morbid information, I found the atmosphere deeply serene. The leafy undergrowth matched the great canopy of leaves up in the sky. Sunlight filtered magically through, like some movie lighting effect which, indeed, it was going to be. We were on the Forest Moon of Endor.

The protective awning created a sort of micro-climate at ground level. It was quite cool, unless you stood in a clearing – there it was sunbathing time. The forest floor was centuries in the making, with decaying vegetation and creepers and ferns contributing to a beautiful, earthy nightmare for Threepio. They laid down floorboards whenever I was on the move. Not so for the poor stormtroopers.

EXT. ENDOR – GENERATOR BUNKER

ACTION!

"I say! Over here! Are you looking for me?"

Stormtroopers were searching the area for rebels. Cued by my amplified voice from a loudspeaker hidden in the undergrowth next to me, the troopers turned in my direction, to see Threepio sticking himself out from behind a gigantic tree trunk. They ran to arrest him. It was scary, then scarier, as one fell over, then a second. The evil in me came to the fore. I turned the scene into a steeple-chase commentary.

"And-Number-Two-Is-Down-But-Number-Six-Is-Coming-Up-On-The-Outside-And-As-He-Takes-A-Tumble-At-The-Fence-It-Is-Number-Twelve-Who-Sprints-For…" sort of thing.

My breathless voice echoed around the forest. I had fun – and no one was hurt. But I wondered why stormtroopers were so clumsy. Picking up an abandoned helmet, I looked through the green plastic eyes. It was like looking through an empty wine bottle. It seemed that troopers could barely see at all. No wonder they were accident prone. It certainly explained why they never hit anyone with their blasters.

The Props Department was ever inventive. But the net proved a challenge – and not only for me. Made of thick rope covered in latex, it was certainly robust enough to hold our group. We were indeed trapped by the crude resourcefulness of the surprisingly all-powerful Ewoks. But once we were all carefully hoisted aloft, it became clear that the camera could barely see us through the hessian mesh. We were ignominiously lowered to the forest floor again. We stood around like cargo waiting to be shipped but were soon winched back up, Props having cut out every alternate square of net, so our faces could peek out.

But the odder thing was what had sprung the trap in the first place. I had time to study it later. The item that had so attracted Chewie's hunger was actually animal. Well, part of an animal – the part at the rear. Days later, as I wandered the delights of the local town, with its grandiose title, I found a souvenir shop. In the window, something very similar to the Wookiee snack I'd seen on set. In a line, the upturned hind quarters of several small deer snarled at me. Their disembodied legs stuck up in the air, like elongated horns. A pair of plastic eyes stuck into the fur above. Below, a set of teeth – framing each sphincter. Deer walk afraid in Crescent City.

Much as I did like the location, my main source of fun was sparring with Ralph Nelson – a highly-regarded stills cameraman. Back in 1976, I had enjoyed working with John Jay. He shot all the stills on *A New Hope*. One of his iconic snaps is of Artoo and Threepio, standing together outside the Homestead. Threepio on the left, my deck shoes clearly peeking out from underneath their gold plastic covers. On the right, Artoo with its legs forgetfully locked in position; the packing struts still screwed in place, having just been hoisted out of its travelling case. Between them on the sand – a cigarette butt. I liked John. He was a seasoned professional but perhaps, sometimes missed the details. He gave me pause during our last scene in the desert.

"Why are you wearing a silver leg today?"

He'd been shooting for two weeks and he'd never noticed George's subtle hint at Threepio's accident-prone history. Mind you, lots of other people missed it, too.

Ralph was very respectful of John's work but less respectful of me. Then I wasn't respectful of him, either. I told him that anyone can take a photo. So he gave me one of his cameras in a soundproof box, a blimp, to try my hand at shooting stills. It was an action scene – the fight outside the bunker. I aimed but didn't manage a single shot. It was harder than it looked. The actors kept moving.

Ralph had a schoolboy's sense of humour. His ability with a toy fartmaker was legendary in the world of hilariously cheap gags. But that wasn't enough for him. One day he poured cold water down inside the leg of my costume, filling my shoe, knowing I couldn't escape. So, when he was dozing on set, I had the FX crew quietly rig an explosive squib under his chair. The effect was rather satisfying. But I shouldn't have done that.

Years later, in a prequel, I had rehearsed a scene and walked past Ralph, back to my number one position. ILM's Don Bies was now my super-skilled, trusted assistant, friend – encasing me in the costume and brilliantly driving Artoo. He was waiting to put my head inside Threepio's. As usual, I closed my eyes as the two halves came together. I heard them clip into place and opened my eyes. Total darkness. Something had gone wrong. I couldn't imagine what. I heard sniggering. Ralph had stuck gaffer tape over the eyeholes inside my mask. He let me out. Eventually. I'll get him back one day.

"What's the red light behind me?"

"Oh. You'd better stop."

I was driving back from dinner in town with my saviour from *Empire* days, Sid Ganis, in the middle of the night, in the middle of nowhere. The cop had been hiding behind a redwood. I was not pleased – especially since I was driving Lucasfilm's Vice President. Would I go to jail and halt production? The company quietly paid my fine and that was the end. Shortly afterwards, some State Troopers visited the set. They said their colleague was a bit embarrassed at having booked See-Threepio for speeding. I toyed whether to send him an autographed photo. I decided not to. The message I considered writing might really have landed me in a cell.

What a joy to see Warwick Davis under the trees. Eleven years old and really cute – as opposed to the other Ewoks, who were meant to be, but weren't. Warwick's mask was the only face that was actually animated, to some extent. It had been planned that several furry friends would have faces capable of expression. Time and budget ran out. So I spent days surrounded by the blank stares of the fur-fringed, goggle-eyed creatures. I felt as if I was in an animal version of *Village of the Damned*. Warwick did manage to get something through his costume. His tongue. He stuck it through the rubber lips of the mask and wiggled it – and with his new-found acting ability, it worked rather well.

It wasn't all work in this compelling landscape. A Sunday fishing trip was arranged for those of a sporting nature. I went anyway. Normally preferring to leave the capture of food to others, I was so glad I tagged along with the group. There were several boats with four or five of us aboard, forming a quirky armada as we were rowed up-river together. It was delightful. After a while, the guide hovered our boat in a spot he thought might be suitably thronged with fish. We cast our lines, plopping them rather noisily into the water. The ripples soon stilled and we sat there in peaceful contemplation. I didn't really care if I caught anything. It was all so beautiful and calm. Nothing happened. We reeled in our empty lines and drifted to another prime spot in the gentle flowing waters. Our hooks once more vanished under the surface. We watched and waited, murmuring to each other, lest we scare off any fish below.

VVVRRROOOMMM!

Harrison careened around the bend in the river. His speedboat roared and swirled around our puny craft, as he laughingly waved greetings to us all. Then he was gone.

The water sloshed and rocked against our boat and lapped to a stillness, the fish presumably fled for the day. It had been a surprise.

Like a visitation from Harrison's other action hero. But now, another surprise. My line was taut. The thrill of the hunt took over. I reeled it in. And there was a fish struggling away from me. I was surprisingly excited as I grabbed a net to scoop up the silvery beauty. The hook dislodged itself and my prize just rested in the net, already exhausted by the brief struggle. I made a decision and took a photo. Gently sliding the net back into the water, I let the fish float away. It lay very still. I felt bad. Then with a gentle flourish of its tail, it was gone. What a sense of relief. But now others in our group were hauling in lines. It was quite a catch – gleaming trophy fish that would provide a generous supper. I had to admit, mine had been something of a tiddler.

EXT. ENDOR - FOREST - DENSE FOLIAGE

ACTION!

"It's against my programming to impersonate a deity!"

I loved the idea of Threepio becoming a god. A chance to get his own back, on one human in particular. We were back at the Ewok village at Elstree Studios. The giant set was raised high above the stage floor. Painted forest backdrops filled in the picture behind the prop trees. The camera could encompass the depth of the forest floor, helped by pumping dry ice into the area below. It gave a lovely, misty quality to the view. And the area didn't go to waste. Out of sight, there were rows of chairs where off-duty Ewoks could relax. It was a few days before they realised that some of our furry friends were in danger of becoming a little too chilled out. Dry ice is the friendly term for a rather unfriendly substance, carbon dioxide. In solid form it's so cold as to burn the skin. As it warms and becomes a gas, it changes the atmosphere, and not in a good way. The Ewoks were in danger of passing out due to lack of oxygen. They moved the chairs.

Meanwhile, I had a throne. But I too felt slightly unsafe. I trusted the crew – but you never know. Wires, front and back, tensed and then winched me up to the studio rafters – the flies. A small length of tracking above, allowed the chair to travel in a circle, as I waved my arms in fear. It was partially real. I was genuinely glad when I landed.

I'm often asked, what is my favourite line from the movies. Han had been bullying and dissing Threepio since their first meeting. Now, hung over a pile of firewood about to be ignited by an Ewok, the cocky young smuggler wondered what was happening. Threepio was always happy to provide information.

EXT. ENDOR – EWOK VILLAGE SQUARE

ACTION!

"It appears, Captain Solo, that you are to be the main course for the banquet given in my honour."

You can read the satisfaction on Threepio's face.

I don't wear the costume in rehearsal. Everyone can see my face and Threepio's emotions writ very large on it. To get anything through the suit, my droid performance has to be slightly larger than life – *Robot World* rather than *World Of Chekhov*. In other words, it's a form of overacting. Without the suit, it's probably quite apparent. But there's no point in rehearsing out of character.

This being the third movie, I had evolved a little. Both as myself and as the droid. Still insecure that I looked and sounded foolish in rehearsal and equally so within the suit, I had to go on in my own way. I now knew what it took to create an effect through the costume; the can and cannots of wearing a suit like that. Still dependent on the script to give him opportunities for new and fresh expression, Threepio was Threepio was Threepio – not everyone's cup of tea – but I liked him. So. Tough.

His character is really an exaggeration of a human. Somehow the audience enjoys human emotions coming from a creature that is not actually flesh and blood. They become quite forgiving and empathetic.

George's script for *A New Hope* had firmly planted Threepio in my head. It was gloriously well-written and defined the basis of his character. I could absorb him. Once absorbed, a character can live in the actor's mind, to the extent that many of its characteristics become instinctive. He was never going to be allowed to be a protagonist, someone who heroically moved the story forward. He would always be re- rather than pro-active. But that allowed the audience to empathise with him. His lot in life is, for the most part, like those of us ultimately watching him on screen. His overt sensitivity and nerves are the raw emotions that humans are taught to hide as they grow up.

I had grown to admire his innate loyalty; a quality I admire in humans, so maybe I was able to relate and play it up a little. But unlike me, the poor creature has no sense of humour, which actually makes him quite funny to watch. He is the ultimate straight man. The fact that he finds human behaviour hard to understand is key to some of his anxieties. Humour and irony are essential to survive living on any planet I know. Without them, Threepio is indeed doomed to suffer.

In spite of the overblown performance, I did need to give Threepio a sense of reality and truth. In his own way, he needs to seem, to feel, real. Then we all can believe in him. It was certainly a challenge from the start, especially relating with the ever-silent Artoo. Thank The Maker for those improv classes at drama school. Then, rather stupidly late, I realised that my stint as the sharp-witted Guildenstern had been a rehearsal for it all. His relationship to Stoppard's more blunt, gung-ho creation, Rosencrantz, was like a mirror of the two droids. Gloriously bonded, interdependent in their unique characters, tempest-torn by events beyond their control. R was Artoo. G was Threepio.

On top of the character play, I did have to continually consider the physical aspects of each scene. I needed to work around the restrictions of the suit, whether it was manual or visual. The hands couldn't touch the face or head. That took away quite a range of human gestures.

The head could only turn a few degrees in the neck. I had to fake eye-lines to avoid peering downwards at Artoo or the Ewoks, which would have made Threepio seem like an old man. I wanted him to stand stoically upright. I only had so much to work with and it was my job to make the best of it. Which, for the most part, I did. With the occasional failing. However, I did rely on everyone else performing as in rehearsal. Which, for the most part, they did.

It didn't help that with all the clicks and squeaks of the costume echoed and amplified up inside the head, it was often hard to hear what the others were saying. Equally hard for them to hear my muffled tones, again deafening me from the inside.

Even in unsuited rehearsal I stand like Threepio, with my arms spread like him – it helps the camera crew understand how much of my physical presence will fill the screen. I speak in his voice. It probably looks and sounds ridiculous without the mask. But it's what I do to help me stay in character.

Marquand had asked me to work it out for myself. So I spent the weekend rehearsing at home. How to mime the story of our adventure that Threepio was tasked with telling the Ewoks, so they would understand our plight and help our cause. Back in the village on Monday morning, I demonstrated my homework to the tiny audience. For this moment, I had written simple lines in English. Later, Ben Burtt and I would re-record the words in Ben's cleverly constructed Ewokese. But for now, it was me delivering some fairly lame stuff.

"Princess Leia put a message in Artoo because there was this really bad human – Darth Vader who built the Death Star. Then we met a Jedi, Obi-Wan Kenobi who fought him with his glow stick. We were attacked by Walkers but Master Luke blew them up. And we flew to Cloud City in the *Millennium Falcon*..." and so on.

Not Shakespeare. But a start. No good being embarrassed, I went at it full tilt. The Ewok faces gazed up at me with their scary dead eyes.

But I caught Harrison's rather disdainful stare from off camera. Clearly he was not impressed with my performance. But with Ben's sound effects of walkers, X-wings and explosions, it became a much-loved scene. Not bad for a character who once apologised for being not very good at telling stories. Subconsciously, that look on Harrison's face may have inspired one of my proudest moments.

INT. ENDOR - CHIEF'S HUT - COUNCIL OF ELDERS

Threepio is in conversation with one of the tribe.

Han rudely taps him on the shoulder, interrupting. The droid turns and gets a peremptory demand, right in his face. He turns back and begins politely translating Han's enquiry. It happens again. Threepio politely listens and turns back to his new little friend. Han taps once more – once too often.

The irritated droid whips his head round, giving this ill-mannered human a furious stare. And another – his emotion clearly written on his golden face. The mask doesn't change. The emotion does. The anger is right there. It took a little planning with my head and torso positions. But I think I managed to communicate Threepio's true feelings.

The torture room was a smaller challenge. How to show absolute horror as the child droid gets pulled apart. I realised that humans do a sort of tortoise thing when they're afraid – hunching shoulders around the ears. I think Threepio's horrified reaction is quite effective. Besides the actual drama, it was a strange scene to shoot. Marquand had his face in the script the whole time. He personally read-in the lines of the chief torturer. At the end of the shot he looked up and asked the cameraman if it was okay. I wasn't sure whether he meant my performance or his. He liked performing. He liked dramatically posing for stills. But it was apparent that it was actually George who was directing – by proxy.

C-Z3

C-3PO

Signings

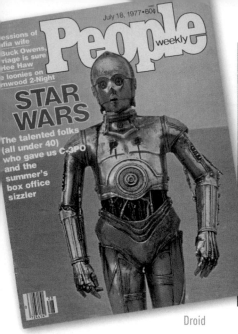

July 18, 1977 • 60¢

# People
weekly

essions of
...dia wife
Buck Owens,
...riage is sure
...Hee Haw
...e loonies on
...rnwood 2-Night

## STAR WARS

The talented folks
(all under 40)
who gave us C-3PO
and the
summer's
box office
sizzler

Droid

Donnie and Marie

Special

the
## STAR WARS
holiday special

Anthony Daniels

295
PROGRAM
PARTICIPANT
ANTHONY DANIELS

ACADEMY
AWARDS

THE BEVERLY HILTON

Golden Anniversary
Board of Governors
Ball

Golden Anniversary

Ben and Oscar

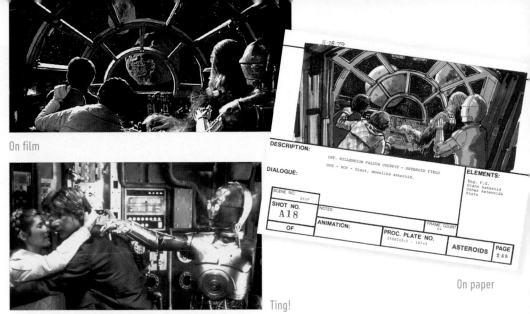

On film

DESCRIPTION:

INT. MILLENNIUM FALCON COCKPIT – ASTEROID FIELD

OVE – POV – Giant, moonlike asteroid.

DIALOGUE:

SCENE NO: 241P

SHOT NO. A18

OF

NOTES:

ANIMATION:

PROC. PLATE NO. 2508183-1 – 107+2

ELEMENTS:
Eng. F.G.
Giant Asteroid
Other Asteroids
Stars

FRAME COUNT 64

ASTEROIDS

PAGE 248

On paper

Ting!

The Pig and friends

The Frog

The Street

Magic

Mmmmm

Kirsh

Cloud City

Sandstorm

The fall

Half apples

Jabba slime

Peter Diamond in lights

Endor with friends

Ewokese

Tony Daniels

BLUE HARVEST

IIM BLUE SCREEN SCHEDUL...

| DY | | SC # | SKETCH #'S | DESCRIPTION |
|---|---|---|---|---|
| DY 1 | | 22,24,pt. | 3,4,5 | |

LUCASFILM Ltd                1.601

VA-ta-ta Rundi Darth Vader!

CHEUKO

TI A TUM DE DEATH STAR...

ODS MEECHI UO JEDI OBI-
WAN KENEOBI. EE MANA
MACHOO VADER CON YUM NURM

~~TORONTO GOSH~~
~~CONTAY MAONNA CONDU~~

MAYTER LUKE A CHIMENY
CHOO DOOOSH

BEN BURTT

84                                              88

        100    AMUY

        LEIA
only takes one to sound the
...rm.

        HAN
        (with a self-confident grin)
...n we'll have to get them out of
...way real quiet like.

...ins what is going on to Wicket and Teebo.
...ter a moment between themselves then
...p and scampers into the underbrush.

        LEIA
        (checking a wrist instrument)
...running out of time.  The
...'s in hyperspace by now.

...eebo where Wicket went and is given a

        THREEPIO
..., Mistress Leia!

        HAN
...own.

        LEIA
...s it, Threepio?

        THREEPIO
...aid our furry companion has
...d done something rash.

        LEIA
...e you talking about?

...NTRANCE

...out of the undergrowth near where the

89

#2 while

G3...
G3? KU CHANNA MA FLATTA ~~FLATAS~~ FLATAS
                              FLUATA
3                             COUTOO...
045 CORROWAY MANNA ...
...                ... WLUN DAY.

...OSS — VA — TA TA RUNDI DARTH VADE...
...UN CHEUKO VAS SKEEMO ...OS
OS/MEECHI UN JEDI - OBASDAO KENOB...

EE MANA MACHOO VADER. CON
YUM NATI

Yeo R2 I ... ful c... ll that

TORONTA GOSH   TORONTO GOSH

...  MASTER LUKE)

A CHIMENY  CHOO DOOH CHOOD...
A CHOODO  CHOODO

Brian Lofthouse

Remains of the *Falcon*

Featuring the Original Cast: R2-D2 · Anthony Daniels as C-3PO

The Ride

Radio Empire

The Message

I had my doubts about this new director from our first meeting. Sitting in his office at Elstree, I mentioned that I sometimes rewrote Threepio's dialogue lines, with a view to improving them. He addressed me like a headmaster in a minor boarding school. He informed me that a scriptwriter had been paid a lot of money to write the words, so I should leave them alone. This man was no Kirsh. When I later saw Marquand's previous effort, *Eye of the Needle*, I phoned lovely co-producer, Robert Watts, questioning if this was the right man for the job. It transpired that George seemed to agree with my assessment. He hadn't planned to be on set for the entire shoot, having a plateful of other stuff to deal with. As he observed the first few days of the shoot, he changed his mind and became a significant presence on the set, although the stitching on his hat didn't actually say "Director".

With the slightly confused focus about who was actually in charge, it seemed that Harrison was also taking a whip hand. It became a maxim on the shoot, that a close-up of Carrie ended up as a two-shot favouring Harrison. I always thought that he would make an excellent director. Too busy being an excellent actor, I suppose.

Marquand seemed to enjoy scapegoating people.

I was watching from the camera position on Jabba's barge. After a couple of takes Marquand was vociferously rude about Billy Dee, wired onto the distant skiff.

"Why couldn't he get the lines right?" he grumbled expletivly for all around to hear. The fact that Harrison had just rejigged the scene with the director and Billy was hanging upside down in the severe heat of Yuma's desert, perhaps had something to do with it.

Marquand tried it with me in the forest. Hearing my name spoken from behind a bush in the adjacent clearing, I was beside the camera in moments.

"That's the second time you've kept us waiting."

"What?"

"Okay. Let's start."

"Wait a minute. What are you accusing me of, in front of the crew?"

"Never mind."

I dropped the exchange because now we were both wasting time. Some days later, the schedule was suddenly changed, so that Harrison could fly to LA for a premiere of his latest, non-*Star Wars* adventure. He had indeed, become the star he truly deserved to be. As we watched him walk, Indiana Jones-like out of the clearing, Marquand turned to me, suddenly his best buddy.

"Now you and I can get on with making this movie together."

"Richard. Throughout the production you have belittled me. Ignored me. Given me no useful direction. Cut takes when I am still performing. I would prefer you not to speak to me for the rest of the shoot."

I turned from his blank expression and walked over to George who was hovering. I gestured behind me.

"I can't dub the movie with him. Okay?"

Lovely Howard Kazanjian produced the whole thing in the most gentlemanly fashion. The attitude of the producer can make a huge difference to the atmosphere on any production. The film business has its own peculiar rules on how people are treated. There has yet to be an HR Department like other industries. It's better simply not to complain – if you want to work again. Howard somehow managed to contain the awkward situation and made a very popular film that audiences love. And many fans loved the Ewoks. And, as I had requested, George directed my ADR sessions.

It was here that we incorporated real Ewok words, covering my place-holder lines recorded on set. It had been huge fun working with Ben on the language. He and I had listened to recordings of weird dialects from around the world. We wrote down sounds and phrases and jiggled them about to make credible-sounding sentences.

*"Princess Leia wassay wad-ma Artoo. Oss va-ta-ta rundi, Darth Vader! – un chemko vaskeemo tee a tum de Death Star. Oss meechi un Jedi, Obi-Wan Kenobi. Ee mana macha Vader con yum num. Toronto Gosh – Toronto Gosh. Master Luke ah chimeny Choo-Do. Choo-Do. Uta Millennium Falcon ah – chimeny Cloud City."* And so on.

*Yum num* still makes me smile. Along with the drama of – *Han Solo, Teekolo Carbon!* We had to stop sometimes, falling about with laughter. Certain sentences sounded too hilariously vulgar. We didn't use them in the end. Ewoks are meant to be cute.

I was shocked. I had wandered into the back-lot behind the stages at Elstree. It was the area where productions could build outdoor sets, do what they wanted here. I remembered seeing the snow-bound gas station from *The Shining* when we'd shared the studios with Stanley Kubrick. Literally tons of salt had been dumped across the whole area to create the right effect; and the same inside the stages. I recalled sneaking into the set of the garden maze. Big signs declared "Closed Set" but there was no one around. Nosey, I pushed open the heavy, sound-proof door.

It was genuinely amazing inside and I shouldn't have been there. Tall green hedges were set against the snow piled on the ground. Even though it was inside Stage Two, next to my dressing room, it seemed genuinely chill as I trespassed on. Then. Horror! I looked down. My trainers had left perfect prints in the fresh fake snow. I froze – in the emotional sense – before working out my escape. So as to limit the damage I'd already done, I carefully walked backwards in my footprints. At last, I reached the edge of the set and walked nonchalantly out of the stage as if I had never been there.

How extraordinary and spine-tingling to see the finished film in the movie theatre. There was the maze. There was the little boy hero escaping from crazy Jack out in the snow. And he did it by walking backwards in his own footprints, exactly as I had done. I wondered if Mr Kubrick had got the idea from seeing my footwork. Probably not.

It was a damp, gloomy day and the gas station and maze were long gone – so was the snow. We were reaching the end on this shoot and I wanted some fresh air, away from the Ewoks and the fuggy atmosphere of Jabba's palace. But now there were clouds of smoke here as well. Two crew members were making a bonfire. I realised what they were doing. But why?

They paused in their destruction to explain. Its huge steel frame had already been sent to a scrap yard. They were disposing of the rest – the wood and painted panels that were flaming and smouldering in front of us. No longer wanted, too expensive to store, the *Millennium Falcon* was finally going down in flames.

I felt a strange emotion as I gazed at the mess. This craft had taken me and my friends on so many exciting journeys. It was a part of our family. It was known and loved around the planet. An icon. What an unfeeling fate – to be wrecked, torn apart, burnt. Immortalised on film but never to exist again in real life. No goodbyes. No speeches. Just this acrid pyre.

I bent down at the edge of the wet grass and picked up some bundles of wiring. I'd seen them lining the *Falcon*'s corridors. It didn't matter what they were for. They looked important – and real. Nearby were some small plastic grills about to be melted down. I picked up this doomed souvenir of a magnificent creation and thumbed mud off the black shape – a word stamped on them. "Ford". And it didn't mean Harrison.

These were car parts.

So it had been pretend after all.

It was the end. George wasn't going to make any more *Star Wars* films. His once-planned trio of trilogies was going to remain just the one. That was okay. My memories were, to say the least, mixed. I had certainly moved up the chain from being ignored to having my name on the poster – and to being a deity – albeit of the Ewoks – and to being included in some publicity bashes. Perhaps there was an enduring, residual emptiness in my mind – feeling trivialised for playing a role in total disguise – inferior to the other cast whose faces could be seen. Also, I had some good times. Made a living. Made friends. Got to know my golden friend.

But I would soon find that my life as Threepio was far from over.

## 42 ride

1986 – Flower Street – Burbank – California.

Tom Fitzgerald sat behind his desk. He was the creative director-producer. He and his fellow Imagineers would combine talents with Lucasfilm and ILM to create a thrilling ride in the Disney theme parks. In his simple office, he conjured the most extraordinary adventure in the air between us, simply with his voice and gestures. He was describing, with vivid energy, the *Star Tours* experience.

Guests would be hurled into space, under the incompetent piloting skills of Captain Rex. Being his first day on the job, there would inevitably be some problems. This meant experiencing many of the most dramatic and exciting moments from the three *Star Wars* movies – the viewport screen constantly alive with a seamless view of the drama, with the passengers seat-belted into the hurtling flight simulator. Thrilling!

Entering the spaceport prior to departure, the guest would be immersed into the world of space travel. While weird announcements and flight information filled the air, passengers followed a snaking path. It led them past a *StarSpeeder 3000,* similar to the vehicle they would soon be boarding. This particular one was currently under repair. Artoo doing the mechanics – Threepio directing from a control platform, up above them. Things would not go well, especially with the craft's space cannons about to explode. This was where I would come in.

I stood before the camera, in front of a mock-up of the control console, in an otherwise empty studio. Tom directed my performance, as I instructed and cajoled an eyeline that was the non-existent Artoo. I was wearing jeans and a shirt – and a sandbag. The latter kept my feet steady, in one place. My left leg would be the conduit for all the wires needed to activate the animatronic figure I would become.

Tom and I had such fun, as we recorded the 12-minute performance that would eventually be an endless loop in the parks. And that would include Paris Disney. So I recorded the lines in French as well. Months later, they realised that the French take twice as long to say anything. So we had to re-record a truncated script to fit with the animatronic programming. But I was concerned that the talented team of Imagineers, the utterly brilliant and inventive team who actually create the experiences at Disney parks, would make Threepio too human. I impertinently briefed the animation programmer, that this droid's movements were unique. David Feiten listened impassively. I just hoped I had made myself clear.

Many months later, in the middle of the night – a time when installations and maintenance are done at Disney parks – I stood in the new but empty spaceport. There was Threepio, going through his procedures. It was uncanny. He was just as real as if I were inside. David had done a stupendously good job. Later I would tell him my ecstatic reaction. He would smile, slightly. He always did a good job.

But now I stood there alone. When we'd filmed the sequence, Tom directed me to put a glance down, towards where the audience would be passing through. Standing there, gazing up at my golden friend, the machinery that was hidden inside turned his face down towards me. He looked straight into my eyes. I felt my soul turn over. We gazed at each other for a moment. Then he looked up and went back to nagging Artoo. It was as memorable a moment as my first encounter with Ralph McQuarrie's concept painting, so many years before.

Opening Night! Well, the rehearsal, anyway. I stood up on my stage, waiting to make an entrance. It was four in the morning. The brilliantly talented David Schaefer, concealed somewhere nearby, was twiddling Artoo's controls. David was still accompanying me too, on all sorts of gigs around the world. I sang his praises to Tom, suggesting Disney could well use his skills. So they gave him a job. Stupid of me – our happy times together were no more. But his talents were clearly made for a higher level responsibility than mopping my face and driving Artoo. But that was later. Now. At Anaheim Disney. All systems ready for the spectacle.

GO!

A giant flying saucer appeared high in the night sky. Its long, delicate arms fringed the rounded body, as it rose up into sight. A sensational theatrical stroke. It flew towards me, so high above. Now it was nearly overhead. My pre-recorded voice sounded out through an array of speakers. Threepio began landing procedures for his arrival with Artoo, ensuring that Mickey was standing by to greet them. As my words echoed through the empty park, the saucer paused – sort of. For now, it was moving away. Now back again, as it started to swing like a giant pendulum. The arms began to flounce as they beat the air. The motion grew stronger. Stronger. Suddenly. Pieces of the craft tumbling. Breaking. Falling. Crashing.

It seemed that the giant prop was suspended on a wire. The blacked-out helicopter supporting it was flying four hundred feet higher. It stopped in the right position and hovered. But the prop had gained its own momentum during the brief flight. It didn't stop. It paused, as if considering the situation, then corrected itself in the opposite direction. And began to oscillate, till it self-destructed and fell to earth.

There was an eerie silence. Just the hammering of the helicopter dropping back down to the car park.

In the sound booth some five hours later, I was recording a new script. This time I would be "beamed down" from space, rather than make a hard landing.

Twenty-two years later, Tom was back. The original intention, when *Star Tours* was launched, was to revise the film every few years with a new adventure. For whatever reason, the original film was still running after all that time. At last, that was all about to change in a massive update. No more celluloid film, rushing endlessly behind the cabin walls, through the projector and back. Solid-state digital was the thing. And in 3D. And with branching storylines from all six *Star Wars* films, providing multiple, randomised adventure combinations which would fly guests to all sorts of destinations. And there were other special effects too. Really special effects. Wow!

Tom paused. He had sad news. It seemed that Captain Rex had retired, due to metal fatigue. *Star Tours* needed a new pilot. And they had found one. See-Threepio.

I was back at Burbank with Tom, recording Threepio's dialogue as pilot, for what was going to be another wild ride. *Star Tours – The Adventures Continue.* I was so amazed at ILM's new footage that, several times, I forgot to speak my lines – so I had to watch it again, which was fun. Earlier, we had actually been filming live-action sequences for the pre-flight monitors. There was the *StarSpeeder 1000*, an earlier model, since it was to encompass events from the prequels. It was actually a larger version than the ride vehicle, so that I could enter while wearing Threepio's rather wider shoulders. I fussed around the hangar and up the ramp to the door. It still wasn't quite wide enough. Rather than rebuild and reschedule the whole shoot, I slid in sideways.

Prior to take-off Threepio would appear on the cabin monitor. Then as the protective shutter rolled down he would spin round to face the passengers. We filmed me in the pilot's chair – for real. Except that the rotation mechanism wasn't quite as state-of-the-art as I'd imagined. It was actually the smallest member of the crew, crammed in a corner under the chair, out of sight. On command, he clutched the seat and whizzed me round. And back again. It looked good on film – looked very funny on set. I tried to insist that protocol demanded Threepio raise his hand in a polite greeting to the guests. This would not be advisable, they said. Given the dynamic movement of the vehicle, lurching through the galaxy, all day, every day, anything not tied down would fall off within a week. With my protective instincts towards my gold chum, I agreed his hands could remain glued to the armrest controls throughout.

Of course, Threepio wasn't meant to be on the flight at all. He was merely doing a maintenance check when Space Traffic Control set him on automatic take-off. Poor thing. After years of racing through the worlds of Hoth, Kashyyyk, Tatooine, Naboo and Coruscant – with a side step through the terrifying Death Star, Tom and the team crafted even more thrills based on the last trilogy of the Saga. Meaning the adventures will continue non-stop for our golden pilot, who is doomed to be terrified on an hourly basis, every day of the year, until metal fatigue finally takes its toll of him, too.

But for me, *Star Tours* was, and is, the best ride of my life.

## 43 radio

It was more than ten years after we had finished the radio version of *The Empire Strikes Back*, when the phone rang.

I remembered the fun Mark and I had, making the original *New Hope* and *Empire* radio series for National Public Radio. I'd felt sad that we never completed this incarnation of the trilogy, otherwise so fully represented in every merchandise-filled bedroom of every *Star Wars* fan across the world.

Given my long association with radio, I was glad to be a part of NPR's adaptations. For a start, I didn't have to wear the gold suit. But more than that, I felt that it presented the wonderful story that George Lucas had created, in a form available to anyone who had a radio. No admission charges, no standing in line, no stink of popcorn. Just the actors' voices, Tom Voegeli's effects, and the imagination. It worked splendidly back in 1985. Then ten years' silence.

But now Highbridge Audio were planning a production of *Return Of The Jedi*, with previously unpublished passages from John Williams' outstanding scores. Three hours of radio need a lot more music to fill out the scenes. Would I care to be involved? Was Brian Daley writing the scripts again? Yes, he was. Yes, I would.

Months later I was sitting in a boardroom in Los Angeles with Tom, once again the editor, and John Madden, who had directed our previous efforts. Brian couldn't join us. He was fighting cancer and sorry not to be with us at the script conference. We were sorry, too. There are always rewrites in any project. We each had lists of comments and suggestions. Many vanished as John and I hammed up the lines out loud and made Brian's writing come alive – just the way he'd written them. Perhaps because we both had jetlag, we were hammier than usual but the room resounded with raucous laughter at Brian's humorous inventions.

Studying Brian's script, it was clear just how difficult it is to describe exotic scenes, only in sound. Imagine trying this with Jabba's palace – a nightmare in all senses of the word. And Brian had given me a problem. He had put much of the scene's description into a conversation between Threepio and another character, lurking in that mass of strange creatures. Unfortunately, he had made my companion Boba Fett. I was against Fett bonding so closely with Threepio. It simply wasn't protocol. So, in a nifty pinch from Timothy Zahn's *Tales From Jabba's Palace*, we changed Boba for Arica, an exotic beauty we assumed to be partying on in the unseemly melee.

Jabba's film subtitles were not a problem, as Threepio naturally made them his own. But sometimes, when the great Jabba is being particularly disgusting, his own Huttese speaks louder than any translation. And, of course, there were my own lines. I'd always loved the way Brian developed Threepio's character in his scripts. He had a real ability to capture the droid's strange mixture of humourless comedy and his oddly bleak but loving personality. No other writer had been able to do this for Threepio – outside his movie incarnation. Only Brian, at the end of the Ewok storytelling scene, could find a radio way of capturing the droid's deeply-felt frustration with Han Solo.

So there we were again – me, Ann Sachs as Leia, and Perry King as Han. Everyone was lying that we didn't look ten years older than the last time we'd met. A happy new addition to the team was Josh Fardon, who had joined us to play Luke Skywalker – at least one member of the cast was the right age for the part. With Ayre Gross playing Lando, I was the only original member of the movie cast present in the studio. Would I be able to restrain myself from giving helpful advice? The question never arose. All the members of team grasped their characters without any assistance from me. Anyway, John patiently masterminded everything with his confident direction, so we all felt comfortably supported by the genial atmosphere he created.

Tom needed to keep everyone's tracks separated for eventual post-production. I spent the days isolated behind glass screens, listening to the drama unfolding around me through headphones. I wasn't the only one. Brock Peters, as Vader, and the even more fearsome Emperor, Paul Hecht, were similarly banished to various undignified corners and cupboards, as Tom ran out of studio space. When you hear the echoingly bleak acoustics of the Emperor's Throne Room, imagine Paul in a tiny store cupboard, draped in sound-deadening blankets. We had to crane our necks down the corridor for a look at Ed Asner, giving an outrageously disgusting rendition of Jabba the Hutt.

It says a lot about the performances, that off-duty members of the cast would cram into the small control room to listen to what was going on in the studio. Tom just kept going, carefully monitoring each take being recorded on his multi-channel desk. He managed to concentrate, in spite of the loud appreciation of the gathering team. In particular, John Lithgow's delightful recreation of Yoda was standing room only.

Of course, there is always a contrast between what you see through the studio window and what it sounds like over the speakers. We all looked particularly silly as we contorted our bodies, trying to suggest we'd been caught up in an Ewok net trap. It sounds convincing, though. So does Han's passionate ardour. At a mere hint from the stage directions, Perry apparently swept a sighing Princess Leia into his arms and lavished her with kisses. The truth was more prosaic. Perry at mike three. Ann at mike four, some feet away. Perry held his script in his left hand while leaning closer to the mike. Ann holding hers and breathing heavily. Perry's right hand came up to his lips, his breathing heavier. He passionately kissed the back of his hand. Ann went, "Mmmmmm." In the control room it sounded like total passion. In the studio everyone rolled around in helpless mirth.

As in the movies, much was left to post-production. Anyone having a conversation with Artoo was on his own – his beeps would be added later.

The Ewoks would similarly arrive on tape from Ben Burtt, their original audio creator. Actually, some things are better heard and not seen. I think Ewoks look great on radio.

It had been intended that crowd tracks would be lifted from existing recordings. Fortunately, John decided to employ a group of actors to cackle and snarl. They were hilarious to hear but even better to watch, as they recreated the scum of Jabba's entourage. Later, they became the crowd of macho pilots in the briefing room with Mon Mothma. Even Howard Roffman, Lucasfilm's Vice President of Licensing, was persuaded to join in as part of the Rebel Alliance. A clever chap, he still couldn't quite understand that, in a radio crowd, everyone speaks at the same time. He kept politely listening to the other actors and nodding. Nodding doesn't work on radio. Howard was not natural radio material.

"It must be easy on radio. You don't have to learn the lines." How many times have I heard that? The truth is quite different. For a start, most films have only some blue-screen effects. Radio is all blue-screen. The actors have to imagine everything. Pretending you are on the verdant Moon of Endor when you are in fact, in a tiny, mirrored recording booth on Beverly Boulevard, takes some doing.

As for learning lines, if you aren't absolutely familiar with them and their position on the page, you'd never be able to take your eyes off the script. Most actors are very insecure people. They need to look at each other. If you're not familiar with the words, you're bound to lose your place, with a resulting, embarrassing pause. My problem was that I never learned to write neatly. All my notes and changes and self-instruction are like hieroglyphs and render the neatly typed pages into pencil labyrinths.

After five days it was over – a wrap. We met for dinner that night in a lively restaurant on Melrose. Strangely, for an LA eatery, we could hear each other speak. Maybe we'd just got used to shouting over intergalactic battle-noises. We raised a glass to absent friends – to Brian. Quite a few glasses were subsequently downed in the happy relief that a wrap party brings. But there is always a tinge of sadness in these occasions. You never know if you will meet again. It had been fun. But for the cast at least, it was over. There would not be another. We left for our various homes and hotels. Maybe someone said, "May the Force be with you." I don't know. I went to bed.

My phone woke me early the next morning. It was John. He'd just heard that Brian had died that night, as we sat in the restaurant, just about the time we were drinking to absent friends – to Brian.

It had become a joke that Threepio usually stole the last line of any scene that included him in Brian's scripts. Without Brian to write the lines for me here, I can only say, I was so happy and proud to have known him.

## 44 smoking

It was an honour to meet Robin Williams. Just as brilliantly energetic in person, as on screen.

I had so long admired his zany character in TV's *Mork and Mindy*. And now I got to stand next to this hilarious and lovely man. A charity event. "Hands Across America". 1986. The idea was to raise awareness and funds for hunger and homelessness in the USA. About six-and-a-half million people tried to form a line across the States by holding hands. Mr Williams held Threepio's hand in West Hollywood. It was May 25. It wasn't my first Public Service Announcement.

I'd donated my time for a different PSA, ten years earlier. American parents weren't getting their kids vaccinated. Measles, polio and whooping cough were taking a toll on young lives. Just as it is today, the message was important but the spot itself was horrible – a sludgy, if informative script. We shot it in a faux sci-fi control room. Most memorable was the way Artoo appeared to pay no attention to the laws of physics.

The control consoles were fairly standard. The floor was large black and white squares. It seemed the director was oblivious, or perhaps magnetised by Threepio's words. Watching the finished piece, Artoo magically changed position in each different camera angle – as though he was playing "hop-scotch" mixed with "grandmother's footsteps". It was a hilarious lesson in continuity failure. But the shoot gave me an idea. Eventually I would try to persuade the US Health Department and Lucasfilm to make an anti-smoking spot. They would. If I wrote it. So I did.

Months later, I was dressing up again. This time in a rather scary electric power installation, in north Los Angeles.

SCARY FACTORY SETTING. THREEPIO AT A MACHINE THAT SPARKS.

                    C-3PO
            Ohh!

THREEPIO LOOKS AROUND FOR HIS COMPANION.

                    C-3PO
        Artoo? Where are you? Artoo?

GOES IN SEARCH. SEES SMOKE FROM BEHIND HUGE BANK OF
MACHINES. HEARING ARTOO BEEPING HAPPILY.
HE TURNS A CORNER

                    R2-D2
        Beeb Beep Be Beeep…

                    C-3PO
        Artoo??

HE FINDS ARTOO WITH SMOKE COMING OUT.

                    C-3PO
        Uh! Artoo, you're on fire!

                    R2-D2
        Beep Dewop!

PULL BACK SHOWS ARTOO WITH A CIGARETTE IN HIS PINCER.

                    C-3PO
        Artoo Detoo! You found a cigarette!

                    R2-D2
        Beep Bop Bap.

                    C-3PO
        Well, I don't think smoking is grown-up at all.

                    R2-D2
        Beep Boo?

                    C-3PO
        Because it's very dangerous.

                    R2-D2
        Beep?

                    C-3PO
        Smoking does dreadful things to your lungs. And
        is very bad for your heart.

                    R2-D2
        Beeep boo!

                    C-3PO
        Oh. Well, I know I don't have one. But humans do.
        And I think we should set a good example.

ARTOO DROPS THE CIGARETTE AND RETRACTS HIS PINCER.

                    C-3PO
        Well done, Artoo.

THREEPIO SEES THE VIEWER.

                    C-3PO
        Oh. Hello. You know smoking is bad for your
        health. And it isn't grown-up at all. So please…
        don't smoke.

CAMERA PULLS BACK.

                    C-3PO
        Artoo. Do you really think I don't have a heart?

                    R2-D2
        Peeeep.

The emotional impact of this tender last moment may have been slightly lessened, for an observant viewer at least. The wonky end-card faded up in a star field.

"A MESSAGE FROM A DISTANT **GALAXAY** FAR, FAR AWAY."

Someone in production had obviously been smoking – something.


## 45 naked

Well I never expected this to happen. I had suddenly learned a new word along with the rest of the world.

It had been so many years since the last production – for me, years filled with the Saga's spin-off activities and stuff with no relation to *Star Wars* at all.

I was amazed and excited to be back.

"You're created by Anakin."

George was detailing a plot-line for, what would become, the first "Prequel". I was at Leavesden Studios. It was 1997. I was pleased and touched. Sir Alec Guinness had been such a lovely, kind colleague. So many years ago now – still remembered with fond respect. How fitting, I thought, that his character should be the one to bring Threepio into existence.

But a few days later, I had a revelation. It had been fourteen years, so I could be forgiven for getting confused. Alec had played Obi-Wan, not Anakin. Dear, sweet, troubled Threepio was created by a bad guy. Maybe that's why he's so anxious.

That was the only piece of the story I learned that day, or later on. I didn't see a script, didn't see George, didn't hear from production for many weeks. I wondered vaguely, how it was all going.

They obviously didn't need me. So I just got on with my life, assuming they would get in touch when they were ready for whatever input I might add. Eventually, I was back at Leavesden. A mere visitor on the set. There was Threepio. But not as I knew him. What a genius idea, to have him built by a little boy. Plastic, bare wires and electric motors created a truly inventive, puppet version of my friend's inner workings.

The life-size doll was rigged onto the body of the immensely skilled prop maker, Michael Lynch, who'd created it. I wondered why they hadn't asked me to try puppeteering the thing. Of course, Michael was familiar with the workings of it all, and was doing a grand job. But I could have learned how to manipulate it. It fed into my sense of always feeling that I wasn't permitted any sense of proprietorship over the character – in spite of what I might have brought to it from the beginning. Impressed though I was, here I felt completely sidelined. No one had thought I might want to have a say in how Threepio began. The film industry can be surprisingly insensitive at times.

Looking back, how amazing to meet Natalie Portman and Jake Lloyd on set. Both so young and fresh and enthusiastic. It was fun to hear how they felt being in a *Star Wars* film. But Michael seemed to avoid me. Normally a perfectly friendly chap from ILM, he apparently felt awkward in knowing how little involvement I'd been allowed into this development in the character I had inhabited for so long. Lucasfilm owned the copyright but, as a creative person himself, he clearly understood my unspoken thoughts. Eventually, in ADR, I would admire his puppeteering skills, as I added my voice to movements that were not mine.

There was a moment I liked.

"My parts are showing!"

Poor Threepio.

Eventually, the film was edited and graphically enhanced. The computers had worked overtime to create overwhelming scenes and landscapes and characters. I'm not sure if my brief stint, mostly in ADR, had really made me feel a connection it. But I was certainly thrilled to be a part of it all. And the expectation, in America at least, was palpable.

Due to geographical issues, I saw the much-awaited, long longed-for Prequel in Salt Lake City. I sat unrecognised in the whooping, whistling crowds as the famous opening sequences shone from the screen. The noise hushed as we read a treatise on galactic political machination – the words rolling yellow, away into space. Certainly I was confused but settled back to enjoy what followed. Or not. Impatiently exiting during the credits, I paused as the audience crowded around me into the street. I overheard a rather sad but telling remark.

"I guess we'll just have to wait till the next episode, to see if it gets any better."

To be fair, the years have been kinder to this, the first Prequel. Many, who were young at the time, still hold it, and Jar Jar Binks as their dearest memory of the Saga.

As for me – I was never the target audience for *The Phantom Menace*.

## 46 celebration

How ironic then, that I had earlier been an element of its long-awaited unveiling.

I'd known Dan Madsen for some years from the days when he ran the *Star Wars* Fan Club. He edited the club's magazine, *Star Wars Insider*, too. I used to write "The Wonder Column", a tongue-in-cheek selection of memories from the first three films. It kept my brain alive. I have no idea what it did to the brains of others but I still get appreciative messages from readers. Dan and I always got on well together. So, when he suggested I might help him produce the event, and host it, I was more than thrilled to agree.

*Star Wars* had been dormant for many years. *Return of the Jedi* seemed to be it, as far as movies went. Now the trilogy was being revitalised by starting another one. From the beginning. *Star Wars* was coming back to life with that hitherto unknown, word. Prequel. Something to celebrate and restore a solid connection with the fans.

"Celebration". I wasn't yet sure what it actually was. It was going to be different from the normal fan conventions that had rapidly sprouted around the world. This one was official. Dan had been brought in by Lucasfilm to mastermind the very first event of its kind.

We collaborated over the months, putting on a show together and it was fun. Me, helping to find guests who'd be willing to come – Dan researching suitable sites. Me, planning the stage sessions – Dan, sub-contracting builders and vendors and getting all the safety permits. My jobs were reasonably easy, as guests eagerly wanted to join in the event that would showcase the upcoming film. And I'd always been fascinated by the art and science of stage management.

Dan's tasks were hard work. Suitable venues had been booked months before. The National Rifle Association was busy setting up their own event, having bagged the biggest indoor venue in Denver, Dan's home town. And now he was running out of time to find anywhere that might work. He doggedly searched on, and eventually found the Wings Over The Rockies Air and Space Museum. Most of the buildings housed various pieces of aviation memorabilia. But there were wide-open spaces, where temporary marquees could be erected for the event. And even more spaces for open-air exhibits and parking. A proper convention centre was simply not available but the ground at the museum site was solid and could take a lot of traffic – both vehicles and people. So huge numbers of fans could be accommodated in safety and comfort in the warm spring air.

I felt quite excited as I arrived in Denver, two weeks before the big event. My seventh-floor hotel room had an excellent view of the sunlit hills beyond the city. And it was great to be working face-to-face with Dan, rather than by phone calls and emails. But whatever our means of communication, all our preparations were going well. I drove to the site and was amazed at the infrastructure that Dan had installed. Two huge marquees and spaces for numerous food outlets. The *Star Wars* Store was housed in a small brick building near what would become the Sky-walker Stage. That was where I'd be spending my time, talking with cast members. The other stage was slightly smaller but would allow for all sorts of different interviews. Scott Chernoff, writer, actor and above all, comedian was hosting that one.

A large space had been made available within the museum build-ing itself. All sorts of artifacts had been shipped in to provide a fascinating array of props and costumes. There was even a life-size X–wing fighter on display. It was all going to work so well. Fans were going to love it.

The midday news was devastating. Thirteen students had been massacred in a shooting at nearby Columbine High School. The two shooters had killed themselves, after wounding many more of their fellow students and teachers.

Putting aside the outrage and grief, Dan had to consider his options. He was wholly responsible for creating this enormous *Star Wars* event. But how could it continue in the face of such tragedy? To go ahead might seem to disrespect the dead and bereaved. To cancel it would be ruinous and a huge disappointment to fans travelling to Denver, liter-ally from around the world. A Lucasfilm executive, indeed, argued that it should be cancelled – everyone would understand the reason. We talked around it for days, still in shock and wondering what was the best that could happen.

The mayor of Denver spoke out. After such an unspeakable event, the community needed to be lifted up. Memories would remain forever but life needed to go on. Denver needed this event.

Though the April sun was pleasant as Dan and I walked around the site, some of the joy had gone out of our footsteps. But we were still excited about tomorrow. And, as it does, tomorrow came.

I drew back the curtains to rejoice in the view. I was stunned. The distant hills were invisible. Rain was crashing down, blotting out the very clouds that were creating this deluge.

Even though it was still early, I anxiously drove to the site. Thousands of fans had arrived there before me. They were standing in already saturated lines, gallantly waiting to get under cover in the giant tents that housed the temporary stages.

The next hours felt like I was wading through forces I could not control. Not just the rain. Thinking what to do. How to fix what I could fix. I wasn't quite finished with setting up the stage area and its lighting grid. I'd planned to do it all this morning before the first panel started. I could only reappraise. I organised the staff to open the doors of the huge marquees. Fans flooded in, already drenched. Some had raincoats and umbrellas. Others had clearly been surprised by the change in the weather. They were in T-shirts. I shook hands with those nearest. They were corpse cold. Shivering. But smiling.

The Fire Marshall told me the place was full. I argued that there were sufficient doors for safety and, in these sodden conditions, even a box of matches couldn't catch fire. By now the seats were all filled but we squeezed hundreds more fans down the side aisles. At least they were out of the pouring skies and chilling wind.

I stood on stage, marshalling the inflow. When, even I felt, we couldn't cram in any more, I pulled a Jedi mind trick. I explained that I was an illusion. I was not actually there. But I would be. Soon. I went backstage, exhausted. And we hadn't even started yet.

When we did begin, the warm welcome from the crowd was in stark contrast to everything else. Dan opened the proceedings by asking for a minute's silence. It was memorably profound, save for the rain lashing us above. We were all wearing buttonholes in the Columbine School's colours of silver and blue – a tiny but heartfelt gesture of sympathy for all those who had been affected by the unspeakable atrocity. But the goodwill and enthusiasm were clearly present on the smiling faces that heard me congratulating Dan and introducing various members from the new cast.

Jake Lloyd was amazingly mature and self-confident. He delighted the fans with his happy banter. We even did a quick lightsaber fight. I think I let him win. Or maybe he just won in his own feisty way. It makes me sad to remember how the little boy, who would epitomise the Dark Side, would go on to suffer dark times in his own future. But for now, Master Ani was a joy.

Ahmed Best came on stage and took it over with his quick-witted humour. I took a moment to relax. I had miscalculated the time I would need to be on stage, introducing and interviewing the guests over three days. I hadn't included any breaks. Not self-sacrifice – just stupid. Now I had a moment to myself. Ahmed was more than capable on his own, as he talked about his new character in *The Phantom Menace* – Jar Jar Binks.

Pernilla August added a touch of serene glamour to the fairly masculine event. She was allowed to admit to playing Jake's mother in the film. An utter professional and seasoned actor, she must have wondered what she was doing in a tent in Denver – in the rain.

Possibly the highlight of the day was Ray Park who stormed the audience with his martial arts routine. He leapt and bounced around the stage in a hugely dynamic and engaging demonstration of his skill. It was the first time everyone got to hear John Williams' signature music for this devilish character, *The Duel of the Fates*. And the fans loved it. So did I. And they loved Ray.

But I did, reluctantly, give him a piece of bad news. No one had thought to tell Ray that his voice had been replaced by the actor,

Peter Serafinowicz. It wasn't my place to do so but I liked him enough to save him from the wound of finding out, as he sat with his friends in the cinema. It would have been kinder if someone in Production had prepared him. Peter is a super actor, with a fine vocal range but I think Ray is probably better with the lightsaber, especially the double one. Darth Maul continues to be one of my favourite characters in the Saga – brief but favourite.

Stepping away from the stage, I was aghast at what the rain was doing. I'd heard it bouncing off the marquee's roof but the pathway to the *Star Wars* Store was a swilling watercourse. The store was packed solid with fans, admiring the new merchandise, but they were all brownly muddied to the knees. In fact, the entire site seemed like a war-torn battlefield. The mud oozed and slopped everywhere. That evening the rain still torrented down as I wearily drove back to the hotel to dry out. At least we had all survived. I wondered what tomorrow would bring.

Tomorrow brought more rain.

The conditions were so bad that city officials had to turn away hundreds of devastated fans. The facilities just couldn't safeguard the crowds against hypothermia and trench foot. Whenever I had the chance, I wandered down the lines of guests outside. The rain fell continuously but everyone I talked to was defiantly cheerful. The weather might have been kinder but all the fans were joyfully supportive of the whole event. They loved *Star Wars*. They loved being there.

Back on stage, I was again wearing the gold jacket I'd had made especially for this Celebration. It was my way of celebrating See-Three-pio and saying, don't take me too seriously. Because I, too, was putting on a brave face. I'd never before been rained on, on stage. For my next entrance, I came on under an umbrella. But worse for me was stepping out into the audience.

I was holding a radio microphone so I could catch reactions from the guests and amplify them around the auditorium. I wondered if I was going to get electrocuted. Then I worked out that they only had batteries inside, the main equipment being at a safe distance from me. As I stooped to point the mike at an enthusiastic fan, I felt something horribly weird. Though I was standing on the fake grass that carpeted the marquee, I was actually in a slight dip. It was filled with water so deep, it was gently flowing over the top of my shoes and filling them. I consciously reflected on my sense of misery as I poked fun at my interviewee, before squishing back up on stage. I leaked for the rest of the show. It was seriously depressing. But the day was over and people seemed to have had a good time. That was the main thing. Back on the seventh floor, I dried my feet and put newspaper in my shoes. I wondered what tomorrow would bring.

It brought sunshine.

I was back on stage, in my damp shoes and equally damp gold jacket. The sun glimpsed inside the marquee, bouncing off the puddles that had yet to drain away in the fake grass. As the programme went on, I realised I was hot and uncomfortable. I looked at my arms. They were actually, visibly steaming. The sunlight on the marquee, mixed with the dampened state of everything inside, was causing a fog bank to rise around us all – because we had all become one. We had all lived through an extraordinary event – even managed to enjoy it. To recall Shakespeare, I felt we few, we happy few, were indeed brothers. That people would hold themselves bereft they were not with us at Celebration.

Dan Madsen would never brag about his achievement. So I will boast on his behalf. Against a series of formidable, unfathomable odds, he created a miraculous event that bolstered the spirit of everyone there. Regrettably, he was left to wring out the pieces by himself as the marquees were dismantled and the flooded fields began to heal. But he had started a tradition.

Celebrations seem to come along like buses now. In Japan. In Europe. In America. Wherever it is held, Celebration brings fans together in a growing family of friends and like-minded individuals, making a global community – because of what Dan Madsen started with his wonderful, admirable spirit.

As I drove to Denver's airport, I passed a huge hoarding, still advertising the NRA's convention. Charlton Heston's stern-faced, noble portrait towered above me as he proudly clasped a rifle. The text below him?

"Join us."

## 47 tchewww

Another prequel.

Somehow, my hoped-for pleasure of being on a *Star Wars* set again, was elusive.

There were many people who were thrilled to be back. It was like a *Star Wars* reunion for the crew every three years. However, from my perspective, the experience was not a joyful one. I felt an uneasy atmosphere. No sense of joy – rather the opposite – a sense of an oppressive management ethos coming from above. George was busy directing the film – the actual production, naturally, being left to others. But there should be more to keeping a project on track than merely making the trains run on time. Considerate and respectful treatment of the cast and crew is equally important. Here, I sadly felt neither of these qualities was present to any degree. I wasn't alone. Though bullying in the workplace is far less tolerated today, back then it seemed to be endemic on many productions, our film unfortunately being no exception.

170

But at least they agreed, this time, I could puppeteer the skeletal Threepio. For me, it made artistic sense. It made economic sense too – they didn't have to fly Michael out.

But there were the pleasures of meeting Ewan McGregor and Sam Jackson. Both separately exclaimed their childlike disbelief at working with See-Threepio. I rather marvelled that I was working with these two friendly and talented actors. Though I was never in a scene with Christopher Lee, I did spend time with him, as we hung around the set, waiting. Here was a real bastion of cinema history. His endless, enthralling stories of his various filmic experiences made the hours pass quickly.

The principal joy was that the production was filming in glorious Australia. I had enjoyed so many previous visits. But it always feels more special if you have a reason to travel, a purpose, a belonging. And here I was, trying to belong.

I was rehearsing in "Creatures" at Fox Studios, surrounded by an eclectic collection of rubber heads and limbs. As I worked, a team of modellers and sculptors were transforming plaster casts into tentacled aliens. The intriguing results were stored all around the workshop like a mad freak show.

Don Bies, Justin Dix and the team attached me to the droid puppet. It was heavy, cumbersome, awkward. I wondered if my taking on the task was a mistake. The contraption was planted on my front, attached at the feet, hips, shoulders and my helmeted head. Sticks in my hands, attached to its elbows. Truly, we were an item.

This time, there were indeed large mirrors, helping me to see the effect of what I was attempting. I spent hours rehearsing in this rig, reminiscent of a Steadicam harness. I remembered the Japanese art of Bunraku – magic theatre created by black-clad puppet masters, ignored behind their exotic creations. They were free-standing while they manipulated their exquisite figurines. Not me. I was conjoined.

My puppet's head movements mirrored mine. Looking down to see where my feet were on the floor, was not an option. Where he didn't look, I didn't see. I would have to trust the crew to keep me upright. Eventually, I learned to walk and stand with reasonable credibility. I was ready.

The first shot had Threepio sitting down. Nice to have been warned. So now I was in Owen's garage, kneeling painfully on the floor, attached to my seated nemesis, nervous – self-inflicted. We began. Padmé looked deliciously serene in her blue nightgown, bathed in the twilight of the room. She had earlier arrived at the Homestead with Anakin. But that was yet to happen, so the, as yet undamaged, puppet was still in one piece.

INT. TATOOINE - HOMESTEAD - GARAGE (FULL MOON) - NIGHT

ACTION!

"Please don't leave us, Miss Padmé. These people need your help."

"I'm not leaving, Threepio. I just can't sleep."

"That's something I cannot relate to. As a protocol droid, I'm either active or inactive. There's no in–between."

"I guess you're lucky."

"Do you really think so...? I suppose I shouldn't expect..."

"You're not happy here?"

"Oh, I'm not unhappy... and my masters here are so kind I wouldn't wish to trouble them, it's just... being like this... well, it's embarrassing."

"Being like what?"

"Naked. If you pardon the expression. You see, when Master Ani made me, he never quite found the time to give me any outer covering. It's so humiliating. How would you like it, if you had to go around with all your circuits showing?"

"I guess I wouldn't like it at all."

"Of course you wouldn't. Nobody would. It's simply not protocol."

"Maybe we can do something about it."

"I don't think so. Only Master Ani..."

"Why not? They seem to have a box of old coverings here."

"Oh? How observant of you, Miss Padmé. Of course, I'm just not mechanically minded... if you see what I mean."

"Let's see, if we put this... here..."

"Ooooh! That tickles."

Sweet. But surely, Threepio was never that unobservant. He'd lived in this space for eighteen years, and never noticed a box of coverings? The scene ended with Natalie offering up a chest piece to the waiting droid.

Cutting back from a different thread, Threepio stood there, nearly whole. Natalie proffered up his golden face. Don had stuck fridge magnets around the back piece, now clamped to my head. I was wearing Threepio's eyes on a special rig that Don had built, too. Natalie had to finesse the face, with opposing magnets, over the wires and lenses, onto the back of the head piece. It wasn't easy, rather like a game show challenge – it took several goes. But now, with a satisfying Click, Threepio was complete, whole, ecstatic. How joyful everyone was – Padmé, Aunt Beru, Uncle Owen. Assuredly, too, the audience who, at last, would recognise the beloved figure of their childhood. The scene was cut. All of it. George said it slowed things down.

Of course, he'd written the scene in the first place. In playing it together with Natalie, the moment became really quite moving. At last you were given a glimpse of Threepio's inner feelings, as well as his inner workings. There was a genuine feeling of pathos, at least for me. Action films can surely benefit from the odd moment of tranquillity. And in this case, the audience already knew Threepio so well, I think they would have appreciated the sensitive insight the sequence revealed.

I'm sorry George decided there wasn't time for it. But before he made that editorial decision, a worse fate awaited the hapless droid. And me.

Thousands of miles away from Fox Studios, in a hole in the ground, I was politely introducing a young Aunt Beru and Uncle Owen to my returning Maker and his girlfriend, Padmé. We were back in the underground dwelling at Matmata, far away from its exterior domed entrance. That was many miles down the road on the salt flats of Tozeur. Movie magic again.

More practically, I assessed the rock floor in front of me. Naturally, it was rather uneven. I suggested it might be prudent to lay down some boards and even out the surface. There weren't any boards. I'd just have to be careful then. And so we began. First, with a wide, establishing shot, then I successfully manipulated the weighty puppet through five set-ups and many takes, without incident. Now it was Threepio's close-up.

INT. TATOOINE - HOMESTEAD - DAY

ACTION!

"Master Owen. May I introduce..."

As before, I stepped forward, looking straight ahead, triangulating on nearby, fixed points. The puppet's face leading me forward, the puppet's doomed feet, pinned to mine. My foot? The puppet's foot? A foot struck a stone. I was falling. Falling. My world was in slow motion, as I fell straight down onto my left side. The puppet's left side. Threepio's left side. The sound was frightening. The ensuing silence, profound. Don's distant voice approaching as he ran.

"Are you okay!"

I wiggled my toes. My spine must still be in one piece. Feet running closer. Don was there, urgently unstrapping me from the giant doll. Others helped me up. I was shocked. Then I looked down. Threepio lay there, abandoned on the stones. His carefully crafted thigh, a shattering of parts. I was doubly shocked. I had smashed a unique prop.

174

The only Threepio puppet in the world, let alone in a Tunisian desert. But my shock was for something else, too. I felt I had wounded my friend, hurt him irretrievably through my clumsiness.

"Hey. It's your close-up."

Don opened his tool kit and took out a pair of metal cutters. He snipped the puppet literally in two.

ACTION!

I stepped forward, confident in my own shoes, balancing just the top half of naked Threepio against my chest.

"Master Owen. May I introduce..."

It was suddenly so easy. But it wasn't the first time I had fallen. It wouldn't be the last.

It was an accepted fact that Threepio had somehow acquired his coverings in between Episodes I and II. Possibly, moisture farming was not Uncle Owen's only talent. Perhaps, in an intense fit of embarrassment, the naked droid had seen the box of parts lying on the garage floor and got dressed by himself. Either way, it was Justin who did an extremely convincing paint job on one of my gold outfits – turning it to rust. We had shot everything with the puppet for real. Now I had to re-enact each scene, wearing brownish grey, on a blue screen, or it might have been green. But the show wasn't over yet. Was this the time I would really break my neck?

They seemed strangely unconcerned that I might damage myself – expecting me to stop dead when I reached the open doorway, some twenty feet above the studio floor. Of course, I couldn't see the edge. But they offered no safety harness, to prevent me crashing onto the pads below. They did briefly consider tying a rope around my waist, attached to a railing at the back of the set. In street clothes, with clear vision, it wouldn't have been too bad. But dressed as I was in rusty Threepio, I was surprised at their seemingly cavalier approach. I would recall the moment, many years later, in a sequel, as I clung to a racing speeder, safely harnessed aboard by a caring team. Here was not so nice. And the scripted lines didn't help either.

INT. GEONOSIS - DROID FACTORY

"Machines making machines! How perverse."

Quite. In the end, George decided to do the fall digitally. The resulting sequence is not ILM's greatest hour, or Threepio's, or mine.

Back, nearer the studio floor, in the world of blue, I was standing on a rolling road, rather like an airport travelator – the kind of transport that makes people forget they have legs as they stand there, just blocking it up. But I had this track all to myself.

ACTION!

The road began to move backwards as I ran forward, shuddering away from imaginary dangers overhead and around me.

CUT!

The road stopped and I walked back to where I started. We did it again. It would make the shortish roller seem much longer in the finished edit. I decided to be helpful. Instead of walking back on a stationary roller, I ran back while it was still moving and repeated my journey forward – two or three times.

CUT!

The road stopped. So did I. At that moment the distraction of concentrating, and the adrenalin, wore off. I found that I couldn't expand my wanting-to-pant lungs at all. No one could see my anguished face inside the mask. I was dying. I managed to use my last breath to yell.

"GET ME OUT!"

Don was there in a moment. He did just that. Perhaps I would be less helpful in future.

But now I had something I'd always wanted. Since gripping anything with my hands was still a challenge, Don had to wire it into my fists – a blaster, of my very own. This was something new for Threepio.

Well, nearly Threepio. I was fully dressed in his rusty outfit. But in the final edit, ILM would replace his head with one from a battle droid. Either way, I stood in a largish sand pit and aimed the weapon past the camera. I got myself into commando mode.

EXT. GEONOSIS – EXECUTION ARENA – DAY

ACTION!

"Die, Jedi dogs! Die!"

CUT!

I had found it impossible not to make Tchewww Tchewww Tchew noises, as I pressed the trigger and faked the gun's recoil – probably be the same if they'd given Threepio a lightsaber – all those Vmmmmm Vmmmm sounds. But the crew were amused – especially by something else. "Die, Jedi dogs! Die!" were the words I eventually recorded in ADR. By the howls of mirth from anyone watching and listening on set, it was obvious that's not what I said at the time. I couldn't resist substituting "Jedi dogs" with another two-word expression. The laughing crew never knew that Threepio's facility with communication included some fairly major expletives.

This was the last shoot day of the, as yet unnamed, Episode II. I'd like to say it had been fun. But here was the crowning tragedy. The wedding of Anakin and Padmé. Curiously, there was a kind of glum humour in the situation. I had always felt I was never allowed to be the bride but here, for real, I was almost officially – a bridesmaid. The other was Artoo. Apparently, Kenny had asked if he could take part in at least one scene of this film, for old time's sake. So here he was, clambering into Artoo for the last time, for this one iconic shot. Sadly, we were not on the beautiful shores of Lake Como, in Italy. Slightly less exotic – we were at Ealing Studios in London. On blue screen.

Of course.

EXT. NABOO – LAKE RETREAT LODGE – GARDEN – LATE DAY

ACTION!

I remembered all the weddings I've attended. They all seemed to have been rather more enjoyable than this one. I gave muted brides-maid, not wishing to upstage the unhappy couple. Two minutes later, like painful dentistry, it was all over.

CUT!

It was a wrap. And being the final shot of the movie, there were actu-ally nibbles and wine to celebrate, just like a real wedding, except something had been missing.

Or someones. The groom and his bride. Anakin and Padmé. Hayden and Natalie had already done the deed by the lake in Italy. Threepio and Artoo's attendance would be down to Industrial Light and Magic. We would be inserted later.

And, inexorably, the third prequel rolled in.


## 48 relationships

The relationship between Threepio and Artoo was an aspect of the original script that I found very appealing.

The strangely believable banter – Threepio says this, Artoo replies or blows a raspberry. Threepio cleverly returns the insult. Charming. I naturally took it for granted that my counterpart and I would be acting out this delightful repartee together, when we eventually shot the film. The reality was a shock.

Much to my surprise, on location in Tunisia, I discovered that I was required to say my lines with no response or feedback at all. Nothing.

Nobody had bothered to mention that I would be working with a silent companion. Artoo's unique voice wouldn't be heard until months later, when it was added in production by Ben Burtt. It was a bit of a blow. I quickly learned to leave pauses for replies that would never be forthcoming. And I soon realised that I had to work out in my mind, and sometimes on paper, what those responses might be. I needed to be able to mime an appropriate reaction, as I pretended to listen. Of course, the editor could move everything around in post. But on the day, I was on my own.

We shot the first six films with many versions of Artoo. For the most part, I worked with mechanical models, packed with motors, batteries and gadgets, depending on what was required in a particular shot. In later films Artoo would, for the most part, be added digitally back at ILM. This was especially useful when he suddenly acquired surprising new talents, like flying and climbing stairs. Otherwise, Artoo moved when he was pulled along on piano wire, or yanked on fishing line, or poked with a broom handle or, hilariously, by Don Bies sticking his hand up through the back panel like a farmyard vet giving an internal exam.

Of course, there was a version of the unit that Kenny could fit inside. This was effective for wobbling, bowing and sometimes, turning the dome. His waddling into the escape pod scene was especially memorable. Otherwise, pinioned in that rigid structure, Kenny had few resources at his command. But he sat in his tiny prison like a trooper. He couldn't hear me at all and could barely see. It was frustrating for me, and most assuredly for him, to work with a fellow performer where we were unable to perform together. But we both got on with what we had been given to do.

The loving, on-screen relationship between the two characters was not mirrored by Kenny and me off screen. It was an unfortunate situation that only worsened with time. He repeatedly asked me if I would tour the world with him, as a human double act, a "reunion" of sorts.

We had never been close friends, but Kenny thought we could make a lot of money by appearing together on stage. It wasn't something I felt at all comfortable about. Perhaps I considered it would trivialise what, I felt, my performance had brought to the Saga.

Over the years, Kenny publicly made comments that hurt me greatly. I know his oft-repeated criticisms gathered a considerable following of believers. For the most part, I refrained from commenting and will resist the temptation to do so here. Kenny adored his association with *Star Wars* and Artoo and the fans. He appeared at countless conventions and the fans loved him. Sadly, our off-screen history prevented me from feeling the same.

## 49 officer

"George. I'd like to have my face somewhere in a *Star Wars* movie. Would it be all right, if I played an extra in some scene?"

"Shurr."

We were filming *Attack of the Clones*. It was great to be working in Australia. But the script didn't give Threepio much to occupy his mind. Or mine. And I suddenly had an urge to be myself for once – to show my face – in this great Saga. The First AD suggested I could be in the bar scene. I looked in the script. Ah, yes. The bit where a beautiful girl, Zam Wesell, played by Leeanna Walsman, turns into a hideous creature, having been lightsabered by Obi-Wan the Younger. Leeanna looked thrilling in her costume. Not so much, when she shape-shifted into her true self, as a Clawdite assassin. But what about my costume? I went to Wardrobe.

"I'm afraid you're a wee bit late."

Michael Mooney was assistant costume designer – assistant to the wondrously talented and eternally modest, Trisha Biggar. The fact that Trisha's superlative designs, including Zam's body-hugging sheen and Padmé's vast array of gowns, and the even more extravagant robes for Palpatine, never won an Oscar, is a matter of regret, and an eternal misjudgement by the Academy. But that would be a year on. Now, it was my turn.

Michael explained, in his gentle Scottish way, that all the costumes had been assigned, except two military-type uniforms. I thought that would be fine. We had a fitting and it was more than fine. Quite dapper, really. However, the blue jacket, picked out with gold trimmings, had been created for someone even smaller than me. I could, at least, fasten the high collar around my neck. Soon, I would be given highly polished boots and a hand-made, Sam Brown holster array. Such detail, for my five minutes of fame. Of course, I didn't know my character enjoyed going to the opera. That was later. However, now there was a snag.

The problem was my arms. They were too long. Or the sleeves were too short, depending on your point of view. From Michael's point of view, this was an easy fix. In an hour, he had added a piece of blue cloth and an exuberance of gold braid to the cuffs. Now my arms were the right length. Even better, the extra detail meant that I had been promoted. I was now an officer.

Many months later, back at Lucasfilm in California, one of the post-production crew, Fay David, was tasked with finding this handsomely clad officer a name. Thanks to the scrambled egg around his wrists, he was clearly a lieutenant – at least. Ah. Daniels became Dannl. Fay joined with Tony, short for Anthony, became Faytonni. He even got a bio. Turned out, I was playing a con man.

INT. CORUSCANT – OUTLANDER CLUB

It was one of those grand party scenes that always, eventually, come along in a *Star Wars* film. Stunning set – lots of wonderful and weird extras.

George thoughtfully positioned me at the bar. That's where all the action was going to be, so my face was guaranteed to make the cut, at some point. The Second AD parked two stunning girls beside me, while Matt Doran was at my other elbow, with his death sticks. His name – Elan Sleazebaggano. With his already long career, Matt was fascinating to talk to. Which was lucky. A party scene like that takes ages to shoot.

It got exciting when Ewan and Leeanna did their thing, as Obi-Wan and Zam. But I hadn't thought of all the coverage George would film, to make the scene as effective as possible. It took a long time. Life as a background artist is harder than it looks. I was standing at the bar all day, with a glass of ginger ale in my hand. I certainly needed a glass of something stronger when I got home that night.

There had been two uniforms. I told Ahmed Best that they were going to let me reveal my face in the movie. Normally, he was in a similar situation to mine, of being disguised. But Jar Jar wasn't in the scene, so he decided to join in on the act. I think he looked better in the outfit than I did, especially with his intricate facial decoration. Turned out, he and Faytonni were a criminal partnership. And he, too, eventually, acquired a character name. Achk Med-Beq. Clearly, Fay was on a roll that day.

## 50 green

This was a job with benefits.

We were back in Australia again to film, what was meant to be, the last and final *Star Wars* movie, *Revenge of the Sith*. It only took me moments reading the script to see that Threepio's role continued to be fairly minimal. So my duties were slight. There were clearly lots of exciting scenes in the continuing storyline of Anakin's fall from grace.

I was never sure about all the political aspects of the drama. But these pages showed promise of something good to come. It seemed like I would be watching from the wings. Threepio's talents were always available to the story but the story was not about him. Maybe he was simply there as a historical reminder of times past – a recognisable figure from everyone's childhood. It didn't matter to me. That I was there at all was a wonder.

If anything, my previous feelings of unease working on *Attack of the Clones* were greater now. As for the rest, the sense of discomfort was worse for some than others. I felt the industrial, rather threatening atmosphere.

As before, the main pleasures of this production were the joys of Sydney, and Sunday lunches with the Design Department, led by Gavin Bocquet. Lovely Trisha was there, too. Again, she had designed another array of wondrous costumes, not just for Padmé. Supreme Chancellor Palpatine's wardrobe bulged with even more gowns and robes of ever-increasing sumptuousness. Lunch was always a relaxed affair, our meal scrutinised by hungry pelicans at the water's edge.

Visitors came out from California. Wonderful, exuberant Lynne Hale, Publicity Head. Howard Roffman, ace Lucasfilm head merchandiser and Yoda in Residence – someone whose wise counsel I would regularly seek and value.

Sydney's restaurants are renowned. And I know why, though I always had to remember that my one-size suit lay waiting for me at the studio, like some dread Nemesis. I maintained my shape with regular workouts in the hotel gym and a certain discipline towards food intake. It was especially difficult to resist the on-set catering at Fox. In general, it's sensible to spend a hefty budget on food, to keep everyone happy. Here it was superb – and tempting. I tried to avoid looking at the dessert buffet. On the last day, they made me a huge pavlova.

That made me happy.

Australians are renowned for being straight-talking. I like that. I like a lot about Australia and Fox Studios was a comfortable, pleasant place to work. My dressing room had a view of a grassy playing field and the trees around it. One day the sun went out. I went to see why night had fallen early. Nothing to do with daylight hours – Ewan had parked his huge camper van, with its chunky motor cycle attachment, right outside my window. I didn't say anything. Right from day one, he'd exclaimed his exuberant joy and disbelief that he was working alongside See-Three-pio. I was always happy to be in scenes with him.

After the camper van moment, I was walking past a group of extras, playing footie on the grass. I stood there in my full-length, purple dressing robe, enjoying the fresh air and fun. They paused to cool down. Seeing me under the trees, they came over, clearly excited, thrilled to be meeting someone who was in this film, and not just as one of the many stormtroopers.

"Hey, mate. You a Jedi Knight?"

I paused, knowing they were about to be amazed. I was modestly prepared for their awed reaction.

"No. Actually, I play the gold robot, See-Threepio."

"Oh."

"No worries."

Their disappointment was palpable. They went back to kicking their ball.

Of course, there were some fun times. The crew were so good at everything they did, and hugely supportive and patient, weaving around each other with all their heavy and delicate gear, always courteous to each other and the cast – a pleasure to work with. I tried to enjoy myself, against the odds. I accepted that this would be the last time I would wear my gold suit, that I was nearing sad farewells to my old friend. I might have hoped for a more satisfying conclusion, than ending up as a discomforted bit-player. Clearly, the future was an unknown country, one I couldn't see, couldn't have dreamed of. Or maybe I'd had enough.

George had become devoted to green-screen technology. Mostly, we seemed to shoot on ever-repainted floors. Gravity planted our feet in semi-reality but everything around us was in George's head, and several other heads at ILM. Only months later, would I know where I had been, and it would be a year before I saw what alien critters had flashed past when I'd opened a door.

It had always been a challenge for me to hit my mark, the position you're meant to go to so that you're in the right place at the right time. It also means that the camera can see you and you're in focus. A mark can be anything – chalk, a pebble, a twig, a sausage sandbag. It had to be something I wouldn't trip over because I couldn't see it as I came close. Often I would rehearse the number of footsteps from my start to my end mark. Then I would toe it, feeling it under Threepio's foot. It was fairly impossible to get it right. As time went on, I seemed to become reticent about approaching obstacles when I couldn't see or judge how close I was. Perhaps Threepio's fears were becoming mine. But the camera crew and the focus-puller were ever patient. They even created an elaborate T-mark in gold and black tape. It made me feel special – Threepio, too – though I still couldn't see it.

Padmé's sitting room was a memorable set. Dreamy pale blue and gold, the drapes moving gently in the breeze from the off-camera fans. Constructed to a height of about forty feet, it was magnificent and tasteful. Obi-Wan's vehicle was parked at the bottom steps. George looked at Artoo in his navigation position, jutting out of the front.

"Take him out. We'll do it digitally."

"Why?" said Don.

"It's too high in the shot."

"I could drop it down for you."

"Hmm. Okay."

George looked miffed. He had grown to prefer digital.

EXT. CORUSCANT – PADMÉ'S APARTMENT – VERANDA –
AFTERNOON

Newly arrived, the serious-faced Ewan mounted the steps, to be greeted by Threepio, who conducted the visitor towards his mistress. Natalie was gazing into a blue screen. Eventually she would be gazing at the Jedi Temple, burning in the distance. Threepio discreetly left them to it. Except there was nothing discreet about it.

The set was a gorgeous design, incorporating elaborate steps that curved in various directions, narrowing at the ends. The two humans spoke of their fears for Anakin and the galaxy. I needed to get out of shot. For once, I hadn't checked where the edge of frame was. I soon found a different edge. I walked into the thin end of the steps. That dread feeling again, as I toppled forward. I managed to stop myself falling through a window, bracing myself on the ledge. I could only watch, as Don sprinted down the side of the set, below. He ran over sheets of hardboard that slid on each other and sent him crashing to the floor. I kept bracing, not wishing to join him. Suddenly.

"Are you all right, Anthony?"

Ewan's concerned voice reminded me how caring some actors can be. But now Don had limped up and rescued me. The actors finally completed the tragic scene. It was the next day that I saw the alternative facts. Recording some of my own lines to picture in the edit suite, that scene came up by accident. It looked beautiful and very moving. Both actors appeared so concerned and fearful. There was Natalie talking earnestly with Ewan; Ewan listening to Natalie's worries. Suddenly, a strange noise. They stopped talking. They looked around. They paused. Their hands flew up over their mouths. Not in shock – in mirth. The camera rolled as they suppressed their giggles. The sight of Three-pio's golden butt sticking out and about to defenestrate was too much, even for two such pros. At last, Ewan managed to control his voice enough to say, "Are you all right, Anthony?" Actors. But we would laugh together some days later.

INT. NABOO - SKIFF

Padmé sat mournfully at my side. I was piloting some kind of flying machine. I didn't know what because it wasn't there – ILM would add it later. We did each have rather splendid pilot seats and a sort of joystick, held down with sand bags. That was it. The rest was green. Natalie just had to look tearful as I pretended to fly.

In a later scene, Ewan would be in my seat and I was looking to leap into the other.

"Don't worry. We can take you from yesterday's scene with Padmé and put you in digitally."

"But Anthony's right here. Why doesn't he just sit down?"

George gave Ewan a look. How we both giggled as we went into action with me sitting beside him. For real.

It was one of the most memorable moments of being on set. Hayden and Ewan were simply marvellous in their lightsaber fight. The two actors were more like dancers, as they played out the scene. Their choreographed steps and sweeping blades got faster and faster. Even without the digital effects that would enhance the whole thing, it was breathtaking to watch, and scary, and disciplined – and beautiful. Though they were both exhausted at the end, no one got hurt. What they did get was a round of loud applause from the crew. And me.

A wistful moment. Jimmy Smits was a delightful addition to the cast as my new master, Bail Organa. He was such pleasant company on set. He fondly talked about his early memories of *Star Wars* and See-Threepio in particular. But he was concerned. He felt bad about it – didn't want to say the lines. It seemed like a personal thing. Certainly, it was for me. But I became devil's advocate and reassured him that it would be okay, that Threepio was no more than a household appliance.

All right, one that had attracted some degree of affection, over the years. But nevertheless, no more sensitive than a dishwasher. He wasn't convinced. But he was a consummate professional.

INT. ALDERAAN STARCRUISER - HALLWAY - SPACE

ACTION!

"Have the protocol droid's mind wiped."

And yes, it was casually insensitive. But it was the script.

On another day.

INT. CORUSCANT - SENATE OFFICE BUILDING - MAIN HALLWAY - LATE AFTERNOON

"I could do with a good tune-up myself."

We were in a sea of green. I rehearsed the simple action of me trotting towards camera, berating Artoo on my right. I was in costume but wasn't yet wearing the head. I walked back to my start mark. Don locked me inside Threepio's face and picked up the Artoo remote. Don is versatile. I turned and clocked the camera.

ACTION!

I busily puttered forward as before. Sudden confusion. My mind told me I was flailing in a giant bowl of breakfast cereal. Lots of snap and crackle. And I was falling. Bewildered. And scared. Don was running. Again.

The rehearsal had shown the crew just how much green was reflected in Threepio's shiny surfaces as I walked straight towards the camera. It would take a lot of retouching in post. Why not place large sheets of black polyboards under the lens, sloping outwards at an angle. They had assumed I would see them, since they were now blocking my path. I didn't. I walked straight into them. Of course they were concerned but, thankfully, I hadn't damaged the costume. This time.

Another time.

"You can just talk. We'll put Artoo in later."

So business as usual, another blue wall, more blue floor. I was so used to working with the Artoo unit that I knew its height and could easily fake the eyeline. I noticed they'd just finished cleaning the carpet and spotted that they'd left the vacuum cleaner nearby. For the camera rehearsal, I dragged the domed machine along by its hose, chatting away as scripted. It was a lot shorter than my usual counterpart but that didn't matter. His name was plastered on his forehead – Henry. He was cute. I thought my new double-act was amusing. So did the crew. Sad, but Henry didn't make it into the movie.

Sad, too – it was all over for me. A sadness tinged with a certain relief. I had survived it all, and now it was finished. As a traditional gesture to an artist's last day on set, the First AD announced that I had completed my role and would be leaving the shoot. The crew made some nice applause noises, and then they were gone, all of them, racing to another set-up on another stage.

I had been involved in all six movies, over many years. Now they were past and done – over. Don took off my Threepio head for the last time. In the quietness of this huge green space, I had thought we were alone. But Tippy Bushkin, our gentle and talented documentary maker, was standing in front of me. She wasn't pointing her camera. She held out a bottle of champagne and a polystyrene cup.

"Congratulations."

2012. It was lying on a bench, on a ferryboat to Manly Harbour, Sydney's nearest surfing shore. Not that I was a surfer, just a tourist back in this great country. And Manly made an interesting sightseeing trip – like stepping back into the 1950s. But there it was. The *Star Observer, Morning Herald* or whatever. A newspaper, abandoned by a fellow passenger, left to flap in the salty breeze. Like a magic effect in some cheesy film, the wind fluttered it open at a page. I read the headline.

"George Lucas sells *Star Wars* to Disney."

2015. I was in New York, lurking round a corner, waiting to make my entrance – listening in shock.

Many years before, I'd been invited to front *The Art Of Star Wars* exhibition, at the Barbican in London – a terrific collection of artifacts from the movies. Here were objects that whizzed by on screen, with no time to admire them. Now guests could stand and stare. They could marvel at the intricate designs and the amount of careful detail, the surprise of the true scale of objects, the tiny Rancor, the huge model of the Star Destroyer that had filled the screen in *A New Hope*. Many of the artists involved were themselves displayed in video format, explaining just how these objects were created.

I felt a little sorry for Threepio, locked inside his glass box. It's not always easy to protect exhibits. Souvenir hunters can reduce an artwork by degrees, unless it's behind a barrier of some kind. Not everyone is respectful – some can't resist pinching a piece of the real thing. And this was Threepio's first appearance in a display case. It was interesting to see him standing so still. But I was on the other side of the glass, so moving about, at this moment, was not an option for him.

Then I noticed something peculiar. His knees were bare, his elbows similarly – just blackened spaces. Against all the laws of protocol, he was incomplete. I pointed out the lapse to the over-worked exhibition designer. She said Threepio always looked like that and nothing could change now. She rushed off. I noticed that the glass wasn't actually locked, after all. I went off and rummaged in a backstage area and found bits of redundant computer cables. I cut and glued gaffer tape patches and sneaked them behind Threepio's knees, slid them into his elbow joints. Now he was fit for the public. They'd never know these wires weren't actually in the film and Threepio wasn't about to tell them.

And the fans loved the exhibit from the moment they saw the stunning poster – Threepio peeking through an extravagant, gold picture frame.

Lucasfilm, under the leadership of their Director of Special Projects, Kathleen Holliday, had asked me to front the opening events which, with the help of the nascent 501st stormtroopers, were full of drama and wonder. Kathleen had seen me speak at an after-hours launch of *Star Wars* toys at FAO Schwarz in New York. Planning a few words of welcome, I narrowly escaped making an embarrassing gaff. Part of my address had been to suggest that guests go down to Broadway and see the stage musical of the film, *Big.* The show featured that giant piano keyboard danced on by Tom Hanks in this world-famous toy store. I ran my words past Howard Roffman. He winced. Apparently, though the ads were still running on TV, the show had suddenly closed as a bit of a flop. I desperately improvised some remarks about how many years it was since I first stood on a distant planet and said those immortal words.

"I am See-Threepio, human-cyborg relations."

Better than any remarks about a defunct musical, the audience loved hearing Threepio's voice in person.

It turned out that I shared his ability as a master of ceremonies, though he would always remain the complete master of etiquette and protocol – two skills rather more useful in the worlds of exhibitions than in the mayhem of the Saga.

Like hosting *Star Wars – In Concert*, live events bridged the gap between my fond memories of work in theatre and my life in films. I loved being able to share with a live audience. And guests seemed to be amused that my beautiful gold costume was locked inside a glass display case so, even if I'd wanted to wear it, I couldn't. And that was fine by me. I had a silky gold tie made to wear at similar events – a gesture – and there were many similar events.

My close connection with the movies and my ability to present, took me around the world. Back in 2002 at The Powerhouse Museum, Sydney, Australia, *Star Wars – The Magic of Myth,* had arrived. And so had an attentive and select group of museum patrons. They were here to marvel at the inaugural event. All beautifully arranged and produced, in the absence of the Museum Director, the production was planned and timed, to the minute. Go. Lights down. Music. Thirty seconds in, lights up. First speaker enters on stage. Three-minute speech. Exits. Next speaker enters. Three-minute speech. Exits. Anthony Daniels enters. Three-minute speech. Exits. Intro Museum Director. Enters. Seven-minute speech. And so on. Being a professional actor, used to following directions, I followed this very tight schedule. I crossed out all the prepared comments and anecdotes I had planned to share with the audience.

With great discipline, I just had time to say that I was thrilled to be back in Australia to celebrate the arrival in Sydney of this superb *Star Wars* exhibition. My time was up. I exited. Polite applause. Now the turn of the Director. He'd literally arrived only moments before, rather jet-lagged from a European trip. He hadn't heard my brief, hello everyone. They stuck his script in his hand as he walked on stage. He started with the words, "Thank you Anthony, for that fascinating insight into the film-making process." Fortunately, I was round the back by then – not sure if the egg was on my face or his. In spite of my failing to share insights, the exhibition did prove hugely popular.

Most enjoyed by me, among the impressive array of costumes and props and videos, was a tiny booth in a quiet corner of the display. There was a miniature stage set in the darkened interior. A beautiful version of Yoda's home forest perfectly replicated the moody scene from the movie. There were the gnarled trees and filthy pond, all wreathed in strands of mist that eerily floated above the surface. And there, half-hidden in the swamp, was Master Luke's X-wing.

The guest was encouraged to raise it from the waters, as Luke had done in *Empire*, to find the Force within them, and use it. It was fascinating to watch adults concentrating on freeing the craft from the tangled clearing. They waved their hands in mystical gestures, thrusting them upwards, in growing frustration. Many of the younger guests, too, would become impatient and saddened that the Force was not with them – for today at least.

Then I would see a child stand and gaze and concentrate their thoughts. And magically, the craft would slowly rise at their unspoken bidding. They were entranced. I was entranced. Of course, I had learned how it all happened. But I wouldn't spoil it for a child, who might have imagined that the Force was strong in them. For adults, I would explain.

The beautiful little scene was fitted with a movement sensor. Nothing would happen – the X-wing would stay water-logged forever – unless you stood very, very still.

I loved fronting another major *Star Wars* exhibition – one that concentrated on aspects taken for granted in the movies. In particular, it was aimed at getting kids to think beyond what was on screen and about the real science that they would come to know in the future of their planet. *Star Wars – Where Science Meets Imagination*, was the brainchild of the Boston Museum of Science, master-minded by Ed Rodley and Jan Crocker. It was hugely popular – and not just with kids. Such a wealth of props and gadgets and experiments and augmented reality gizmos to play with. How could Luke's hover landspeeder actually work – because there was the real one from the movies and you could see the wheels. Could you construct a robot like See-Threepio – because there he was in his 'naked' state, inside a glass box, thankfully having been reassembled after his unfortunate experience in Matmata.

Dr Cynthia Breazeal was one of the expert brains behind the exhibit. Born in 1976, her work at MIT had been inspired by seeing *A New Hope*.

In particular, she had been delighted by Artoo and Threepio. From that moment she wanted them to exist in her world – not just on the screen. Movie makers are only limited by their imaginations. Their inventions don't actually have to work. Dr Breazeal has become a world expert in the field of socially intelligent, personal robots that can interact and communicate with humans. It was delightful to be working with her on the exhibit. But I was concerned that her astonishing research and development would put me out of a job. Reassuringly, she thought that Threepio was a hundred years ahead of his time. Good. I need the work. But now I'm not sure she was right. Robotics seems to be fast-tracking itself into the near future. But in her case, it all started with George's imagination.

The whole exhibition experience was all educational fun. The kids asked lots of questions, mixing science and fantasy and their own imaginative ideas. They wanted to know if you can really hear explosions in the vacuum of space. Of course you can – but only in *Star Wars* space.

And here I was, November 2015, back in New York, at the Discovery Times Square. *Star Wars and the Power of Costume* had arrived. Again there were lots of museum patrons and friends. Naturally, it's proper for the host to welcome the guests and thank everyone involved – of course it is – but when the guests have had quite a go at the fancy snacks and cocktails, it is possibly not the best time to rabbit on. There was nice applause for the host, when she eventually handed over the microphone, but the preliminaries weren't over yet. A representative from another sponsor did the same thing in different words. By the time the Lucasfilm producer had waded through several prepared thoughts and pages, the crowd was quite raucous. They were having a good time – quite right, too.

But there was a problem. I was on last.

Next.

Now.

Those who noticed my arrival, applauded when I came out of my hiding space. Some of them listened briefly. They were simply not following the appropriate etiquette. I realised that drastic action was needed. I began to speak. They could see my lips were moving. Gradually they began to take notice.

"You will listen to Anthony's opening remarks."

They looked puzzled. I had to explain the process. Some guests needed individual training – to the amusement of others. Eventually they managed to intone together.

"We will listen to Anthony's opening remarks."

They had all remembered that scene from the movie – the one where Obi-Wan does his gesture thing to the inquisitive stormtrooper. After that, they listened and laughed and still had a good time. So did I – but I certainly needed a glass of whatever they'd been drinking, afterwards. Doing a Jedi mind trick is harder than it looks.

But that was later.

The day before, arriving at its new venue just off Times Square, I was hugely impressed by this latest iteration of the costume exhibit. Thrilling reflections of stormtrooper helmets suspended in an eternity of mirrors, dynamic postures of Darth Maul defiant with his double-edged sword, dramatic theatrical lighting and at last – the Droid Room. The Force had finally awakened and enough time had passed, that a new member of the droid family had joined us.

Oh dear.

Artoo and the normally exuberant BB-8 stared vacantly, head-on into the void behind me. No sense of movement. No attitude. Simply objects. But there was worse. With the opening events just a few hours away, the production crew had rushed to other areas for final touch-ups – there were mirrors to polish. I needed to help. If I thought the two shorter droids had a sad, unloved air, they were rolling drunk happy compared with Threepio. He slumped there in his own spotlight as if institutionalised, waiting for his meds. I'd have to have been switched off, to give a performance like that in the movies. I couldn't leave him in that state. His propensity to view the future, or indeed the present, as doomed, was one thing – but his forlorn stance here was too much. I stepped in, took off my shoes and jumped up onto the black shine of his stage.

First were his arms. I gently uncovered the wire armature that held him in this droopy posture. Anxious that I might snap something, I twisted and pushed and adjusted. An arm raised up, an elbow bent, a hand suddenly gestured. Now the other side. His shoulders were immovable as he gazed forlornly at the floor. Threepio always looks directly at humans, employing a particular choice of his six million forms of communication – eye contact.

I'd noticed some production off-cuts so, as before, I scavenged and manufactured several foam inserts. Under his chin, inside his neck – nothing snapped. Eventually I slid off the stage, looked back. There was Threepio, as we know him. I put on my shoes, glad I was there to help my friend. I glanced back as I left. I'd like to think he smiled at me.

But that would have been weird.

I should admit it – I just don't get Bobble Heads.

I find them mildly disturbing but they're bought by thousands of delighted fans around the planet. The much collected Funko Pops, too. What's all that thing about giving these toys huge heads? On the other hand, I love my softly golden, Beanie Baby Threepio. A squidgy caricature of the character.

Merchandise. Merch. George almost invented it. Everything *Star Wars*, from bath soap to dangly earrings, and many a stuffed alien and action figure on the way. He famously created a "sandbox" concept. He wanted fans to use his film as a launch pad for their imagination, for them to be inventive with his story and with the merchandise – always within the laws of copyright, of course. *Star Wars* was his sandbox but everyone was welcome to come and play in it.

I was overcome with wonder at the creativity I saw on the film set. But now it came in miniature form – the toys. How amazing to receive boxes of them, that I would give away to friends or the local hospital. Amazing, since their value has now multiplied many, many times.

I was lucky to be in all sorts of TV commercial shoots, often for the superb Kenner toys. Making ads is serious business but under the leadership of feisty, funny producer, Barbara Barrow, we were a bunch of adults having fun. On a non-toy shoot with her, I did learn something useful. It was an ad for Puffs. Little boy in bed in the stars has a bad cold and can't sleep. Artoo and Threepio arrive, bearing a box of the eponymous facial tissues. Problem solved. Except there was another problem.

The set was a real bed with real pillows and blankets and a real child. The rest was blue walls and floor. The stars would not be real. They wheeled an Artoo into position and keyed in the star-field effect, on camera. Anything blue became part of the galaxy, including Artoo.

It was as though he was being X-rayed. The stars shone brightly through his arms and his head – and other bits. There were some red faces. Barbara was not happy. I got the morning off while they repainted the entire place green. That's where I first learned about the use of blue screen, and its limitations. Little did I know that over the oncoming decades, I would see a lot more blue – and a lot of green too.

I don't live in a See-Threepio-*Star Wars* shrine – it's not my thing. Stuff takes up a lot of room. But I loved the honour of Threepio being part of the *Star Wars* postage stamp collection. Cute design, practical, self-adhesive, so no licking required. Flat, too, for easy storage in a drawer. There too, rather more bulky – but it makes me laugh – is the show-off, giant, shiny Pez dispenser. Monumental. But not to be shown-off too often.

Only one item stands discretely on a corner table. Over several years, I had been lucky to be involved in various animation series. *Droids, Rebels, Clone Wars* – they went on to become wildly popular in their own right. Such fun to perform. Usually I was on my own in a London studio. The director might or might not be on a laptop screen at my side, watching me on Skype. Sometimes it was just their voice through a headset. Threepio is already a slight exaggeration of a personality so there was no need to augment the simple graphics too much. But the dramatic situations could be even more extreme than in the movies. The cartoons were broadcast but also available on disc, for endless replays. I so enjoyed being a part of them all. In particular, under the expert and creative direction of Dave Filoni, the animation in *Clones* was exceptional.

But for me, it was the hysterically funny and well-observed *The Yoda Chronicles* that I cherish. I loved them so much, I would have done that job for no charge – but I didn't tell them that. It was all in Lego characters and was just such hilarious fun.

The two Michaels and I would often be tearful with mirth. Usually I was in a London studio while director, Michael Donovan was in his in

San Francisco. Brilliant and inventive writer, Michael Price, was often on speaker phone in his car on the 40 freeway in LA, driving to his other job – writing scripts for *The Simpsons*.

Once we'd done the voice work, the animators got involved. I so enjoyed seeing the rough-cut animations and being able to spot some additional speech opportunities that I could add. It wasn't always perfect – a whole gag was based on the fact that Lego Chewie was too plump to follow Lego Threepio and squeeze through a gap in the Lego wall. Oops! Rewrite – all Lego characters are the same size.

We adored working together – jolly script conferences on the phone, followed by intense recording sessions. Eventually we would meet up on stage at Celebration. Such a joy to show off our stuff in front of a live audience. But now, a surprise gift from Michael and Michael and our Lego masters. A twenty-pound, twenty-inch high Lego likeness of Threepio – a wondrous piece of chunky pop art, in yellow bricks. It made it all the way back to London, in spite of some curious questions from British Airways. He stands there on a table as a key – a reminder of magic times.

And what a thrill to be in *The Lego Movie* – an action-packed cast of super heroes, all made of plastic brick. I eventually saw it in a state-of-the-art theatre on 42nd Street in New York. It seemed somehow a fitting place for such a whacky production. For me, it had been a very brief recording session back in London. Now I would see the results. The packed audience loved the ingenious film. But when Threepio briefly yelled from the Lego *Falcon*, the cheers drowned out the theatre's super multi-track audio system – before the craft jumped to Lego light speed and was gone. It reminded me just how much people love *Star Wars*.

And I loved the association with Lego. They invited me to their production facilities in Billund in Denmark. I flew in their private aircraft, slightly amused at the Lego logo on the tail fin. The implication that I was in a plane made of bricks was briefly unnerving. But what an honour.

I had such a good time addressing the teams. But an even better one, visiting the factory. Amazing to see machines relating to each other, stamping plastic, delivering supplies, collecting parts. Each one travelling smoothly on concealed tracks. All in complete harmony. Threepio would have been impressed. It was possibly proof of my growing empathetic relationship with him that I noticed my host switching off the lights as we left, leaving those poor droids to work in the dark.

At another Celebration, in London, I signed something that wasn't quite the usual collectable. An airplane – not a real one but a sleek, fifteen-foot model. What a respectful homage to the character. All Nippon Airlines – ANA – were already flying a real plane in the style of Artoo-Detoo, all white with blue bands, that was instantly recognisable. It had flown us all back to London from the Los Angeles premiere of *The Force Awakens*. I knew there was a BB-8 version – white, with his signature orange decals. And now Threepio. Apparently, it had been a major challenge to turn the humanoid droid into a plane-shaped design. Early attempts left him looking as if he'd dropped dead and been placed in a coffin between two wings. So ANA's inventive design team and Lucasfilm's Howard Roffman rethought the whole thing. They cleverly placed iconic elements of Threepio's "look" around the fuselage. Time passed. Now I had a beautiful plane to keep for myself – not a real one. But a four feet long model. A gift from ANA.

Time passed again. Now, I was addressing two hundred guests and press and television crews way below me as I stood at the door of the ANA Threepio plane. A real one – a brand new, shiny, yellow one, parked in a huge hangar in Tokyo. What a thrill, as I welcomed the crowd in fluent Japanese – days in the phonetic learning but also written in big black marker across the top step, just in case. Then I autographed the fuselage of the spectacular craft. Seeing the essence of Threepio on such a grand scale made me feel quite emotional. But here was a craft simply too big to take home. I can just about accommodate the four-foot version.

Rather smaller is the sat-nav I recorded. What a strange script. Just a list of words – pages and pages of words. The computer would eventually stitch them together with brilliant algorithms. They gave me a gizmo for my own use. It worked extremely efficiently and some drivers found it fun to have Threepio on board, as their navigator. But how weird to hear myself telling me where to go, in places I'd never visited before. I'll admit that, in the end, the uncanniness of it all began to unnerve me. Eventually, I switched to another voice. Please don't tell Threepio.

Another favourite piece. A beautiful blue box. Golden Threepio proudly presenting a bowl of fruit and cereal. Kellogg's "C-3POs". I have a pack of the original product – unopened. I wonder what it would taste like some thirty years later? Probably the same. The snack had started life as totally unsweetened and healthy, and they were indeed "O" shaped. It was a fun play on words and we shot amusing commercials around exotic Mono Lake in California. Those few tourists visiting this National Park were clearly astounded to find Threepio wandering about with a bunch of Rock Monsters.

They would have been amused, too, to see me taking a break in the open air. The crew suddenly arrived with a silver tray, bearing all the china necessities for serving tea and biscuits. They'd wanted me to feel at home in the middle of this lunar landscape. A thoughtful team effort. Threepio would really have appreciated the proper rules of etiquette that they exhibited towards me.

Less proper – it snowed. Fortunately, someone had a hair dryer. On full blast, it stopped me from freezing to a halt. The ads were great, the product not so great. They added sugar to the recipe and stuck two Os together. "Twin rings of honey sweetened oats fused together for a truly galactic breakfast." We shot some more commercials in the sandy wastes around Las Vegas. It was warmer, but the producers were not amused when I insisted the shapes were "C-3P8s".

For the product launch in Tampa, lights and lasers revealed an eight-foot box revolving on stage. It stopped in a whirl of smoke and colour in front of the applauding throng. It opened and out stepped Threepio, waving and smiling at the sheer whackyness of what I was doing. Of course, you couldn't see I was smiling – but I was. Back at home, the "hero" box is the star – the hand-painted art box from the stills shoot. Wearing only the top half of Threepio, I clutched a delicious bowl of healthy-looking breakfast items. But there was a problem. The milk made the product go soggy as we shot. The solution – a gloopy white mixture purchased from a local pharmacy. The art director kept repositioning the fruit and the cereal. He used a cotton bud to push the white stuff around for the best effect, and kept sucking it clean – again and again. I knew he was flying home the next day. I wondered if he'd be okay – the gloop was a laxative.

It's hidden in a drawer somewhere, out of sight – an example of possibly the worst piece of *Star Wars* merch, ever. I know it's somewhere. It's made of glazed ceramic in yellow and white. It haunts my dreams. Threepio reclines with his hands resting on his knees. His legs are parted to allow the insertion of a roll of sticky tape. It's meant to sit on a desk – possibly a gynaecologist's desk. I did enquire if they were ever going to make a sister version – Threepio on his hands and knees with a rather larger roll inserted behind.

Perhaps to be found in a bathroom.

# 53 forgery

I was amazed to receive fan mail. Amazed and flattered.

People, whom I had never met, were taking the trouble to write to me. To tell me how much they liked what I did in *A New Hope*. It was music to my ears. And every other bit of me. In my experience, there was not a lot of time for praise on set. Getting the next shot was paramount. But neither was there much appreciation afterwards. How lovely then, to receive through the post, unsolicited praise for Threepio, albeit attached to a request for an autograph. I tried to oblige, if there was a photo enclosed. I had nothing to send. No one supplied me with a stock of official photos.

Eventually, my sense of embarrassment was strong enough to make me create hundreds of cheap prints. My face on the left. Threepio's on the right. Or maybe the other way. It was long ago. I left a space in the middle. Some fans enclosed a photo and an envelope already addressed to towns across America. As the film's distribution continued over the months, these addresses would become more exotic – a simple indication of its global popularity. I signed the cards, addressed the envelopes, licked the stamps and slid them into the red letter box in the street. It seemed the right thing to do.

Then I found out that other members of the cast were actually selling their autograph. It sounds ridiculously naïve, but I was shocked. It didn't seem right at all. Here were fans wanting some kind of innocent souvenir of their wondrous *Star Wars* experience – they were showing me their appreciation. The least I could do was to respond. Even now that feels quaintly innocent. Because I would gradually learn the facts.

Of course, many fans appreciate an autograph as a record of a meeting. But the growth in collecting scribbled names seems to be massive. The hobby attracts thousands, or maybe millions, of collectors – all craving the complete set. The commercial side of it has rocketed.

Now, I too charge fans for my signature. I'd be crazy not to. I still sign many things as a courtesy but I occasionally attend conventions where it is clearly a commercial event.

I do try to give a few moments of real time to fans who have stood in long lines to meet me and others. But there's always the concern of taking a pen to some treasured piece of memorabilia, often already emblazoned with signatures, hoping it's not going to spatter and blob and ruin the cherished item. It's quite a challenge, as I see the queue stretching away and my brain hurts, along with my hand.

My website, www.anthonydaniels.com, has never been commercial. No autographs to purchase through the mail – nothing but goodwill. I'm occasionally bothered by seeing fans encouraged to send requests to addresses, supplied by companies claiming to know my contact details. Their information is useless and simply serves to frustrate fans.

What my site does demonstrate, is a large gallery of forgeries gleaned from the Web. A glance over the small images shows the range of attempts to forge my signature. Some are quite close. Others add insult to injury in their pathetic attempts, dashed off with a Sharpie. But these fakes go on sale for alarmingly large sums. Maybe it doesn't matter that it's not the real thing, if a fan believes it is. I remember learning that, in medieval times, conmen would roam the country selling bits of St. Peter's shinbone or pieces of the "True Cross" to Christian believers – chicken bones and wood shavings. There have always been scams, the unscrupulous taking advantage of the innocent, but the Internet has multiplied the issue by many, many times over.

FBI? A message from agent X. I was about to dump it in the Spam, along with offers to launder the inheritance dollars of a Nigerian prince. Then I noticed there was a phone number. I left it for a couple of days before I rang.

"Federal Bureau of Investigation. How may I direct your call?"

Gosh. This was really real.

I was soon talking with a real FBI agent, part of Operation Bullpen. They'd appreciate it if I would help them in the trial of an accused forger. They didn't want to subpoena me – just asking nicely. Weeks later I was studying a large family bible. Each page was devoted to a name. Below were repeated attempts at an acceptable signature. The sides of the pages decorated with swipes of a suitably coloured Sharpie, where the accused had tested each pen. Now, I was in a courtroom in San Diego, witnessing that my signature had been faked on an item sold by the accused, standing there in dock. Somehow the sheer size of the projected image made me even more troubled. I could certainly confirm that it wasn't my writing. His counsel asked how I could tell. Perhaps the fact that I had signed my name many times over the years gave me some kind of expert knowledge. But I did give the court a few technical pointers which strongly suggested that a hand, other than mine, had written my name. But mine wasn't the only forgery in evidence that day. The room was filled with boxes of hundreds of pictures of any personality you could name – as yet unsigned. All – claimed the accused – for his personal use.

Operation Bullpen had begun with an undercover FBI agent sending the accused a marked poster and payment, with a request that it be signed, in person by Sir Alec Guinness. It eventually arrived back in the post, duly signed by Sir Alec who sadly, had been dead for many years. The perp got just three.

There have been all sorts of attempts to verify autographs. Certificates of Authenticity are just as easy to fake as the signature they testify. They are not worth the paper they're written on – literally. Holographic stickers mean little. Really, the best way to know you have a genuine autograph is to see it written in person by that person. Impossible most of the time, but the only sure way.

On the other hand, if you believe what you have is real, then for you – it is.

"Hello. My name is Kathy Kennedy and I'm the producer of the next *Star Wars* film. Would it be all right if J.J. Abrams called you? He's the director."

I have had some phone calls in my time but this was one of the more exquisite. Then silence for a month. What was going on? The phone rang. It was like speaking with an excited school boy. J.J. had seen *A New Hope* when he was ten years old. Eventually I said – enough of the adulation. What did he want?

"Would you like to be in my movie?"

"Yes."

"Would you like just to do the voice?"

"No."

"Quite right."

"But I would like a new suit."

"Of course."

It was a great start. Such full-on enthusiasm.

Now I was at Pinewood – wondering what was next.

"And please give me your phone."

"Why?"

"So you can't take photos of the pages."

I was surprised. I can barely use my phone as a phone, let alone a spy camera. I handed it over to the Guardian of the Scripts who showed me into a small office. The room had a security camera peering down. And a young woman reading a book. She looked up.

"Hello. I'm Daisy. I'm playing Rey."

Of course, it meant nothing to me. But there was a black book on the other desk. Perhaps I would find out a little more. I sat down and opened the cover. It was a shock – every page inside the thick volume was deep red, with black lettering, my name writ large, spread diagonally across the words. This was "The Script".

It wasn't easy. The dense story was hard to absorb. The red security pages made it worse – headachingly hard to focus on. It was a long read, but an intriguing one. Finally, I got an overall view and thankfully, and a little sadly, closed the book. I accepted Threepio had very little to do in this story. But at least he was there – and so was I.

Daisy was still reading as I left – young enough to be at least my granddaughter – and lovely. Now, I knew who Rey was, and what that would mean. I turned back, interrupting her concentration.

"Your life will never be the same again."

Unoriginal – but true.

David Merryweather arrived at the flat with an exploded-view version of my suit, on his laptop. An electro-mechanical CAD genius, he was in charge of the redesign. It looked wonderfully hopeful on screen. The days of torture inside my "Iron Maiden" might be over at last. Eventually, we moved on to first fittings at Pinewood. No more glass fibre. The costume was 3D printed.

I stood there in various pieces of white plastic, as we discussed which bits worked, and the other bits that didn't. Suddenly, J.J. rushed in. He dashed off numerous selfies, even though I was wearing an early prototype. He was still in schoolboy mode. His genius enthusiasm was overt and infectious. But we didn't agree about everything. In particular, the arm. Threepio's left arm. It was going to be red.

"Why?"

"It shows history. A back story."

"Like the silver calf in *A New Hope*?"

"Exactly."

"But that was so subtle that few people notice it."

"Exactly."

There was certainly nothing subtle about red. Clearly J.J. had got a thing about that colour. But he was the director. I eventually, in desperation, mocked up an idea in Photoshop. An arm with metal Band-Aid patches, riveted on. I liked it.

"No. Red."

So the design team carried on, until I had a passable copy of the original suit. Though that vital artifact was locked in Lucasfilm's archive, some communication problem between them and Disney barred David from seeing and measuring it accurately. Which was a shame. The lack of exact data added greatly to the task. David had to use a lot of guess-work and intuition. Most of which worked.

The best part was his rethinking of Threepio's head fixings. The thirty-minute horror of lining up various screws and holes was gone. A simple fix had me encased in six seconds. Uncased in three. Now I would be able to see and breathe and cool down between each shot. What a gift.

Less of a gift for me was the script. I accepted that Threepio was very much on the periphery but I recognised that J.J. had a huge, difficult balancing act – getting everyone back into the story. I would have liked it if my friend had more opportunities to show off his talents and vulnerabilities. I thought Threepio was worth more. But I was already more than pleased to be part of this new enterprise.

And what a transformation from prequels to sequel. I would never forget the experience of working on the former. Here was utterly different. J.J.'s enthusiasm flowed all over and around the set. Everyone seemed so happy to be there. Every member of the crew had grown up with *Star Wars* – many not born at the time of the original. Whatever blockbusters they had worked on, they were so pleased to be a part of this one. It made for a real family atmosphere. That included hosts of background artists. J.J. would always welcome the Crowd with genuine affection and respect. He asked them not to share what they saw or heard – not to ruin the surprise. I don't believe anyone ever did. They would tell me how proud they were to be part of a story so vividly remembered from childhood. They were angry at the drones that tried to snap spoiler photos of the sets and costumes for the newspapers.

It was a thrill to watch the ranks of stormtroopers going to set, each one draped in a black cloak against prying eyes, each with a concealing black bag in their hand – their helmet. They had the aura of a sinister religious sect on the movie, almost as thrilling a sight as their new white uniforms worn underneath, only revealed for the shoot itself. And the sets were thrilling, too. Where had all the green screen gone? We had reality – no more pretend. We had the real thing all around us.

But before that, there was the read-through. We sat in a large circle. I don't know if the others felt as self-conscious as I did, but there was Peter studying the script. Harrison being hilarious and Carrie eventually retiring to a back seat, and Mark sitting next to me. An Artoo unit was in an open packing case on the far side of the group. Eventually, a select photo of the whole thing sped around the world. There we all were. Laughing. Smiling. Talking. Reading. Sadly, the only one with his back to the camera was me. How typical. But I was just amazed to be back again – and touched at the little round of applause from the team, when I chipped in with the first of Threepio's few lines.

Carrie took us out to dinner that night. Her now-constant companion, Gary, joined us at the table. His tail wagged briefly as his tongue lolled flaccidly over the menu that he could only dream of being served. The meal was like a therapy session. Both actors were appalled at their roles – Mark in particular. He had brilliantly read the stage directions for us all that day at Pinewood – brilliantly, thrillingly, sight-read them – because he had no lines of his own in the script. He seemed traumatised in the hubbub of The Firehouse restaurant.

I tried to explain that this was surely the biggest build-up to an entrance – ever. He was still not convinced. Me? I understood that we were there to serve the story, the bigger picture, literally. I had developed the protective mantra of taking what I'm given, to a certain degree.

Though it was nice to be back with the originals, I had hoped that somehow Threepio would return to be with his companion, Master Luke. But it was not to be. Though I rarely saw Mark again during the shoot, it was good to have Carrie back on set once more.

Threepio's first task was to pull the covers off Artoo. He had been forgotten in a dusty corner of the bunker. This was the moment J.J. first saw the golden droid for real. He was delightfully excited, as one of his fondly remembered childhood figures came to life. Sadly, that innocent moment would be shattered.

In spite of the brilliant redesign, some parts of the suit still had little functionality, the hands in particular. There was Artoo draped in tarpaulins, there was Threepio reaching forward, there were the steps leading to sunlight above, there was their daylight brightness dazzling straight into my eyes – there was me swearing loudly, as I groped in the blinding darkness. Time after time. There was J.J. listening to my voice, expleting with frustration through his headphones. Simply not correct etiquette at all – it was a side of Threepio the young J.J. could never have imagined in his boyhood wonder.

How brilliant to meet Brian Herring and BB-8, the magnificent new droid he was puppeteering. I quickly labelled Brian, "Man In Green", since he was dressed head-to-toe in a coloured suit that would eventually be wiped out in post. His co-operator, David Chapman, was remotely controlling the droid's perky head from a distance. He was dressed in jeans. I labelled him "Dave". Brian called me "MIG", the original "Man In Gold". Silly stuff – but much in keeping with our larky relationship on set.

Brian's scripted, but extemporised, burblings and whistles were whimsical magic. The daft sounds he made were simply hilarious and, in context, completely understandable. I wanted J.J. to sample Brian's vocal performance for BB-8's screen voice. That didn't happen. But it made scenes between us such fun. The only problem was that I had to remember to look at the little round droid at my feet, rather than at Brian's animated face next to mine. Also, I had to try not to giggle.

However realistic was the set of the underground Rebel Bunker, it got a bit old after a while.

EXT. D'QAR – REBEL BASE – DAY

It was a joy. Daylight. Fresh air. Greenham Common – another Anglo-American production. During the Cold War, it had been the local American nuclear weapons launch pad. Our perimeter fence now protected the set from snoopers, rather than the thousands of anti-nuclear protesters who had tried to storm the facility, back then. The missiles gone now, the more benign *Falcon* parked on the runway instead, the detritus of rebel conflict and giant vine roots dressing the manmade landscape where once, nuclear conflict had threatened to end our world. And yes, to my surprise and a twinge of guilt, there was the *Millennium Falcon* apparently risen from the ashes at Elstree decades ago. Should I return the pieces I had rescued, now mouldering in my attic? I decided not to mention it. But it was a sweet moment to see the iconic craft once more.

And a sweet recollection, revisited. A sudden harking back to that interrupted kiss, so long ago, another gooseberry moment, as Threepio obliviously crashed an emotional reunion between Leia and Han – Carrie and Harrison. Would Threepio never learn?

But here was one of J.J.'s master strokes.

EXT. TAKODANA – MAZ'S CASTLE RUINS – DAY

ACTION!

"You probably don't recognise me because of the red arm."

I so loved that moment, so typical of Threepio's misreading of the moment, so typical of J.J.'s inventive thinking. And it seemed as if he had, indeed, heard me.

Throughout the shoot I had greeted him daily with the phrase, "No Forgiveness!" It was the red arm thing. I still didn't approve. He was the director. He got his way. Eventually I created some large buttons – badges with a sinister blood-red arm suspended in the dark and those warning words across in red letters. J.J. laughed. But maybe he heeded the warning after all. How amazing – seeing the finished film for the first time at the premiere. There was Threepio, waving to the departing *Falcon* with his left arm – his once more, gold left arm. A gift from J.J. in post – a sweet and final gift, I thought – wrongly.

Eventually they wrote the story of the red arm as a comic book – *The Phantom Limb*. It was a sensitive tale, with some profound thoughts – a story of loyalty and understanding – of memories of memories – of self-sacrifice. I was genuinely touched when I read it. Later, at a Celebration, I was gave a dramatised reading. The audience listened in entranced silence. I think they liked it. So I'm surprised that many fans ask me about the genesis of the notorious red arm. Don't they know it is touchingly memorialised in this moving account of droids with feelings?

A phone call. Customs officers at London's Heathrow Airport were intrigued. What exactly was inside the package addressed to me? Package? What package? I had no idea. I wasn't expecting anything. It seemed that a company, suspiciously called "Bad Robot", was sending me something from California. I asked what it said on the customs declaration. There was a pause.

"Fudge Brownie Mix."

Suddenly, I understood why the authorities were suspicious. I could hear the approaching police sirens. Jail time threatened. I laughingly explained who I was, what Bad Robot was, who J.J. was, and about his persistent generosity. They seemed to believe me and the box duly arrived. Indeed, it contained everything required to make a batch of delicious chocolate treats – with nothing added.

J.J. denied trying to get me arrested. Well, he would, wouldn't he?

It was Lucasfilm. I wasn't expecting a call.

"He's a huge, huge *Star Wars* fan and he'd love to meet you."

It seemed they were making a *Star Wars* spin-off story. The director was a chap called Gareth Edwards – a huge fan. I assumed he wanted an autograph, or a selfie.

"Why doesn't he come round to the flat for a cup of tea?"

And so he did. What a lovely man, so exuberant, full of boyish enthusiasm for his new project. I didn't ask what it was about – these things are hush-hush. But he couldn't contain himself, in his need to lay out the full story for me, and it was really full. I didn't time his flow of words. I managed to hold on to the plot for a while, but eventually just let the whole, darkly exciting thing wash over me. Then I suddenly caught up.

"Sorry. What did you say?"

"And I'd really love you to be in it. Just to have Threepio walk through a scene…"

"What a neat idea."

"Because you are so much an icon of the Saga, it would be really important…"

"I'd love to do it."

"It would be just a cameo but I'd be really, really grateful…"

"I'm saying, yes."

"I know it's not what you would normally do but…"

"I said YES."

He stopped. He had arrived under the assumption that it would be a difficult sell. He'd wound himself up to having to convince me. Now, he was stunned that I had been a pushover. But I loved the idea of this Hitchcockian moment. Why would I ever have said no to him? He looked relieved.

"Now would you like a cup of tea?"

It would just be one day at Cardington, deep in the English country-side. We drove up to the huge, imposing structure – a giant, lofty tin shed 180 feet tall. It had been a zeppelin hangar in the days when air-ships were the thing. On a dreary, grey day, it looked rather threatening – in keeping with what was happening inside.

The scene they were shooting was clearly very serious – lots of pilot types discussing strategy. I wandered off to find the two master-brains and helpers, David and Jonathan, in my E-Z UP tent. What a joy to see them again after our fun together on *The Force Awakens*. As ever, David couldn't wait to show me the little refinements he had added to the suit. For a better effect, I got fully dressed and eyes lit to walk out of my tent. Very few people had seen me arrive in the morning. Now, heading towards sunset, the whole population of the colossal shed seemed to pause, to gaze – many seeing Threepio live for the first time. The effect was palpable, and very reassuring to my sense of pride in the character.

We shot various set-ups of troops running towards the giant exit doors, me just trying to keep up. Magically the grey skies cleared for a lovely sunset. The exit faced west. Finally, I stood there as the beautiful gold light flooded in and hit my suit. I said my two cents' worth. Gareth's lines, completely in character, leaving Threepio confused, bewildered and irritated – as ever.

INT. YAVIN 4 – HANGAR – DAY

ACTION!

"Why does nobody tell me anything, Artoo?"

Typical. But now I was out of a job, again. Sad – it had been such fun.

Fun too, earlier. Gareth had told me there was another droid in his film – K-2SO. Sounded like some dry-cleaning product to me. But I had a tinge of concern. Was I about to be upstaged by another BB-8-type ball?

Alan Tudyk was cruising the food truck. Actors can generally be found near food outlets. Never sure of where the next meal is coming from, it's wise to stock up when you have the chance – and it's free. Now we were both nibbling away at some comfort junk.

So, this was the new droid on the block. Should I have felt threatened? No chance. Tall, elegant Alan was a hoot from the start. We hit it off together. I loved our bantering encounter there, and at the wondrous premiere, that would be many months away. Of course, he had to admit that ILM would paint over his physical performance, so he wasn't actually real, like me. It seemed some people are happy to go digital. I said that wasn't quite the thing. He winced. I was just being jealous.

I liked *Rogue One*. A lot. With one exception. The young Carrie Fisher moment. Inside my head, I was silently shouting at the back of her white dress and bunned hair – begging her not to turn around. But I did like the reaction from a surprised audience when Threepio turned up. He would have been proud. I know I gave Gareth a hug. Not sure if he ever got an autograph.

Or a selfie.

## 56 lost

After the rollercoaster of *The Force Awakens*, it was interesting to see each scene in *The Last Jedi*, fully written and plotted in advance.

Rian Johnson, the gentlest of directors with a Teddy Bear quality, had a way of listening to the cast with great respect and kindness. Of course, he didn't always follow suggestions, especially if it was me.

He always wore a face of quiet content. As a fan, he was living the dream; thrilled and excited to be directing this latest episode of the Saga.

But he was so self-contained that it was Jamie Christopher, the ebullient First AD, who was a memorably jolly voice on the set. And we had real scenery again. Once more, the Design Department had excelled in their creativity. Always my favourite set – any one with a flat floor.

INT. RADDUS – CONTROL ROOM

Such a super spaceship setting, with Billie Lourd being wickedly funny during rehearsals. She'd clearly inherited her sense of humour from Carrie. And there was Oscar Isaac again. Watching through Threepio's eyes, I could study his acting technique, just so natural, chatting away as we rolled up to "Action!" gently segueing into whatever the scripted lines were. I delighted in being part of the scene with him and Laura Dern, so lovely, in spite of the cocktail dress and mad blue hair. The chemistry between them on set was visible. Though I had very little to do, I felt very much included in their scenes together. And it was fun to see the script build up Poe's gentle irritation with "Shiny". It made us both laugh.

More awesome than funny, was to stand close to a stunt guy. Hit by Leia's blaster, he was smashed backwards into the wall, yanked on a hydraulic harness. Each time he picked himself up, ready for the next shot – literally. Each time, Threepio raised his hands in surrender. He is in awe of stunt actors. So am I.

Other sets were spectacular but not easy. Filming in the tunnels was horrible, underfoot was horrible, bumping into the chiselled walls was horrible. Even with the hidden red LEDs marking the path, it was horrible. It was a real labyrinth, okay when lit and peopled with crew, but returning from an on-set press interview, all the lights were out, the crew gone home. I was actually lost inside a sound stage – a bewildering moment. But, thinking back over the day's scenes, where I had stumbled around, I eventually managed to navigate myself out, and home.

INT. CRAIT – MINE ENTRANCE – DAY

The surface was awful for Threepio to walk on, and probably also for everyone else, including BB-8. Eventually, it would be changed for the glossy glamour of Canto Bight. But that was later. And I wouldn't be on that set – well, not in the usual way. How good to see Carrie back, happier with her script than last time. Nice to see Mark, too, but he seemed less happy perhaps. He was mostly doing his thing on a Celtic island, or on the back lot surrounded by shipping containers pretending to be a Celtic island. These massive steel boxes formed easy walls around different open-air sets. They had proved to be a good defence against prying eyes and peeking drones. There was no group read-through this time.

My first encounter with Carrie was in the medical centre on day one. Shot first in the schedule, this moment would come after Leia's out-of-ship, in-vacuo experience. So now she was lying there in recovery, as Oscar, John, Kelly Marie and Threepio argued whether to mutiny – or not. I peered over at the cot, on the far side of the set. Was it Carrie? It certainly looked like her. But surely they wouldn't have her asleep all day? What if she started snoring? Of course, it was a prop figure.

So perfect, so still in its tranquillity.

It was eerie.

# 57 Carrie

Of course, Carrie did die, tragically and unexpectedly, not that long after we finished filming – before she could see the results of her own brilliant work in *The Last Jedi*.

Quite frankly, in those latter days, Carrie seemed to glory in arriving for a walk-through on set first thing, looking like – well, let's say she was not a morning person. When we began the glorious task of filming *The Force Awakens* she would arrive, papoosed in a down jacket against the chill of an unlit stage, her latest signature coiffure bound up in a matronly hair net. As ever, she clutched her comfort drink like a curious product commercial. It was part of her support system. Permanently grasped or stuffed, last minute, behind a concealing piece of scenery, that can of Diet Coke was a reminder that the secret location of our rebel base was in fact at Pinewood Studios, UK, planet Earth.

Her character hadn't appeared in the prequels. I'd rather missed her, and the familiar presence of Mark and Harrison. But those productions were long gone. Now it was the seventh story in the canon. Life and times had moved on for all of us. We had become Legacy Players. I kept saying "heritage" but was told that applied to varieties of vegetables.

I sensed Carrie took some reassurance that there was at least one old face on set, a face she knew – mine – Threepio's. At one point, Leia generously awarded him a warm oil bath as a gesture of thanks for a job well done. He was very happy. That scene never made it. But we had other moments together.

We quietly rehearsed our marks and lines. It was difficult to read our sides – the day's script – printed black on red on tiny pages stuffed inside a plastic holder with our names loudly proclaiming our right to see these "eyes only" words. It was all surreal – chill and gloomy in the bleak work lights. But J.J. brought along his big brain and warm heart.

We wandered through the scene, as he transferred what was playing inside his head to the actuality of the stage floor. Once everyone got the rough idea, we went back to our trailers for a couple of hours and breakfast. We relaxed while the lighting crew did their work. But I realised that Carrie was far removed from the fresh-eyed girl I'd met decades before. I found it a little unnerving. But I find looking in the mirror equally so, these days.

On set once more, there she was, beautiful, quietly commanding. Makeup and Hair had returned Carrie to the Princess I knew – a General now. Her eyes still spoke so softly, so eloquently. But the lines were sometimes elusive. I could certainly empathise. Relaxing back in our trailer-park world, she would be her gently funny self, sadly admitting that it was all more of a challenge than it used to be.

And so it continued into *The Last Jedi* in a similar way. At least now I was prepared for this gradual decline. What never seemed to change was her gentle, kind personality, her wit and amused self-deprecation. The loving affection from Rian and the cast and crew hopefully helped her to be as comfortable as was possible in her determination to get it right.

I can't actually remember the first time or the last time we met. On set, at a party, over dinner, over dinner with Gary, her canine companion. It doesn't matter. But back in 1976, trotting next to her in another rebel base, running to congratulate Luke for his heroic deeds, she giggled, clutching her bouncing boobs – more X-Rated than PG-13.

We laughed again, when it transpired that the crowd artists had no idea who Luke was or what he had done to a bad thing called the Death Star. They hadn't seen the movie yet – no one had. Poor Mark jumped down from his X-wing and was forced to congratulate them as they ran past, as opposed to the other way round. The second take was better. Lots of well-dones and back-slappings for Mark and less boob from Carrie.

And we both laughed over a delicious pastilla a year later. The fancy-dressed maître d' at Dar Maghreb on Hollywood Boulevard, robed like an extra from *The Desert Song*, fulsomely praised her performance in *A New Hope*. He slightly spoilt the moment for me. He added, that the only thing he hadn't liked in the film was that silly gold robot. The man was English. Carrie doubled the tip. She was always generous and seemed very at home with English people in general. She'd studied at London's Central School of Drama. I had auditioned for a place there, too. They'd turned me down.

It had been such a giggle, that night in Hollywood. And I slept well in my room in Westwood. Strangely, I didn't dream of the Princess or the tubby English guy in his djellaba. I dreamed of my new culinary experience – the amazing Moroccan invention of pigeon and sugar and spices. And nuts.

After *A New Hope* shattered box office records, I watched Carrie and the others being interviewed and fêted around the world's press. By the time we met again for *Empire*, she was a bright international star. She was just as kooky and kind as ever – but now in a different league. The kookiness started, first thing. The ADs gave her a call one hour earlier than normal, so her driver could wake her up with a pot of coffee, and get her to the studio and on set on time. As I said, Carrie had never been a morning person.

But I am one of the few who have looked into her beautiful eyes and had them look directly, deeply, warmly back into mine – and back into See-Threepio's eyes, too. Like Mark, the reality and honesty of her performance coaxed the audience to believe my gold man was a real, valued companion, even though she would brutally switch me off in the *Falcon*'s cockpit.

She loved a live audience and played up mercilessly. I couldn't ever get used to the glitter thing. At conventions she would sprinkle fans with the stuff – Pixie Dust. It got everywhere for days. It seemed like she wanted those encounters to go on for ever. Her fans loved it. Fan I might have been, but I found the stubborn sparkles more than irritating – or maybe she was paying me back for the time I greeted her on stage. With a hug.

I was hosting another Celebration somewhere, and interviewing all sorts of cast and crew. There was a great atmosphere, though it was a little hot, with all the stage lights aimed at me and the guests. Memorably, my introduction of Oscar-winning special effects maestro, Lorne Peterson, was hysterical, for me at least. It was a very wide stage and I gave him an appropriately grand intro for the lovely and talented man he is. The applause rose. And died. Nothing happened. I walked to the wings. There was Lorne happily waiting to be introduced. I hadn't realised he was a little hard of hearing. So we started his bit with quite a giggle. He fascinated us all with his tales of being the head modeller on so many of the *Star Wars* sets. Hearing about his inventive creations was fascinating but I kept glancing down at my hand, to check we were on schedule. I'd written the afternoon's sequence on my palm in blue Sharpie. It was all so simple then – no earpiece from Production, no video cue screen, no countdown clock. Just my hand and a Sharpie. Eventually, I waved goodbye to Lorne and went for the next intro. It was Carrie.

She was bang on cue when she heard her name and the ovation that greeted it. She came on stage to face her loving fans, looking sweetly casual in a sleeveless linen shirt. I walked across to usher her to the little interview set in the centre. I warmly placed my hands on her shoulders and gave her a friendly peck on the cheek. But I was horrified as we pulled away from each other. There on her little, suntanned shoulder was a perfect print of my schedule, in reverse. My sweaty palm had given her a rather odd tattoo. She loved it.

Her honesty and humanity overcame her much-discussed psychological issues, apparently inspiring countless others in the process.

Her vulnerability and endless determination created one of the greatest screen icons, beloved by millions. Her abilities and talent surmounted her feelings of being, "more a writer than an actor". Certainly her books showed her to be as thoughtful, incisive and witty in prose, as she was in person.

It's sad to think that I will never see her again, except on screen – where she will live forever.

## 58 droids

Well, I wasn't overburdened with Threepio. He did not figure large in Rian's script.

After the prequels and *The Force Awakens*, I was used to being a side order; feeling like a beloved decoration that was brought out once a year to dress the Christmas tree – familiar but with no real purpose. There, for nostalgia's sake only. So why not? And I was flattered to be asked.

Pierre Bohanna had been such a kind and generous mastermind in coordinating my suit's rebuild that I was happy to get involved in his project. "Droid School". Would I be willing to give a master-class to some of the cast? The Casino sequence was going to be huge, thronged with exotic characters and aliens. And there would be five waiter droids. The actors inside might have earned a living as waiters at some time, but it was doubtful they'd been droids before. Would I help them? Of course.

It was fun. We met in a cluttered section of Wardrobe and cleared some space in front of a large mirror – Nathan, George, Lucas, Zsole, Juan and me. For *The Force Awakens* shoot my code name on set was

"Skinny Guy". Of course, for my own comfort, I had got back into shape for each production. The gaps between films were temptingly filled with bouts of overindulgence. But here were five actors who really were slim, and naturally fitter than me, being considerably younger and very enthusiastic. At least we had that in common. I gave some chat about isolation techniques; being aware of what bits of your body were doing at any point – or not doing. Just as important, was how to navigate onto their marks, with no peripheral vision to guide them. Triangulation – find a prop, a person, a thing and use it as a location device, although other people would have to be hitting their marks at the same time. Then we played at dressing up.

They became elegant black knights. The edges of their dapper suits of armour were picked out in gold. Their illuminated wrists gave an extravagantly inventive effect to the cuffs – stunning. My planning notes had me thinking of them, not as mere waiters, but as head waiters, with their noses in the air. Now seeing their outfits for the first time, I was too late. Costume designer, Michael Kaplan, had already achieved the effect with a snooty upturn of their shiny black masks, a really neat personification of an aloof attitude. So all good – till we tried playing with some props.

The trays were strangely heavy – nothing cheap about this production – the glassware, heavier. And as for the decanters... So I had a word with Props and we found plastic versions of most things. Carrying weighty, fragile loads in a droid outfit is asking for trouble. Carrying a tray on your fingertips is bad enough, but perilous when those tips are not your own. Eventually, we stuck Velcro patches on the gloves and underneath the tray. That took care of the accident statistics. Most of the time.

I had been flattered to be their tutor. But Pierre went even further in asking, would I be the on-set Droid AD? A new experience for me. Of course, I said yes.

The once cindered grittiness of the Crait mines had been swept away. Now Pinewood's 007 Stage was filled with such elegant magnificence. Not only the cavernous opulence of the scenery, but also the huge gaming tables, the resplendent pageant of strange and wondrous creatures, wearing the most imaginative evening attire Michael had ever created. In each direction, my gaze was captured by some outrageously creative stroke. Surely a Best Costume Oscar here – certainly an inspiration to the high street fashion industry. I was thrilled to be there. Especially since I wasn't actually in the scene. I wasn't in costume. This time I was Crew – equally grateful that the real Crew seemed happy to accept me as a novice member of their own.

Each droid waiter had two dressers. I was their AD. Amongst other responsibilities, making sure they portrayed the right degree of arrogance, helping to place them in shot, watching out for their comfort and safety. What a wonderful chance to pay back the care and attention I had received over the years. From Maxi and Brian and Don and Justin and, more recently, David and Jonathan and Sophie and Joe. So many patient kindnesses. Now it was my turn to care.

It was exhausting. Looking after five hot and disorientated individuals was a physical and emotional workout. The 007 Stage is the biggest in Europe. With the camera at one end and the gang of five spread all over the vast set, it was a four-hundred-yard dash there and back, on each take. At least I was wearing jeans. The hard-working quintet was steaming up inside their elegant plastic outfits. Forget peripheral vision – they couldn't see in front either. And, of course, I quickly forgot who was inside. Which was Nathan? Where was Lucas? The droids were identical. But since I was minding all of them, it made no difference to me or, I hope, to them. But my main moment of fear came from something else.

Sound can be heavy on the budget if it's added after the event, in post. Stuart Wilson was determined to record as much clean track as possible during each take. All the human characters had body mikes, and there was always Orin Beaton, gently hefting the long microphone boom above us. I had a go with it once, raising my arms above my head and pointing the mike, some twenty feet away. It was quite a workout, and I only did it for a moment. He was doing it on every take without ever getting the mike in frame.

Poor Stuart would go crazy listening to Threepio's squeaks and clanks, as plastic clashed and rubbed with plastic. If he thought it was bad on the outside, Stuart should have experienced what I was hearing. Every noise carried straight to my ear through the fabric of the suit. I lived in perpetual cacophony, a situation exacerbated if I was wearing my tiny earpiece. Essential for hearing the other actors, I was tuned-in to anyone whose mike channel was open – whether they were acting the scene or merely keeping up their own energy levels by loudly singing or gossiping at full tilt. Then there were the times that my hearing aid – inserted in the side of my head – would explode with brain-piercing white noise. The effect was regularly fiendish. Stuart said it might be a transmitter issue, said he was sorry, would have denied it was pay-back for my squeaking and ruining his recordings. We had got on joyously together, after I'd told him to stuff his suggestion that I mime a complicated exchange with Oscar, after we'd just rewritten it. I snapped that I had enough on my plate with the suit and so – no. Remembering it now, I think he was right. I won't tell him though.

But I did have to point out that if we turned off the tiny, tiny fans inside the masks of our waiter-droid team, they would steam up and die. A slight exaggeration but he got the point. In their search for perfect sound, his team laid carpet pieces wherever the floor wasn't in shot. It cut down on the foot noise but health and safety became an issue. Nathan, or possibly George, was doing his thing when I saw his foot catch the edge of one of Stuart's rugs. As the elegant droid shimmied forward, his foot went further underneath. He wasn't aware inside his plastic suit. But I could see that he would shortly be enrolled in flooring material, resulting in a noisy crash to the ground thereby spoiling Stuart's recording and risking severe damage to man and droid. Moments before I was about to do a lifeguard thing and leap to the rescue in shot, they cut the take. He was saved. I could finally unwrap him.

But that wasn't the only tense situation for me.

For the opening shot, the camera hung below a bridge that stretched laterally across the elaborate gaming tables. It was supported on two wheeled columns, pushed by camera Grips. The crane raced forward. Crowd artists casually moved out of the way, as it shot past them. They had learned in rehearsal that moving out of the way saved them being smacked in the face by the speeding equipment. The elaborately choreographed move started as an elegant guest took a drink, before another guest swiped a glass flute of champagne off Zsole's tray – right in front of the already hurrying lens. I steadied the tray as he held it in position then, at the last moment, left it in the Velcro-attached hands of my droid friend.

INT. CANTO BIGHT – CASINO

ACTION!

SMACK!

CUT!

They cleaned up the broken glass and wiped up the liquid, as the camera bridge returned to its start mark. Next take we used plastic. But my heart was pounding as we set off again, and again, and again.

The movie industry can be an unfeeling mistress – so much shot, so much cut away. How sad that a scene I so hoped to admire in the finished film, was edited so savagely. There was some speech about arms dealers but then only a few of the iconic dresses flashed by. Several extraordinary headpieces flourished briefly. The tiny croupier's part was now even smaller. The eerily compelling two-headed girl was gone. And our diligent brigade of waiter droids – reduced to a mere hint of snoot.

A *Star Wars* film without Threepio! It was against the lore.

It seemed there was no place for even a hint of gold in this side story, featuring a beloved smuggler. I had taken part in every episode in the Saga but with *Solo: A Star Wars Story*, suddenly my trivial claim to fame was lost. Then, a new idea. I'd done it before. CZ-3, Lieutenant Fay-tonni – I could be an extra, crowd cameo, bit part player. The producers were thrilled at the idea.

And here I was, being chauffeured through the outskirts of London to the more rural setting of the flourishing Pinewood Studios. And there was my trailer. It had a name on the door, not mine. I was used to the security title I had been gifted on the previous films, along with all the other cast. They had fake names like "Keith" or "Tall Guy". As we now know, I was "Skinny Guy". But this was a spin-off story and so a different name on the door – "Human Slave".

I had been called in for costume and makeup tests – all this for a slave, human or otherwise. But first I went on set to meet the two directors. Two sounded quite a novel idea but it must be working because they had almost finished principal photography – the actual filming part of a film. Phil Lord and Christopher Miller were so excited that I was joining their shoot. I was thrilled, too. Hugely welcoming, they introduced me to everyone around. Alden Ehrenreich was playing the lead character and equally friendly with his charming smile. And here was Chewie, Tall Guy, Joonas Suotamo, clad in his usual yak-fur suit. So good to see him again after the fun we'd shared on the previous shoots. And then I became tongue-tied. I had never been star struck before. No offence to the various stars I had encountered over the years – but this was special. Thandie Newton shook my hand warmly. I could only mumble a besotted, garbled hello before I tore myself away and an AD led me back to my trailer.

My costume was hanging in the little wardrobe. It seemed extremely complicated. Undershirt, overshirt, coat, bandages, scarf, hat, ugly boots – all mangled and filthy. Newly filthy. These were no ordinary threads, these were designer rags. Costume had spent ages drawing and cobbling together my ensemble. We laughed as they gleefully tore extra tatters in it all. Finally, I looked shipwrecked enough to go to Makeup.

I had been growing a beard. Well, stubble at least. I didn't like it. It was a little itchy, and grey. However, it looked the part, but not enough. My face was gradually decorated with bruises and lines and scars. Then, the crowning glory, a disgusting straggle of a wig. It had been carefully crafted to look this way and it fitted me perfectly. As I stared at him in the full-length mirror I could see Human Slave was complete. Everyone around me in the trailer laughed and applauded my new look.

Back on set once more, it was show-and-tell time. Chris and Phil loved it. Costume, Makeup and I had passed the test. I would come back next week to add Human Slave to the scene. However, it would be two months before that actually happened.

Chris and Phil had left the production the next day – over "artistic differences". None of my business. I had enjoyed our brief knowing but wondered what was next, as I scrambled my diary, clearing space for something I still assumed would happen. Eventually it did. Back again, I was surprised and amused. Human Slave was no more. My trailer was labelled "Tak". I stood in front of the new, replacement director in my tatters, scars and newly regrown grey stubble. Ron Howard was a pleasure to meet, one of Hollywood's stalwarts, ever since starring in TV's *Happy Days*. He had arrived to pick up the shoot from where it had been interrupted. He approved of my "look" but wanted more grime. I would finally appear on set – in just a few more weeks. My diary was now officially a mess. But it was all fun. It was going to happen.

Weeks indeed passed when, for the third time, I had been transformed into the hapless Tak. Shrouded in my ghastly rags, I was driven from my trailer to set – another brilliant creation from the Art and Construction departments.

Murky yellow tunnels were thronged with people attired in clothes even more ghastly than mine. Various burrowing machines added to the threatening drama as I raced forward with my team. One was a tall, thin Wookiee but my friend Joonas was at the front, pushing a heavy cargo as I ran by. I passed into blinding white fog. I did manage not to fall down the steps, rendered invisible by the effect. After several takes it was over.

But now we were coming out of the tunnels into another extraordinary landscape. Cliffs of yellow stone towered over slimy, bubbling rock pools. Sulphurous gases belched across the surface, the ground a sandy, yellow mess. It was wonderful. And here on the back lot we were in daylight – a welcome relief from the steam-filled atmosphere below. And now I developed a new game.

Picking out various faces from my recent and not-so-recent past, I first approached our fanatical sound recordist, Stuart. Standing right in front of him, I said hello, in a voice he might not recognise. He looked at this ragged creature before him and politely returned the greeting. I stayed staring at him. He began to look uncomfortable. Then his eyes widened. He laughed in amazement.

"It's YOU!"

It was such a joyful trick that I did it around the set, surprising everyone with my uncharacteristic appearance. Then it was time to work.

The script had been waiting in my trailer. Even with Ron Howard's grip on the direction, I wasn't sure about the scene. It was confusing. It was meant to be confusion. But Ron was very patient in explaining everything – almost. Who was Sagwa? What was he to Tak, or Tak to him? Did they have a history together? Perhaps a sequel would explain.

EXT. KESSEL – MINES – DAY

ACTION!

"Sagwa! This way. Come on!"

Yelling, I bounced through and off the crowd of human slaves and alien creatures, with their strange, improvised weapons. The steam hissed and bubbled. Special Effects fired blaster hits to spark off the rock walls – careful to miss any passing actor.

CUT!

Of course we did it several times. Being a slave was exhausting. Some of the Crowd were growing rather tired and the ADs had to work equally hard to maintain the desired level of mayhem. Everyone escaped in the end but I would return for yet another day to ride upwards, with my fellow escapees, in a large freight elevator. That scene never made it. But I did. I had finally arrived at a legendary place of dread – for Threepio, at least. I had been sent to the Spice Mines of Kessel.

## 60 joy

Well, it was a free dinner. At my favourite restaurant, in London.

So I changed my tickets and got back to the UK, just in time to change my clothes. The Ivy has long been a sort of second home to me. This night, it was something of a family reunion. There was an empty seat next to mine but there was J.J. and Kathy, Oscar, Daisy and John and Kelly Marie. I was pleased to see them again. But what fun to meet Naomi Ackie and Keri Russell and all sorts of other jolly colleagues around the table. As always, lovely food and wine but I was trying to be careful, fat-shaming myself on a daily basis. Rumours were that we would be making Episode IX. Soon. Very.

I was delighted at the prospect of working with J.J. again. I just didn't know what to expect after *The Last Jedi*. I knew nothing of the plot. Where could the story be going? How could anyone wrap up all the strands and tatters and make something complete and satisfying? Would Threepio's last hurrah be a faint cry of disappointment? He and I were inured to being marginalised. But it really was nice to be asked back. And to be invited to dinner with the stars.

I muttered to the elegant Richard E. Grant that I had yet to see a script. He too. Worse. At least I had a name. He didn't even know what he'd been cast as. Probably, he would be a baddie. But he didn't have a name. So we had a drink. It was a great way to start what, for me at least, must be drawing to a conclusion. Those in the know at dinner, said warm words about Threepio's role in this film. That merely increased my frustration at not seeing even an outline draft.

The empty seat next to mine at least had a name card – Chris Terrio. He wasn't feeling well. He wasn't coming. He was the writer. Was he avoiding me? I would have enjoyed discussing his excellent script for *Argo*, one of my favourite films. So inventive, funny and exciting – with more than a hint of *Star Wars* in the plot. I would have loved the opportunity to praise him. And ask him about his most recent work, *Star Wars*: Episode IX. It seemed I would have to wait.

Days passed. Still no script. I learned that J.J. wanted me to have the latest version from Chris, who was feeling better but who was chained to his laptop, tapping away. I would quickly learn what "latest version" meant. There would be many latest versions lying in my trailer each morning. Fresh new words for a new day. Each one a thoughtful, inventive improvement. Over the ensuing months, various updates would follow on coloured paper – Blue Version, Green Version, Pink Version, Beige Version and my favourite, pages with a yellow tint, "Golden Rod Version".

I had emailed J.J. some months before it all started.

**Sent:** Wed, Jan 23, 2018, at 9:11 AM
**From:** Anthony Daniels
**To:** J.J. Abrams
**Subject:**

I'm getting antsy, since I have heard nothing about youknowwhat.
Who do I talk to about my upcoming, finale role in a grand finale
epic that will restore balance to the Force; asking questions like...
How can I see my script pages (both of them) to get a feel of where/
what in, 3PO is involved and get over any shock/surprise at external
design modifications, especially paint finish! (Personally, I liked my
rivet-sticking-plaster design from way back. Oh well...

Has the Director remembered that...

3PO works best in Conflict situations as a Useful Part of a Team
where he is Personally (though a machine, a sentient one) in Danger;
where he is the Voice of Reason, reflecting the audience's concerns,
and not just the sound of worry from a cupboard in a remote office;

that he shows up well, to the benefit of the humorous element of any
epic, in well-crafted, wryly comic, characterful, (for ref, see Eps IV, V,
VI, VII) scripted lines in interpersonal relations (benign or otherwise)
with humans or machines with attitude; that in TLJ he showed signs of
determination to stand up for the Cause of Proper Behavior against a
human behaving badly (in his opinion); that his prognostications are
always ignored, (he would be floored if anyone finally listened to him);
that he regrets the passing of his favourite human – Master Luke;

that he longs for a peaceful life where he can gently translate and
make tea;

that the audience enjoys references, in lines, attitude or otherwise,
to his previous experiences in the Saga;

that he has accompanied that audience for 40 familiar years, over
3 generations, and should not leave either party feeling let down at
the end of the Epic.

There must be more but I haven't got there yet. Anyway, that's
enough homework for you today. And for me.

A
XX

Nothing. For weeks.

**Sent:** Sat, 21 Apr 2018 18:16:54 +0000
**From:** J.J. Abrams
**To:** Anthony Daniels
**Subject:**

You're either going to love or hate how much you have to do in this new movie.

J.J.
XoXo

So who knew what was coming?

**Sent:** Sat, Apr 21, 2018, at 11:28 AM
**From:** Anthony Daniels
**To:** J.J. Abrams
**Subject:**

I'll settle for hate. It'll be quicker.

A
XX

And nothing happened.

I would send out feelers but always got the response that J.J. wanted me to have the latest version. I tried to relax about it all. I trusted J.J.'s instincts. It was still rather frustrating.

Finally. A script. The only place allowed to read this precious text was in the security-ringed studios at Pinewood. Fortunately, Sean O'Connor was available to take me there in comfort. Sean – always my favourite driver over the last two movies. Mark had pinched him from me on several occasions but he wasn't around today.

I sat on the terrace of the new Carrie Fisher Building on the East Lot. It seemed sweetly appropriate that I was reading the script there. A gentle softness to the day mixed with the sun, dappling through the newly planted greenery. I paused for a moment of bitter-sweet reflection, then realised that I had no idea how to work the electronic reader they'd given me. The spell was slightly spoilt as I went in search of someone more tech savvy, to explain.

Back in my spot, I began to read. And read. And suddenly three-and-a-half hours of my life had gone by. Never to return. Just like that. But it had been time well spent. And there was a distinct possibility that either J.J. had indeed read my words or that he already knew exactly what to do. I suspect both.

I loved the script. Chris had clearly steeped himself in the lore of the Saga – certainly, as far as my metallic friend was concerned. Threepio had been away a long time. Now he was back.

For some time, I'd made the mistake of watching YouTube rants about the previous two films – *The Force Awakens* and *The Last Jedi*. I could acknowledge some of the bloggers' points. But so much vicious negativity. I knew that the fans had lovingly attached themselves to the Saga. I was genuinely sad that they felt their loyalty had been slighted.

This was the third time I was there to be part of a final Episode. A curious situation. Each one had enjoyed its own dynamic – some more happily remembered than others. The froideur of the Prequels was irrevocably archived in my mind. Here was a new start. To a final end.

Arriving at Pinewood for the first day's shoot, I wondered what doom-laden atmosphere awaited me.

I found a warm bath of enthusiastic affection. So many old faces, colleagues from the past, all working on a terrific script that seemed heading for a very satisfying conclusion. I stopped watching YouTube.

I'd made several visits to the Costume FX Department at Pinewood to try out various new adjustments to the suit. While David Merryweather was still being his wonderful, enthusiastic creative self, Pierre Bohanna, head of the department, had asked Sophie Allen and Joe Fysh, from *The Last Jedi*, to come back in as my on-set team.

It was terrific to be working with such familiar and attentive companions again. They carefully dressed me up and I stuttered around the workshop, remembering that first try-out at Elstree around forty years before. The whole team seemed thrilled to watch Threepio trotting past their work stations. Someone's pet dog was very intrigued. I suspect he thought I was a lamp-post – but the moment passed without incident.

And now I was on set. And like most films, we were shooting in an order that fitted practicality rather than linearality. It took a while to get the sequences in their proper order in my head, essential to avoid confusion. But at least being Threepio was familiar to me – well it would be, wouldn't it? But here was a challenge of a different kind. It was our first scene.

The set looked so real and atmospheric. However, the terrain was hopelessly difficult to navigate, with its unstable and varied surface. Being enclosed, the temperature rapidly reached sauna levels. Joe was instantly there to mop my face. There was a new addition to the costume, a capillary cooling vest – a thin undershirt, woven with small plastic tubes. This could be attached to a bag filled with ice and water and a circulating pump. The effect was almost instantaneous and rather alarmingly efficient. With the desert location in mind, it was going to be a welcome gift.

We struggled through the terrain, all the actors quite fluent and in character as they shared the drama. I had been slightly unsettled at the last-minute arrival of any script. Lines don't get remembered as they used to, in earlier times. The simplest phrases stumped me. Thousands of repetitions still didn't get it into my head and out of my mouth inside the costume. So I gargled place-holder sounds, much to Oscar's amused, arched eyebrow. The next day, I could say it all fluently without a pause. The three words that had eluded me – "a common emblem".

It seemed I was having a memory wipe on a daily basis – a devastating thought for man and droid. Later, I could see the team brace themselves for a complicated conversation with Threepio. Surely they'd be there all day in that sweltering, claustrophobic set. They were amazed. Not a fluff. Not a hesitation. Word perfect. I was amazed, too. So, I suspect, was J.J.

And I was also amazed by the astounding creativity that was all around me. I'd now read about the huge, malevolent creature. I'd assumed it would be CG – computer graphics, created at ILM in San Francisco. I thought that we'd all be looking into empty space, maybe with a cardboard cutout for reference – perhaps a mop head. In reality, it was real. A giant, living thing that towered and menaced right in front of me.

Even more astounding, I finally had hands that corresponded to my own. Pierre's team had worked hard to give me what I had lacked before. Threepio could pick up objects with ease. He could gesture freely. No more flapping and flailing at props, smacking them with double-sided tape to get a grip. If I could see it, I could grasp it. This proved vital from the start. The gruesome tunnels soon revealed their secret and I was there to handle it.

Suddenly, over the weekend, the entire unit had upped and dumped itself deep in the English countryside. Though it might only appear in documentaries, the sheer scale of this troop movement was literally as awesome as anything we were filming. And difficult. We were at the top of a wondrous escarpment, a huge hill shoved upwards by giant forces millions of years earlier. More prosaically, it meant the food and toilets and home comforts were far off, on flatter terrain. My trailer had been transported along with the others. Its home comforts of bedroom, shower, sitting room and kitchen were fifteen minutes away in Sean's car. Like a child asking permission to leave the room, we all had to ask for a vehicle to take us to the less distant honey wagons – the toilets. A great leveller.

It was strangely grounding, too, to be performing a dramatic moment and seeing white van man casually driving down the main road below. Traffic whizzed by, seemingly unaware of the magic that was being created far above. For the most part we kept our privacy, thanks to the team of vigilant security guards. They did discover one infiltrator lurking in the bushes with a camera – "bird watching" apparently. She wouldn't have got much. It was mostly the gang admiring the view with interest, and me trying to keep upright. Even the orbaks weren't looking themselves yet as they thundered up and down – their silky, grey coats flying in the wind. But they and everything else was stunning and would be more so in the finished film, with ILM painting over the distant pastures. It was all so magical. Before it turned rather horrid.

The clear sky was suddenly filled with tiny flying things. A plague had descended, not biblical, just unpleasant. The tiny insects swarmed around us, cast and crew, they made no distinction. Now everyone was slapping themselves or waving. It was mildly funny but very irritating. The bugs were relentless. Joe and Sophie were draped in scarves as they put Threepio's head around mine. I was madly blowing into the face as it came together, ensuring there'd be no bugs joining me inside.

Back in the studio, my star support team had suddenly disappeared. Daisy, John and Oscar had already raced away, as I tried to rush after them down the ramp of our transport. Slamming my arm into the low-slung architrave avoided making a mess of Threepio and me on the polished floor. I wished it could have been designed with a more droid-friendly slope. We did six takes as, each time, I grew more frightened and self-protective. I could never be a Stunt person – a fact enforced by chatting with Andy Wareham, who was.

We were on our marks in front of the lens, shortly after my hurtling descent experience. Threepio had recovered his poise but Andy's chest was dressed with squibs and a wire, attached to a hydraulic ram. In mid-sentence, he vanished from sight so fast, my surprise was genuine – I didn't have to act at all. Of course, I had to replace the live recording of my vocal reaction. The original was heartfelt but a bit… how rude.

It was thrilling to meet the *Falcon* again. Always in some different environment – outdoors in Blackwood or in a sound stage some fifteen minutes away at the ever-expanding Pinewood Studios. But now the star attraction was The Base, where our small band of fighters could gather their resources. It was so enormous that we indeed had an interior and exterior in different locations. Utterly believable in its natural grandeur, the interior was inside Stage Five. A bleakly silver box on the outside, an astonishment of scenic craft on the in. It was a daily treat to be working in such stunning surroundings. All achieved with scaffolding, timber, polystyrene, paint and plaster – and huge amounts of creativity from the Production Designers, Rick Carter and Kevin Jenkins. They had gone to extraordinary lengths to create a brilliantly believable reality. However, they obviously hadn't had Threepio in mind.

Somehow, I had hoped for the solid floor from *The Force Awakens* set – the inside of a space station, flat, and not too highly polished. It was not to be. Mulch speaks to the gardener in me. But underfoot, when it is under Threepio's foot, it is an accident in waiting. Any bump or rut can have him toppling within a nanosecond. Daisy and John would regularly leap forward to catch me, as I hit a tussock or a rock. In days to come, Daisy was right there to disentangle me from the extravagant clutches of the local transport – the treadible. John, marooned with me on a speeder twenty feet up and far from any external assistance, reattaching my fingers, sipping me water, relocating my busted shoulder, being my carer.

Most of the sets were a minefield of trip hazards for poor Threepio. Acres of highly polished black flooring were an unexpected death trap, with their very slightly raised panels, almost invisible. But if it's there, Threepio's toe will find it. And all the time, J.J.'s encouraging direction.

"Very good. Let's do it again."

And, by the magic of air travel and this magnificent production,

I was suddenly back in a desert. Not Tunisia, not Arizona – we had arrived in the Kingdom of Jordan. How nostalgic to see again the corals where I had scuba-dived so long ago – this time, looking through the glass walls of a tourist boat in the Gulf of Aqaba, rather than finning myself through the warm and clear waters. But that wasn't the set. Our set was sand. Our world was the desert planet of Pasaana.

Once again, I was staggered by the gigantic infrastructure that had been plonked down in this no-man's land. Towering cranes and giant lighting rigs, huge tents that were Catering or Crowd wardrobe, kitchens, trailers housing Production and Cast and Makeup. The honey wagon was, as always, too remote for casual relief. Coffee intake had to be restricted. Peeing had to be planned. And the miles of road track had to be carved and constantly steamrollered into submission. But how insistently the winds tried to heal these scars back into the rippling wastes. This desert couldn't wait for us to leave.

Our daily trek from the city eventually opened up to huge vistas on each side, the unearthly miasma of white dust bridging the red sand below to the craggy darkness of rocky outcrops above. Each escarpment ranged grey and greyer in the distant reaches, fading into infinity. This land, where civilisation flourished a thousand years before the West was ever thought of, was now our playground. Everything, a wondrous surprise.

But driving out to location on that first day, I got a strange feeling of déjà vu. This new terrain was unlike Tatooine, with its flowing dunes. The stretching vistas, more than ever before, in all the previous episodes of *Star Wars*, evoked the spirit of Ralph McQuarrie's original concept painting; that work of art which had so shackled me to this story.

The flat, sandy wastes. The high, jutting mountain ranges. There were no planets visible in the cloudless morning sky, but leaving the location that evening, a full moon bathed the landscape in its cruel, bleak light.

And strange, and sad to tell, there by the roadside in our headlights, a dead dog, just as on my first journey with Mark into the wastes of Tozeur, so many years before. It seemed like an omen for *The Rise of Skywalker*. A good one. Not so much for the dog, of course.

This was dawn on day two, on a new planet. I had forgotten just how persistent fine desert sand could be. It was hard to recognise anyone in their bandanas and shades. The cast had to remove anything protective for each shot. For once my suit was useful in shielding me from the sun and the cutting, flying sand. And Michael Byrch, my stunt double, protected me in other ways.

It was Michael, in a rubber copy of Threepio, batting along at seventy-five miles an hour – with no restraints, lest the vehicle tumble and he be trapped while attached. Me? Later, I stood tethered onto the most inventive fairground ride that hurled us around on the spot. In spite of the sun's heat, I was nicely cooled by the array of wind machines that blasted us as we flew.

I had been roped in by Eunice Huthart, the Stunt Coordinator. I liked her brutal, loving, no-nonsense approach to her job. A voice like a dockyard crane on Liverpool's quayside, she had the sweetest temperament but meant business. I so enjoyed working with her. She was determined to keep everyone safe. How different from my experience in *Attack of the Clones*. I was certainly glad of my daily workouts in the gym. My left biceps worked overtime to keep control of the rest of me. I couldn't actually fall off the crazy ride but it was my left arm that kept me upright.

With one exception.

Tatooine Australia

Tatooine Tunisia

Face time with Padmé

Dan Madsen

Rusty

Faytonni

Old master – George

New master – Jimmy

Green

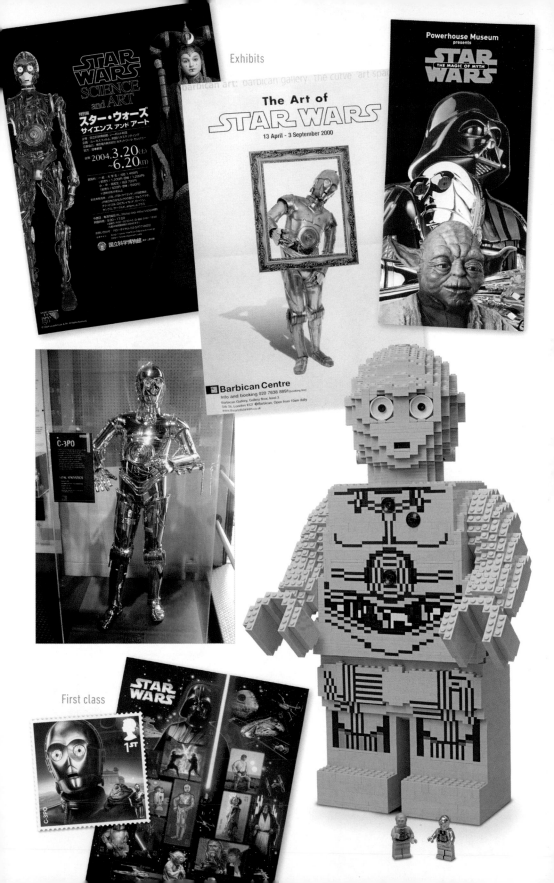

Exhibits

barbican art: barbican gallery, the curve 'art space

The Art of
**STAR WARS**
13 April - 3 September 2000

**Barbican Centre**
Info and booking 020 7638 8891 (booking line)
Barbican Gallery, Gallery floor, level 3
Silk St, London EC2 ● Barbican. Open from 10am daily
www.thcbarbicanart.co.uk

**STAR WARS**
SCIENCE and ART
スター・ウォーズ
サイエンス アンド アート
2004.3.20(土)
~6.20(日)
国立科学博物館

Powerhouse Museum
presents
**STAR WARS**
THE MAGIC OF MYTH

C-3PO

First class

**STAR WARS**

1ST

C-3PO

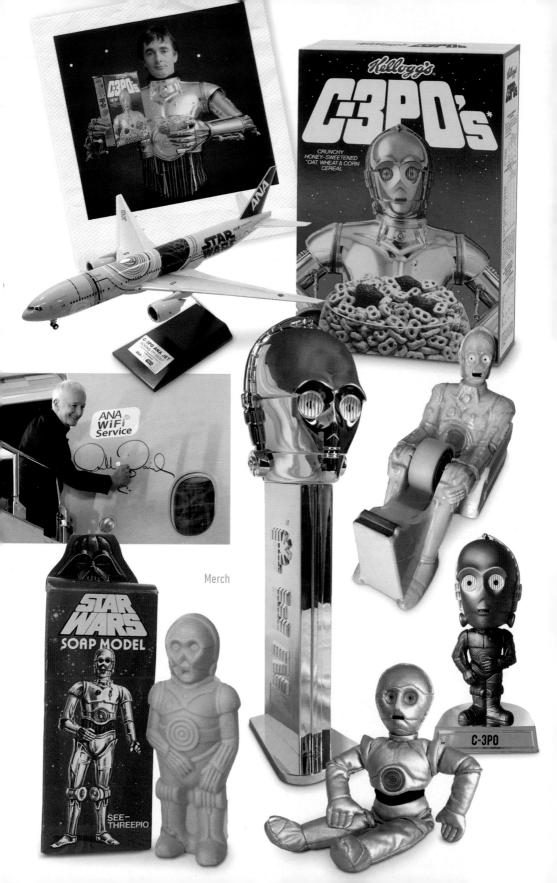

Kellogg's C-3PO's*

CRUNCHY HONEY-SWEETENED *OAT, WHEAT & CORN CEREAL

STAR WARS

ANA WiFi Service

STAR WARS SOAP MODEL

SEE-THREEPIO

Merch

C-3PO

J.J. and friends

Gareth

Rian

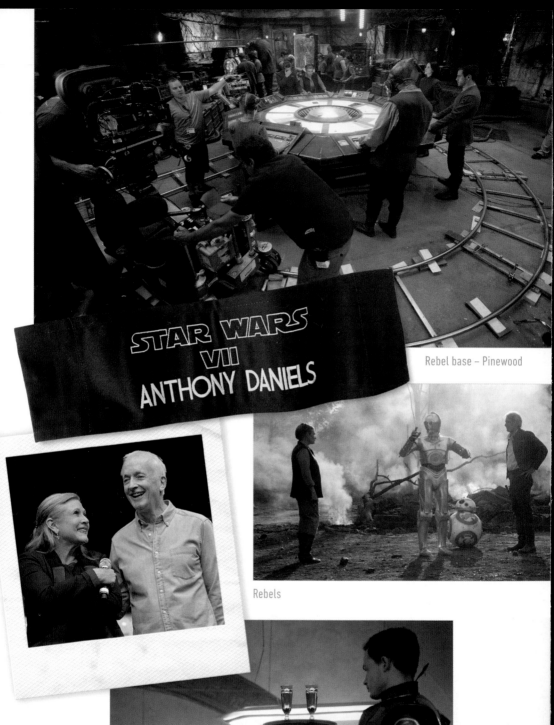

STAR WARS
VII
ANTHONY DANIELS

Rebel base – Pinewood

Rebels

Droid waiter
Zsole

The LSO

The Maestro

The Bowl

Tak and friends

Old friends

New friends

J.J. K.K. A.D.

Simon and Joe

and Sophie

and BB-8

On a different rig, John and I had taken off, with Oscar driving at the front.

ACTION!

Fly, fly, fly.

CUT!

We braked so fast, in a wooosh of sand that I careened forward in a direction we hadn't prepared for. My muscles ached loudly for the few seconds before our ride actually stopped and we ricocheted upright. Not so much whiplash as total bodylash. It wasn't Oscar's fault but the man on the clutch beneath him, who actually was doing the driving. I politely asked if we could park the thing a little less violently next time. And so he did.

It was all good fun. But careening around on a speeder for three days left me with sea legs. Talk about the planet being unstable, I was swaying everywhere. Of course, after sundown, maybe it was the arak. But it really did take a while to regain my balance. How reassuring, the next day, to be back on terra firma, even if it was a bit rocky.

But now the wind obliterated the distant vistas. Standing there, doing lines off-camera for Daisy's close-up, I saw her eyes narrow against the sandy sunlight. She suggested J.J. and I remove our sun glasses, in sympathy. Being team players, we did. Moments later, we put them back on again. Daisy was on her own.

The script was as ever-changing as the terrain. Each new rewrite on a different paper of rainbow hue. I soon stopped mourning over cut lines, favourite moments, that I had loved from the first moment of seeing them on the page. One lost exchange with Poe haunts me still. The verbal attrition grew on a daily basis. Even hourly. Beloved scenes, gone. Much enjoyed and memorised lines, erased. All in the spirit of making a film of a reasonable length and on an affordable budget, with a wonderful outcome. I did fret that some of the script's warmer moments were being too ruthlessly decimated but they were always substituted by something even better. I came to appreciate each thoughtful rewrite and addition that Chris and J.J. had wrestled over. I delighted in the playful rhythm of exchanges between the characters as we shot take after take.

The vastness of our play area was well secured with police at the roadside and soldiers, as part of the production. Careful navigation in these wastes was essential. Obscure code names pointed into the distance – signposts in the sand. Candelabra. XY. Coloured Sands. New Orleans. Bakersfield. Don't Stop Gulch. Ship Rock – this was a thrilling treasure hunt on a grand scale.

In New Orleans I had ample time to consider my lot in life. As soon as I was dressed for the next shot, a sandstorm blew up at us – far more real than anything we'd attempted at Elstree, some forty years before. This had the crew scuttling for cover. We all thought it would blow through in moments. I stood alone on the rocky ledge as Joe and Sophie watched me from their tented shelter, clearly debating whether to brave it and come to undress me. Threepio gave them the thumbs up. I waved that it was all okay. I'm sure they were relieved.

I felt curiously safe inside Threepio. The wind pierced through in several places but the sand stayed mostly on the outside. I did feel a sort of Shackleton moment as the blasting air shrieked past. I stood and waited with my back to the onslaught. At least at Elstree they had been able to shut down the fans. Turn off the wind. Here it was an hour before the gale slowed and died. The crew crawled out of whatever protection they had found and we got the shot, as if nothing had happened. I'm not sure one hour had ever felt so long.

And every day, Mohammed's four-wheel drive took me from my glossy hotel and the civilised streets of ancient Aqaba out into the desert wastes. His hacking cough was accompanied by the constant four-tone ring of his mobile phone. He was a good driver. He didn't answer it – once he'd noticed my frown. So it kept ringing and he kept coughing.

But both noises would be muted as the muezzin's call to morning prayers filled the car with incomprehensible wailings; ancient religion delivered by an app.

Back in Aqaba, the producers surprised us all with a truly stunning party. The vast waterfront terrace of the Al Manara Hotel was turned into a lavish setting to celebrate the halfway mark in the schedule. A thank you to everyone involved. Food, and drinks, and dancers, and music and dramatic lighting and giant visuals which set off the hotel's walls and the sandstone buildings across the inlet. Finally, a spectacular firework display coloured the skies above us – illuminating Egypt and Israel across the water. It was a seriously generous gift to us all. But a few nights later, some of us were treated even more royally.

How extraordinary to be invited to dinner with King Abdullah II and Queen Rania. With two of their family, they hosted fourteen of us round the table at the palace. I'd worried at not having packed fancy clothes for such an unexpected experience. Her Royal Highness looked stunningly serene in a beautiful dress. His Majesty wore jeans and sweater. Just like me. They were the most natural, charming down-to-earth hosts. We always ate well on the set but here the elaborate dinner was beyond exceptional, beyond exquisite. Memorable. Conversation was easy; ranging from the recent devastating floods through studies in ancient Japanese literature and the thriving film industry in Jordan. King Abdullah had helicoptered onto the set the day before and was truly, endearingly happy to see a *Star Wars* movie being filmed in his own back yard. And early the next day, we were back in the yard.

Till now we had been a small band of heroes. How thrilling to see the mass of strange species. Many were brought to life by soldiers, seconded away from their military role, to dress up and prance. It was all rather spectacular and vibrant. Until I got lost.

Poe and friends could always walk faster than Threepio. I could probably out-distance them on the flat in running gear but here,

I had no chance. They raced through the colourful crowd of droopy-jowled Aki-Aki, as I did my best to keep up. But curse my metal body, I wasn't fast enough. I'd suddenly lost them. I was adrift in a sea of wafting creatures. I turned around trying to catch sight of my friends. Where was Rey? Where was Finn? Surely Chewie would be noticeable. And yes. There he was – Joonas towering like a hairy beacon. I set off in my new direction and rejoined the gang. I barged into a few performers on my unrehearsed route. I mumbled sorry but I don't think they could have heard me, as they swayed and sashayed to an ancestral beat.

From a distance, it looked too challenging. It was a wise choice to leave the climb to Michael. But as the set-up took so long, I had time to rethink. It felt wrong to not be inside the costume. I was happy enough to let Michael do the dangerous stuff but this was different. I took the long way round, to avoid footprints in the between the camera and Ship Rock. Now close up to the climb, it didn't look so steep. I apologised to Michael for swiping his job away. He didn't mind. He could relax, as Sophie dressed me in the bikini version, which allowed Threepio to romp up the rock surface. Well, sort of romp. I never actually made it to the flag pole.

What a glorious time in Jordan, shooting against extraordinary, unique vistas. What wonder to spend time off, driving along the rift valley and hiking through Petra. But alas, it was time to go home. Our charter waited patiently on the tarmac at King Hussein International Airport. We were VIPs. We didn't have to stand in line with two hundred crew members. We were politely directed across the compound to the VIP entrance. Behind plate glass, a guard gestured. We followed his pointings to a glass wall. We pushed. We tried to slide it. We banged. Nothing. Our friend was still gesturing. This was not VIP at all. We stood there in the sun, in plain sight of the crew who were filtering smoothly through the non-VIP check-in lines. We acted nonchalant.

Then a glass sliding on its own. A space beyond was revealed by two surprised guards. Lots of fro-ing and to-ing and eventually we – Daisy, John, J.J., Oscar and team – were shuffled through to a bleak box room. A man was reluctantly making coffee and offering water. Reluctantly too, we had given up our passports. We were suddenly stateless, without papers.

Time passed.

In an impatient attack of cabin fever, Victoria Mahoney, our glamorous second unit director, dared to turn back into the Kafkaesque corridor. Brave soul. We sipped water and coffee and waited. Would we ever see her again? I began to wish I had asked for His Majesty's phone number, in case of emergencies. It felt like one was unfolding around us.

The door opened. Victoria was back, laden with smiles and duty free. She had found the path. Left out of the door, second left, she had discovered something that actually looked like an airport terminal. We excitedly followed her breadcrumbs, making our bid for freedom from the cell that was the VIP lounge. The crew watched us finally arriving in their lounge. They didn't snigger. Well, I don't think they sniggered. They may have smiled.

It was a shock to arrive back in London. Christmas had been all but invisible in Jordan. England was festooned and baubled in every direction. But we had work to do before the holiday. The schedule became extraordinary. A late morning start had us on B Stage, in a tiny, cluttered interior set. It was packed with stuff. But one area was particularly interesting. It seemed to be a sort of shrine. No doubt all would be explained in due course. The claustrophobic set was utterly different from what awaited us for the night shoots. That was at the other end of the studio. Outside. What an astounding contrast!

They had built a totally convincing environment on the wasteland that was the back lot. This was Kijimi. A dangerous place, but Gosh! It was childishly exciting to explore the elaborate setting and revel in its design and construction. The team had created a marvel for us to wander in. But as evening turned to night, the December chill set in.

The wintriness was somewhat enhanced by the massive special effects units, blasting gusts of snow at us from all angles. As we crept through the cobbled passageways there was a real sense of tension, especially as the Knights of Ren were rumoured to be in the vicinity. It was dark and threatening and so exciting. And here was Keri Russell again, looking so different from our first meeting at The Ivy some six months before. I couldn't imagine how she stayed warm in Zorri's body-hugging outfit. Her costume's tin hat may have helped but how droll to see our heroes, and me, clutching hot water bottles between takes. For me, it was quite cold enough. For Daisy, it would be a mild audition for what she would soon be facing in the crashing waves that would form the background of a terrifying encounter with Adam Driver. But now the real weather joined in, as heavy rain turned our surroundings into a swamp. Exciting as it was, we were all glad to finish at ten o'clock. That was the curfew – so as not to annoy the neighbours. Here we were, on a magnificently exotic planet and we were worried about the folks living next door. It was a lovely reminder that our film-makers were creating out-of-this-world, out-of-this-galaxy, magic moments, a few miles southwest of London. To finally finish with that wondrous set, we actually worked till eleven one night. But very quietly.

Indoors once again, it was a real memory-jogger to see swathes of red sand. Slightly irritating, too, since I'd only just cleared my wardrobe of the stuff, secreted in the folds of my clothes and seams of my shoes, from their travels in Jordan. Grainy souvenirs of a wonderful time. Now back at Pinewood, the crew had replicated the dazzling desert light as well as the sandy floor. An extraordinary recreation that refreshed my unforgettable, middle-eastern experiences. But here was something new.

The gritty interior of this grungy spacecraft was an amusing contrast to the whacky jumpers and Santa hats that the crew were delightfully boasting. I felt bereft at not owning a glittery Christmas sweater myself. But I enjoyed the outrageous outfits around me. Particularly, Simon White, a recent addition to my team. His energetic enthusiasm and complete dedication to my well-being was matched by his bravery in wearing something truly ghastly. It was like the last day of term. Which it was. Production was shutting down, going home for a seriously needed break.

The Santa hats were gone. We were back where we'd left off that night before Christmas; back on this ingenious set, with all its intriguing rubbish. Props had done another spectacular job. It was hard not to go up and finger various remembered objects. I paid a brief homage to a familiar droid – abandoned in the corner. Perhaps all droids are abandoned in the end. It's their lot in existence. I was again astounded at the patient skill it must have taken to create this masterpiece, junk-filled place.

Then a pause. A wait. A major costume continuity error. Thank The Maker, someone was watching and remembering. Soon, costumes arrived. We were back in action.

I was suddenly finding the rhythm of the lines difficult, words so hard to remember, with a vocabulary I would not have chosen. I came up with a bunch of alternatives that we might eventually replace in post. Dear Daisy and John, my part-time first-aid team, were more loudly frolicsome than usual. Actors have different ways of preparing for a take. Personally, I like a few minutes of quiet to consider the what and where and how of the next scene. So I tried hard to concentrate as finally, the cameras moved around to my close-up. For Threepio, this was going to be a telling moment in his existence. Because, suddenly, I had uttered his last line in a *Star Wars* film. We weren't finished shooting but in the cat's cradle, mixed-up schedule, I was now silenced – for ever.

Back on another set, the next day, forgetting I had seen and heard myself for the last time, it was filming as usual. Of course, it was all out of sequence but in the final edit, we had shot the closing moments of the film itself. It was a rather moving experience. Especially for me. I could see that my future was changing. But as the end of this trilogy, it all felt so right and so fulfilling. Chris and J.J. had gathered in all the threads and tatters of the previous episodes and spun a mystery of their own; a wondrous coup of creative storytelling, a fulfilling and reward-ing closure, for everyone.

And for me – it was over. A Monday night, the beginning of a week, the ending of a journey. Threepio's last scene was in the company of two of his favourite companions, two of his favourite humans. How ironic that he had no lines. He, who had spoken the first words of the original story, who was ever loquacious and verbose, should be speech-less, at the last.

It was a difficult moment. I could hear J.J. and the crew saying their warm goodbyes to Oscar. It was his last day, too. I was sorry not to be there in the group but Sophie and Joe were still helping me out of Threepio. Finally, for the last time, they handed me my tracksuit and trainers. I laced them carefully. I didn't want to trip and fall on the stairs, as I came down from this iconic set, a place that had become so familiar over forty years and more. There was a strange almost silence around the stage. An AD whispered into her radio as I passed.

"He's here."

I had a sense of dread, that something I had known was coming, was finally here. It felt like an execution, a long anticipated, long denied – end. They had made a space. J.J. was talking into a microphone. His warm voice spread across the studio floor as the crew saw me coming closer, walking alone. No escape. I found a space. And stood. J.J. said kind, nice, thoughtful words about me. I couldn't listen. I heard only warm sounds. He went on. I wanted him to stop because I wasn't sure

I could go on. My eyes were hot. I had never been embarrassed to be emotional as Threepio. But here, it was me. In front of people I admired, liked, respected and loved. Please let him stop.

And so he did. We hugged. He pushed the microphone into my hand, telling me which button to press, his last act of directing me in a film studio. I pressed the button. I managed to speak briefly of this, my third ending, of my thanks to Joe and Sophie for their patience and kindness, to the crew for their support and understanding, forgetting Tommy Gormley in my haste to hide myself away from a mounting bit-ter-sweet emotion that was filling my throat and choking my words. Tommy, our First AD who had so successfully masterminded each day's shoot, commanding the set with a gentle and kind professionalism, keeping everything on track, albeit in an incomprehensible Glaswegian accent. How could I have left him out, as I thanked Kathy and her fellow producers, Callum Green and Michelle Rejwan?

But there, standing in front of me was my lighthouse, my beacon, my wayfinder. Someone who had shown me that making films could be a joy – a real joy.

J.J.

Everyone remembers that moment. The giant imperial Star Destroyer filling the screen above us.

I know I ducked down in my seat. I'm sure I wasn't the only one. It was an astounding piece of film magic. But it wasn't the first dramatic moment, the first impact. Minutes before, the symphonic might of the *Star Wars Main Title* had crashed in. That music became instantly and eternally iconic.

1977. I hadn't met John Williams until it was suggested I help promote an evening of symphonic space music. We met outside the Royal Albert Hall in London. It was winter – and cold. The gels inside Three-pio's eyes immediately clouded over with condensation. Decades later, in the scary, snowy streets of Kijimi, I would experience the same loss of sensation. John was now a blur. But the press photos did the job. It would be a sell-out, gala evening.

A day earlier, I stood on the podium, as myself. I'd never faced an orchestra before. Rather a scruffy lot, I thought. And this was the LSO, the famed London Symphony Orchestra that had scored *A New Hope*. So many talented musicians. And they were all peering at me, expectantly, waiting.

A music lover I may be, but no player. But this was that *Main Title*, a march, so played in a regular beat that even I could follow. But how to know when to end it all? When to sever that last chord? The orchestra were a little surprised that I asked them to play the last few bars several times. A different sort of bar was open backstage. Playing is thirsty work, apparently.

But that was the day before the day.

Now, I was concealed behind the centre stage entrance, dressed in gold – and nervous. More than five thousand music and *Star Wars* lovers had already thrilled to John conducting his other works this evening.

I was the encore.

Ushers opened the doors and I walked out into the vast rotunda. The sound of the crowd was huge, all around me and high above. I felt like a victorious gladiator, though the fight had yet to start. I stopped and I stared. I forgot what we had rehearsed. I just stood there, absorbing it all. The musicians, all dressed up now, smart in black tie; the flowers, the brass railings, the spotlights and the joyful and elaborate warmth of it all. The giddy moment passed and I trotted forward.

John was there to usher me onto the podium. I stood, acknowledging the huge audience and their vociferous welcome. Then I turned to face the orchestra. The raging applause abruptly ceased. Silence. Control. A feeling of absolute power came over me, immediately followed by one of sheer panic. Once I made a down beat with the baton, so safely taped to my fingers, ninety musicians would be off and playing – no brakes, no turning back. But – down it went.

It was thrilling. A loud, wild ride. Obviously, the orchestra was following their leader, the First Violin. I was merely waving my arms in time to the music, faking that I was in charge. It was a breathless experience I thought would never end. But eventually we stopped, all at the same time. Relief.

Now the applause was extraordinary – overwhelming, joyous. I bowed. Then, remembering the etiquette I'd observed as a concert goer, I gestured to the entire orchestra to stand and take a bow too. They were all smiling. I shook hands with the leader. I smiled too. You couldn't see that bit. There was John. I could certainly see his smile.

"I think you'd better do it again."

And so we did. Now greater than before, the rapturous reaction. Me, with more élan. I was on a roll. Power suited me fine, and I had not earned it from a Jedi, either. I mumbled through the mask.

"Shall I do it again?"

"No. I think that's enough now."

With a better sense of timing than my own, John was still smiling.

And so it was over.

Power spent, I went home.

It was the greatest night of my life.

We did the same for John's debut as director of the Boston Pops Orchestra. Over the years, I was lucky enough to attend his scoring sessions in London. I would watch him gentle the superb LSO into following his creative leadership. Sometimes, he halted proceedings to change a major to a minor or a crotchet to a quaver, or to add some strange new instrument into his inventive mix, such was musicianship.

George hadn't ever wanted an electronic score for his film. John had suggested that an audience watching a strange space-orientated world would feel comforted by a classical style of music; scores written on the kind of structures employed by Beethoven and Holst. The influence of Erich Korngold too, one of the original and revered film composers. Rich, lush intricate music; easy to absorb, movingly melodic and thrillingly dramatic, John's compositions would stir the emotions with every note. His music is as great a movie character as any Vader or Princess, his leitmotif themes enhancing the stature of every character they graced. He brought the timeless quality of classical structure and his genius, to enhance and complete George's visions on screen.

Many years passed. I was hosting another performance of the magnificent touring event that was *Star Wars – In Concert*. Every show, I was thrilled again and again at John's sensational compositions. Legendary Californian music producer, Gregg Perloff had created this magical event through his aptly named company, *Another Planet*. His belief in this mammoth project had paid off in delighting many thousands of music fans across continents.

Saturday, June 4, 2011. Tonight I was narrating on stage, at The Hollywood Bowl. Another sold-out performance. A surprise. Our maestro and delightful tour companion, Dirk Brossé, happily concluded the evening's thrilling performance by handing over his baton, with heart-felt respect, to a very special guest.

The audience gave John such an ecstatic welcome, that he looked completely, genuinely, dazed. Evidently a much-loved and respected man. Also, one of the most humble, endearing, kind and thoughtful humans I ever met through the Saga. He stepped onto the podium. They played his tune.

1977 in London, I had been John's encore. Tonight, at the iconic Hollywood Bowl, he had been mine. Neat. An honour.

A sadness.

George never asked him to write a theme for my friend, See-Threepio.

I was attending a fan event, amazed that there was a group dressed up as stormtroopers.

Play acting. In time, it would be officially recognised as Cosplay. They were terrific. Their white plastic uniforms immediately brought back the threat they posed in *A New Hope*. Okay, they didn't really seem to hurt anyone, but they could if they wanted to – and if they learned to shoot straight. The costumes said it all. And here were a bunch of friends enjoying being the bad guys, but careful not to frighten the kids. The kids loved them.

I enjoyed watching their interaction with the fans. They made quite an impact. I was bold enough to give them a few pointers about their posture and attitude. Their performance got even better. Knowing I was about to work on *The Art of Star Wars* exhibition, I called Kathleen Holliday, Lucasfilm's Director of Special Projects at the time, to see if they could take part. And so they did. Their squad of white-clad troopers instantly added drama to the opening events at The Barbican in London. From then on, no *Star Wars* event is complete without the 501st.

The premiere of *Rogue One* made me gasp. As we entered the vast halls of the Tate Modern in London, the motionless white-clad soldiers, lining the blue, up-lit walkway was a theatrical coup. Hugely professional, they were doing it for fun. At various Celebrations, I've been awestruck by the Battalion, as they all come together in what looks like an army. But discipline can go too far.

I was hosting the launch of the *Star Wars* Special Edition in 1977. This re-release of the original trilogy was on disc and would divide fan opinions ever after. George had returned to the simple, innocent movies and reworked them in various ways, enhancing them with newly available, and rather expensive, digital improvements. Not everyone approved. Personally speaking, the issue of "who shot first" was not something that kept me awake at night. But for now, our presentation press event was being held at the British Academy building in London.

A group of troopers would again add to the drama. It was going to be a fun experience – Carrie would join me. Rehearsing by myself on stage, I was distracted by the eye-catching trooper that menaced from the auditorium floor, below me. I knew that such a magnetic image would distract the audience, too. I hopped off the stage and spoke to this daunting figure.

"It might be better if you stood by the entrance at the top of the theatre. Up there. If that's all right."

The trooper's helmet turned slowly towards me. His dark lenses stared impassively. Then muffled words.

"I'll have to ask my platoon commander for permission."

Such devotion to duty.

I backed away.

Slowly.

The 501st is a magnificent organisation. They have great fun together. They make friends. They add drama to live events. They collect for charities. They regularly cheer up young hospital patients. I admire them. Hugely. Members come from all walks of life – doctors, truck drivers, meteorologists, surgeons, teachers, oceanographers, students, traffic consultants, builders – anybody who wants to take time away from their normal world. And, of course, the group welcomes all shapes and sizes; towering Ewoks and miniature Vaders, all having fun, with great respect to The Maker. George has famously allowed fans to play in his sandbox, to let their imaginations run riot with the inspiration that he'd given them through his films.

Back in 1975, I had been privileged to watch John Stears and his brilliant team construct the early Artoo units at Elstree Studios

– fascinating stuff. I'd noticed the reference photos of Huey, Dewey and Louie on the workshop wall. *Silent Running* had been on my favourite-films list for years. Still is. Artoo did look to be out of a similar mould as that chunky trio. It was a clever piece of engineering but would go on to famously malfunction from time to time – actually, most of the time.

Increasingly over the years, I would see home-made Artoos at fan events. As time moved forward, these devices grew in numbers and in their mechanical competence. Totally reliable machines, often with added gadgets, unimagined in those early days. Most of them were better than the real thing, in a manner of speaking, and all made for the love of it. It's fascinating to visit the R2-D2 Builders Club when they set up their displays at events around the world. Its status was confirmed when producer Kathy Kennedy hired two of its members, Lee Towersey and Oliver Steeples, to build and operate the little astromech droid in *The Force Awakens* and beyond.

Besides anything else they do, I am amazed that members of the 501st and the Builders Club have made replica See-Threepio suits. And they wear them. For fun.

So many fans share the same stories with me. I know each one is a unique experience that will always be special. Whatever age they first saw a *Star Wars* film, it somehow lodges in the memory as a seminal moment. But often, it's the reminiscences from those early days that resonate the most.

Of course, many stories involve the whole family having fun together. Bunches of kids, parents, grandparents, all able to share the adventure. Each one finding something specific, just for them. Maybe they admire the Dark Side or have a crush on the Princess or Luke Skywalker. But some fans adopt the Saga for sadder reasons. Not everyone comes from a picture-perfect family.

Fans would often tell me the most personal things – an only child saw Luke and Leia as the brother and sister they had always wanted;

Obi-Wan seemed like a comforting figure to a fatherless boy; Han was the older brother they craved. Other children immersed themselves in the whole story as a refuge from a home threatened with violence, divorce and trauma – a girl, doomed to months in hospital chemo units, was swept up in the heroic tale, in a galaxy where she was not in pain; a veteran wept on my shoulder as he told me how watching the Saga had kept him sane in the horrors of fighting in the Iraq War. And equally painful to read, in a tweet – "Your role in the Saga has helped me battle depression and bullying since I was young. Even when I didn't have any friends, C-3PO made me feel like maybe I did."

When *A New Hope* first hit the screens, that's all it could hit. The local cinema screen, some smaller than others, all reflected the bright images that George had created. Often the projector's beam echoed the lightsabers, as it turned the smoke-filled air into a solid ray of light. Parents puffed away on their cigarettes, as if the dramatic action wasn't enough. It didn't need nicotine. But they were hooked on both. The only way to see this film, or others less fêted, was at the cinema. Not such a bad thing. It added to the excitement of a shared experience with fellow fans. Friendships were formed, debate flourished. Dark Side or not, a huge camaraderie was born.

Video and discs would quickly make multiple viewings an easier option. The pause button allowing a close-up inspection of any moment – sometimes too close up. But favourite sequences could be played and replayed, and replayed again. Less well-loved scenes could be sped through, on fast forward. At least discs didn't wear out like tape. Technology rapidly allowed fans to revel and dwell where they wanted.

Nostalgically speaking, somehow 1977 was a more innocent time as far as *Star Wars* was concerned. It was an unexpected boost after the depressing events of the previous years, with the Vietnam War hanging over everything.

I've never been to a drive-in. I still think I've missed out on the experience. I love the stories of too many kids, happily crammed in the back of the family saloon, getting their parents' money's worth out of the ticket price, jumbling up to get the best view of the screen outside, hearing the soundtrack on tiny, tinny speakers; the car's window somehow becoming the *Falcon*'s viewport.

I love hearing about the police called out for a boy, missing all day, to see him casually come home by himself. He'd watched the first showing and was so excited, he'd hidden in the washrooms before sneaking out to watch the second and the third and the fourth. I didn't learn what his worried parents had to say, or the police. I bet they understood. I hope they forgave.

For one young fan, life became even more thrilling. He lived a *Star Wars* moment. Amazed with what they had just experienced on screen, he and his dad got back in the car and set off for home. It was snowing. As they speeded up, the snow fell more heavily. Now it seemed the white flakes were flying towards them, bright in the headlights. And suddenly the boy was there, inside their cockpit with his dad – jumping to lightspeed.

And I enjoy seeing fans at conventions. I am astounded by their dedication and patience. But what I really like to see are friendships being born between strangers in the line; acquaintances made during the wait, interests and opinions shared, lasting bonds created.

Fans often thank me for their childhood, frequently becoming quite emotional, as they recall their first memory of seeing *Star Wars* with dad, or mother, or pals. It may have been a refuge – sometimes an inspiration. Eternally now, a part of their family history. All of their stories touch me. No matter how many times I hear those words, "Thank you for my childhood," I honestly say back, "Thank you for being there."

And I mean it.

It had been so easy to bond with Mark.

The challenge of working in the desert wastes and ghastly delights of our hotel in Tunisia brought us together – much like the relationship between Threepio and Luke. His bright Californian energy was infectious and charming. He was always "on", which was a new experience for me – I'm not sure I have ever "joshed". But I so admired his easy acting style. He was clearly at home in front of a camera. His warmth was natural, whether or not it was called for in George's script. I truly felt that his attitude towards Threepio helped the audience believe that the golden droid was his real companion.

It was a pleasure, too, to meet Harrison, once Mark and I returned to the UK. His nonchalant sparkiness was a delight, as was his sharp intelligence. We shared vindaloos and stuffed naans together at Khan's, my local good-value Indian restaurant. We ate rather more poshly French, with Sir Alec at La Poule au Pot.

Alec was always the most generous, gentle host, enlivening our meals with tales from his memories and interest in our futures. He may have regretted hosting a meal in a London taverna, where we all got a bit carried away, dancing and smashing plates. They don't do that anymore, even in Greece. But it was brilliant fun.

The last addition to the group of heroes was, of course, Carrie. Totally at home in the English culture, she was always a lively delight – sweet, friendly, courteous and spunky. It was all good. But in the days following her arrival, I noticed a gradual change.

It was hard for me to be a part of the team. They were American. They had a common culture, language, terms of reference. They could see the expression on their faces, as they acted our scenes together. They could relate to each other. They wore clothes that made relaxing together easy, over a coffee break. Their hairstyles, constantly tweaked.

They wore makeup that made them look good all day. I was British –
pedantic. I wore a disgustingly hot costume that took ages to engineer
me into, and out of, and left me looking boiled alive. They were far
down the road in their cars before I limped damply from my dressing
room.

I began to see a distance growing between us. They were a team, on
film and in life. Good for them. Their raucous camaraderie was not just
for their weekends and evenings. It continued on set – sometimes with
rather distracting results.

All that joshing made it hard for me to concentrate. It was clear that,
whatever the demands of acting face-to-face with another character, it
was a lot harder if you were in a rigid suit with restricted vision. I had to
rehearse and remember precisely where objects were placed and where
other characters were standing – and remember the strange dialogue.
I had a lot to say, more than others on screen, and it wasn't easy dialogue to get inside your head. It all really did need my full attention. Of
course, the gang would be a little louder as the effects of the night
before wore off. They were usually friendly and courteous, though, on
occasion, when pushed by various tensions that would not always be the
case.

I do remember a fun time when Lucasfilm arranged for Mark to
show me round Disneyland for the day. Excited at the thought of visiting this iconic American institution, I was a little apprehensive about
meeting him again. I'd heard about his horrible car accident – his facial
scarring. Luckily, I spotted him before he saw me. I got over the slight
change in his looks. We didn't mention it as we drifted and laughed
through "It's A Small World". For me, the endless parade of dolls twirl-
ing and miming to a hypnotically simple song was something far worse
than a car crash. It still rattles around my brain some four decades
later. But I so admired Mark's fortitude and constant enthusiasm and
energy. My day at Disneyland was a revelation. And how quaint to think

that neither of us could ever have foreseen the major connection that was waiting for us. But before that, we would share other good times together.

The prequels were different. The old gang absent. As we passed by each other on the set of *The Rise of Skywalker*, the final chapter in his family's Saga, I gave Mark a quick hug. Kathy and J.J. had given him a lovely, appreciative speech in front of the assembled crew. It was his last day. His participation was complete. His role as Luke, done – at least as far as movies were concerned. I guessed how he felt. I had to dash off to dress for my next scene.

That night, I emailed him a fuller goodbye.

He replied.

**From:** Mark Hamill
**To:** Anthony Daniels
**Sent:** Wed, 19 Dec 2018 9.28pm
**Subject:** Re: Today

Thanks for the more than kind words, Tony. I grew so fond of our fictional relationship; it was hard to be separated in this new trilogy. You & R2 were my family & they certainly didn't dare take Chewie away from Han. I was appalled that in the original script for VIII, I just walked by without even acknowledging you! I was grateful Rian let us at least have that brief farewell moment, even if it was only a nod & a wink. Perhaps it was fitting, as there are no words to convey the depth of Luke's gratitude to his faithful sidekick, just as there are no words to express mine for you.

Thank you for a lifetime of fond memories, friend.

xoxo, mh

It was possibly the most touching message I and Threepio ever had.

I realised that for some time I had harboured a kind of resentment. Well, several resentments.

"Did you get the part 'cos you fitted the costume?"

How many times had I felt trivialised – and not just by news reporters, often treated as not being much of an actor – that the suit did the performance – that there was no acknowledged connection between the droid and me – that I felt inferior to my fellow actors, lauded for their visible performances – that personally, I was not worth anything at all.

Everything around that first film had taken away my self-confidence and replaced it with anger. I also recognised that I had the extraordinary chance to work with a genius; a genius who could be socially awkward, neither particularly comfortable directing actors – nor generous with his praise of their work. But unquestionably a visionary. He created a profound and moving mythology for our time, a legend that still powerfully resonates, decades after its birth.

Notwithstanding his brilliant creation of a galaxy filled with fantastic creatures and droids, it transpired that even a visionary genius can make sensitive human life forms – such as myself – feel significantly under-appreciated.

Many months after *A New Hope* had opened, I asked to speak with him. He invited me to breakfast in London. We sat in the Richoux coffee shop on Piccadilly, near his favourite Hard Rock Cafe. We looked at the menu and ordered a croissant each. I had come to talk rather than eat.

I asked him why I felt so neglected, after what I had put into his film.

I wish I could remember George's answer. I think he intimated that working with Threepio, and therefore me, had been difficult. I was thunderstruck. Hurt again. I must have wondered if he had ever tried on the ill-constructed fibreglass costume in the cold of the desert and the heat of Elstree.

"And you never said anything nice about my performance."

George muttered.

"You were terrific."

Astounded.

"Pardon?"

Louder.

"You were terrific."

Shocked, I may have mumbled, thank you – but I was distracted by the waiter. The menu was out of date. The price of croissants had risen by a penny, over the weekend. Such is the reality of life outside the movies.

Whatever my hurts, I wouldn't be writing here without the inspiration of George Lucas's inspiration. He has shown me kindnesses over the years since that day. Sincerely grateful that I am, it's perhaps understandable that I would have preferred to feel that respect from the start. But that morning in London, George did insist on paying for my croissant.

It became public knowledge that Sir Alec had grown a little resentful, that he was known only as Obi-Wan. His fabled career on stage and film seemed eclipsed; his versatile talents, shown in so many thrilling, touching, amusing, dramatic roles, were as nothing compared to the popularity of his performance of an old guru in a dressing gown. In spite of all the good things *Star Wars* had brought him, he regretted the way his triumphs had been subsumed. Alec had achieved so much. He wanted to be remembered for it all. I understood. I would never, could never approach his abilities but, in my own small way, I empathised.

Time passed.

Gradually, slowly, my mood changed. I began to realise the luck of it all. In spite of my initial reluctance to be a part of this endeavour, something grand but humbling had come out of it. I had been given the opportunity to use my skills as an actor, my profession, my passion, to create a character that would become one of the most iconic and beloved of our time. Also, I'd been given the gift of being part of something, much bigger than any one person, touching the lives of millions around the world, inspiring and uniting them. The appreciation I sought was there, day after day, from the fans – the audience. They liked the one thing I offered them. I had achieved something that few are given the opportunity to do. For that I must be – I am – eternally grateful.

I was in a limo in New York, trying to adjust the TV, with its irritating supermarket commercial about "wieners being 39 cents the pound".

Suddenly. Loudly. Breaking News!

"Great Britain's Sir Alec Guinness actor Obi-Wan Kenobi dies at eighty-six."

I was saddened.

Alec had been kind to me and encouraging. He had given me a gentle friendship at the time I really needed it. I had spent weekends with him and Merula at their country home, with the dog and the goat. We had laughed over dinners and breakfasts. He had explained that *Star Wars* was an unusual project. I would find others would be different – better. He was like an uncle, with a very dry sense of humour and a waspish tongue, when appropriate.

Over the years, our knowing each other thinned to a whisper, as friendships often do. People move on. Up. Down. Sideways, like doors in a *Star Wars* film, opening and closing. It had been an honour. Now he was gone. I was moved to think that he had died before reaching that stage of acquiescence and understanding that I was finally approaching.

I had survived long enough to pass through those negative shallows and rise up. I was grateful that my offering of Threepio was enjoyed by so many, over generations. The fans had become friends, whether we'd met or not. They liked Threepio. I like him, too.

I have been proud to know him.

"Is it hot in the costume?"

"I do wish someone would ask me a question I've never been asked before."

"What would that be?"

Smart kid.

But then.

"What will happen to Threepio in the end?"

I was stunned.

Silenced.

After his token presence in the later films, I suggested to J.J. that he should give Threepio a fitting, meaningful end in *The Rise of Skywalker*. A melting down, perhaps – a careless scrapping. In human terms, a death, for the Cause. He looked at me.

"Not on my watch."

I surely recognise, I will someday leave the stage. I hope that I will do so in the knowledge that I have imbued See-Threepio with enough life that, with the love of the fans, he will go on without me.

an end

# droidography

## FILMS

1977 ***Star Wars*: Episode IV – A New Hope** (film)
1977 *Star Wars*: Episode IV – A New Hope: Deleted Scenes (film addition)
1980 ***Star Wars*: Episode V – The Empire Strikes Back** (film)
1980 *Star Wars*: Episode V – The Empire Strikes Back: Deleted Scenes
(film addition)
1982 Return of the Ewok (short film)
1983 ***Star Wars*: Episode VI – Return of the Jedi** (film)
1983 *Star Wars*: Episode VI – Return of the Jedi: Deleted Scenes (film addition)
1996 Special Effects: Anything Can Happen (IMAX short film)
1999 ***Star Wars*: Episode I – The Phantom Menace** (film)
2000 *Star Wars* Episode II: The Saga Continues (film addition)
2002 ***Star Wars*: Episode II – Attack of the Clones** (film)
2004 The Characters of *Star Wars* (film addition)
2005 ***Star Wars*: Episode III – Revenge of the Sith** (film)
2008 *Star Wars*: The Clone Wars (animated film)
2012 Cosplaygirl (Short film)
2014 The *Lego* Movie (film)
2015 ***Star Wars*: Episode VII – The Force Awakens**
2016 Secrets of the Force Awakens: A Cinematic Journey (film addition)
2016 The Force Awakens: Force for Change (film addition)
2016 The Force Awakens: Building BB-8 (film addition)
2016 **Rogue One: A *Star Wars* Story** (film)
2017 ***Star Wars*: Episode VIII – The Last Jedi** (film)
2018 **Solo: A *Star Wars* Story** (film)
2018 The Director and the Jedi (film addition documentary)
2018 Ralph breaks the Internet (animated film)
2019 ***Star Wars*: Episode IX – The Rise of Skywalker** (film)

## TELEVISION

1977 The Making of *Star Wars* (TV movie documentary)
1977 Donny and Marie (TV series)
1978 The 50th Annual Academy Awards (TV special)
1978 The *Star Wars* Holiday Special (TV movie)
1980 The Making of 'The Empire Strikes Back' (TV movie documentary)
1980 The Muppet Show (TV series)
      The Stars of *Star Wars* (1980)
1980 Sesame Street (TV series)
      1364 (1980)
      1396 (1980)
1980 *Star Wars* Underoos (TV commercial)

1981 Multi-Coloured Swap Shop (TV series)
1983 Classic Creatures: Return of the Jedi (TV movie documentary)
1983 From *Star Wars* to Jedi: The Making of a Saga (TV movie documentary)
1984 Donald Duck's 50th Birthday (TV special short)
1985-1986 *Star Wars*: Droids (TV series)
     The White Witch (1985)
     Escape Into Terror (1985)
     The Trigon Unleashed (1985)
     A Race to the Finish (1985)
     The Lost Prince (1985)
     The New King (1985)
     The Pirates of Tarnoonga (1985)
     The Revenge of Kybo Ren (1985)
     Coby and the Starhunters (1985)
     Tail of the Roon Comets (1985)
     The Roon Games (1985)
     Across the Roon Sea (1985)
     The Frozen Citadel (1985)
     The Great Heep (1986)
1990 The Magical World of Disney (TV series)
     Disneyland's 35th Anniversary Special (1990)
1996 Showbiz Today (TV series)
1997 *Star Wars*: The Magic and the Mystery (TV movie documentary)
1998 The Best of Hollywood (TV movie documentary)
1999 The Unauthorised *Star Wars* Story (video documentary)
1999 The Stars of *Star Wars:* Interviews from the Cast (video documentary)
2001 SF:UK (TV series documentary)
     No More Heroes (2001)
2001 R2-D2: Beneath the Dome (TV special short)
2002 Hollywood History (TV series documentary)
2002 *Star Wars*: Connections (TV short)
2004-2005 *Star Wars*: Clone Wars (TV series)
     Chapter 15 (2004)
     Chapter 16 (2004)
     Chapter 21 (2005)
     Chapter 23 (2005)
2004 Empire of Dreams: The Story of the *Star Wars* Trilogy (video documentary)
2004 Ultimate Sci-Fi Top 10 (TV mini-series documentary)
2004 When *Star Wars* Ruled the World (TV movie documentary)
2004 The Story of *Star Wars* (video documentary)
2005 Science of *Star Wars* (TV mini-series documentary)
     War, Weapons and the Force
     Space Cowboys
     Man and Machines

2005 *Star Wars*: Feel the Force (TV movie documentary)
2005 Only Human (TV series documentary)
2005 The 100 Greatest Family Films (TV movie documentary)
2005 *Star Wars* Heroes & Villains (documentary)
2005-2006 Jeopardy! (TV series)
2007 *Star Wars* at 30 (TV movie)
2008-2011 *Star Wars*: The Clone Wars (TV series)
  Destroy *Malevolence* (2008)
  Bombad Jedi (2008)
  Trespass (2009)
  Blue Shadow Virus (2009)
  Hostage Crisis (2009)
  Senate Spy (2009)
  The Zillo Beast Strikes Back (2010)
  Evil Plans (2010)
  The Citadel (2011)
  Mercy Mission (2011)
  Nomad Droids (2011)
2009 The *Star Wars* Comic Con 09 Spectacular (TV special)
2009 The Making of *Star Wars* – In Concert (TV movie documentary)
2010 Robot Chicken: *Star Wars* III (TV movie)
2011 *Lego Star Wars*: The Padawan Menace (TV short)
2012 *Lego Star Wars*: The Empire Strikes Out (TV short)
2012 *Star Wars*: Detours (unreleased TV series)
2013 Words with Warwick (TV mini-series)
2013-2014 *Lego Star Wars*: The Yoda Chronicles (TV series)
  The Phantom Clone (2013)
  Menace of the Sith (2013)
  Attack of the Jedi (2013)
  Escape from the Jedi Temple (2014)
  Race for the Holocrons (2014)
  Raid on Coruscant (2014)
  Clash of the Skywalkers (2014)
2014 *Star Wars* Rebels (TV series)
  Droids in Distress (2014)
2014-2017 Rebels Recon (TV series)
  Inside "Spark of Rebellion" (2014)
  Inside "Droids in Distress" (2014)
  Inside "Double Agent Droid" (2017)
2015 *Star Wars* Celebration 2015 (TV mini-series)
2015 *Star Wars*: The Force Awakens World Premiere Red Carpet (TV movie)
2015 *Star Wars*: Greatest Moments (TV movie documentary)
2015 *Lego Star Wars*: Droid Tales (TV mini-series)
  Exit from Endor (2015)

Crisis on Coruscant (2015)
Mission to Mos Eisley (2015)
Flight of the *Falcon* (2015)
Gambit on Geonosis (2015)
2016 The Oscars (TV special)
2016 *Lego Star Wars*: The Resistance Rises (TV mini-series)
Poe to the Rescue (2016)
2016 Rogue One: A *Star Wars* Story – World Premiere (TV special documentary)
2016-2017 The *Star Wars* Show (TV series short)
2017 *Star Wars* Celebration 2017 (TV mini-series)
Day 1 (2017) Himself – Special Guest
Day 2 (2017) Himself – Special Guest
Day 3 (2017) Himself – Special Guest
2017 Science and *Star Wars* (TV series)
2017 Live from the Red Carpet of *Star Wars*: The Last Jedi (TV movie)
2017 The Oh My Disney Show (TV series)
2017 *Star Wars*: Forces of Destiny (TV series)
Beasts of Echo Base (2017)
2018 *Star Wars* Resistance (TV series)
The Recruit (2018)

# MUSIC

1977 The story of *Star Wars* (album)
1980 Christmas In The Stars (album)

# GAMES

1997 Monopoly *Star Wars* (video game)
1999 *Star Wars*: Yoda's Challenge Activity Center (video game)
1999 *Star Wars*: Pit Droids (video game)
2008 *Star Wars*: The Clone Wars – Lightsaber Duels (video game)
2009 *Star Wars*: The Force Unleashed – Ultimate Sith Edition (video game)
2015 Disney Infinity 3.0 (video game)
2015 *Star Wars*: Battlefront (video game)
2016 *Lego Star Wars*: The Force Awakens (video game)

# MISCELLANEOUS

1987 *Star Tours* (Disneyland ride short video)
2011 *Star Tours*: The Adventures Continue (Disneyland ride short video)
2015 BuzzFeed Video (internet series short)

# index

# picture credits

The publisher would like to thank the following for their kind permission to reproduce their photographs:
(Key: a-above; b-below/bottom; c-centre; f-far; l-left; r-right; t-top)

p1 Dorling Kindersley / Lucasfilm Ltd. / Anthony and Christine Daniels (t); Dorling Kindersley / Lucasfilm Ltd. / Anthony and Christine Daniels (cl); Dorling Kindersley / Anthony and Christine Daniels (cr); Lucasfilm Ltd. (b). p2 akg-images: Horst von Harbou – Stiftung Deutsche Kinemathek (tl); Alamy Stock Photo: Keystone Press (tr); Lucasfilm Ltd. (cl, cr, bl, br). p3 Lucasfilm Ltd. (t, cl, cr, c); Anthony and Christine Daniels (bl); Dorling Kindersley / Lucasfilm / Anthony and Christine Daniels (br). p4 Lucasfilm Ltd. (t, cl, cr); Dorling Kindersley / Lucasfilm Ltd. / Anthony and Christine Daniels (b). p5 Lucasfilm (t, cl, cr, b). p6 Lucasfilm Ltd. (t, cl, cr, bl, br). p7 Lucasfilm Ltd. (t, cl, r); akg-images: Album / Lucasfilm Ltd. / 20th Century Fox (bl); Anthony and Christine Daniels (br). p8 Lucasfilm Ltd. (t); Lucasfilm Ltd. / Anthony and Christine Daniels (c); Lucasfilm Ltd. (cr, br). p9 Lucasfilm Ltd. (t, tl); Getty Images: Sygma / Tony Korody (cr); Photofest: (cl); Lucasfilm Ltd. / Anthony and Christine Daniels (bl); Anthony and Christine Daniels (br). p10 Dorling Kindersley / Meredith Corporation / Anthony and Christine Daniels (tl); ABC Photo Archives / Walt Disney Television (tr); CBS Photo Archive (cl); 20th Century Fox Television / Lucasfilm Ltd. / Anthony and Christine Daniels (cr); Anthony and Christine Daniels / Academy of Motion Picture Arts and Sciences (abr); Dorling Kindersley / Academy of Motion Picture Arts and Sciences (br, bc); Getty Images: ABC Photo Archives / Walt Disney Television (br). p11 Lucasfilm (tl, tr, tbl); Alamy Stock Photo: United Archives (c); Disney / The Jim Henson Company (br) Sesame Workshop (br). p12 Lucasfilm Ltd. (tl, tr, cl, cr, b). p13 Lucasfilm Ltd. (tl, tr, c, bl, br). p14 Lucasfilm Ltd. (t); Dorling Kindersley / Lucasfilm Ltd. / Anthony and Christine Daniels (c, bl), Dorling Kindersley / Anthony and Christine Daniels (cr, br). p15 Dorling Kindersley /Lucasfilm Ltd. / Anthony and Christine Daniels (tl, c); Lucasfilm Ltd. (tr); Dorling Kindersley / Lucasfilm Ltd. / Anthony and Christine Daniels (b) p16 Dorling Kindersley / Disney / Anthony and Christine Daniels (tr); Disney (tl); Dorling Kindersley / Disney / Anthony and Christine Daniels (cl) Dorling Kindersley / RSO Records / Anthony and Christine Daniels (cr); Steve Smith (bl). U.S. National Library of Medicine, History of Medicine Division: Prints and Photographs Collection (br). p17 Lucasfilm Ltd. (tl); Lucasfilm Ltd. / Anthony and Christine Daniels (tr); Lucasfilm Ltd. (cl); Anthony and Christine Daniels (cr); Lucasfilm Ltd. / Anthony and Christine Daniels (bl); Dorling Kindersley / Lucasfilm Ltd. / Anthony and Christine Daniels (br). p18 Lucasfilm Ltd. (tl, tr, cl, cr, b). p19 Dorling Kindersley / Lucasfilm Ltd. /Museum of Science, Boston / Anthony and Christine Daniels (tl); The Barbican Centre (tc); The Powerhouse Museum: Museum of Applied Arts & Sciences (tr) Alamy Stock Photo: Jonathan O'Rourke (cl); Dorling Kindersley / Anthony and Christine Daniels/ Royal Mail Group Limited 2019 (bl); Dorling Kindersley / Anthony and Christine Daniels/ United States Postal Service (bc); Dorling Kindersley / Anthony and Christine Daniels / ©2019 The LEGO Group (br). p20 Dorling Kindersley / Anthony and Christine Daniels / Kellogg Company (tl, tr); Alamy Stock Photo: Aflo Co. Ltd. (cl); Nippon Airways Ltd. (cla); Anthony and Christine Daniels / Cliro Products (bl); Anthony and Christine Daniels / PEZ Candy Inc (c); Anthony and Christine Daniels / Sigma Japan (cr); Anthony and Christine Daniels / Kenner Products (cbr)/ Anthony and Christine Daniels / Funko (br). p21 Lucasfilm Ltd. (t, cl, cr, br); Dorling Kindersley / Lucasfilm Ltd. / Anthony and Christine Daniels (bl). p22 Lucasfilm Ltd. (t, cr, b); Anthony and Christine Daniels (cal); Getty Images: Disney / Alberto E. Rodrigue (clb). p23 Associated Newspapers (t); Rex by Shutterstock: Shutterstock / Sendtoppo (clb); Anthony and Christine Daniels (cr); Lucasfilm Ltd. (bl); Getty Images: Dave J Hogan (br). p24 Getty Images: Barry Brecheisen (tl); Anthony and Christine Daniels (tr); Lucasfilm Ltd. (cl,cr,b).

Front cover and spine Lucasfilm Ltd. Back cover Dorling Kindersley.
Hardback edition: Jacket back flap Dorling Kindersley / Lucasfilm Ltd.